Rick Steves

IRELAND
2003

LEGEND

═╪═	Freeway/Motorway	**Dingle** Recommended location*
───	Major Rail Line	Sligo Just passing through**
✈	Airport	■ Ruin, Museum, other Point of Interest
▲	National Park/ Natural Wonder	♜ Castle/Monument/Palace

* Black locations are places of interest to tourists, sized by importance. Many are covered in this guidebook.

** Gray locations are places of little or no interest to tourists and are sized by population.

0 km   50 kilometers

0 miles   50 miles

Aran Island

Donega

MAYO

Achill Island

Ballina

Clare Island

Drumcliff ■ Sligo

Lough Gill

N15

N16

IRE

Carrick-on-Shannon

Longfor

Westport

Croagh Patrick

Knock

N5

N17

Leenane

Kylemore Abbey

Clifden

CONNEMARA

Cong

Roscommon

Lou
Ree

N59

N17

N59

Lough Corrib

N84

Galway

Athlone

N6

Rossaveel

Dun Aenghus ■ **Kilronan**

Dunguaire ♜

Ballyvaughan **Kinvarra**

Aran Islands

Doolin

THE BURREN

CLIFFS OF MOHER

Lisdoonvarna

River Shannon

N18

Lough Derg

Ennis

Kilkee

CLARE

N67

N68

N7

N8

Shannon ✈

Killimer

Limerick

Tarbert

N24

DINGLE PEN.

Gallarus Oratory

Slea Head

Great Blasket Island

N86

Dingle

N70

Tralee

Kerry Airport ✈

N72

KERRY

Killarney

Limerick Junction

Tipperary

Rock of Cashel ■ **Cashel**

N20

N8

Caher

Clonmel

N69

N21

Mallow

N72

N72

N25

RING OF KERRY

■ *Muckross House*

Blarney ♜

Dungarvan

Youghal

Sneem

Kenmare

Macroom

N22

N8

Cork ✈

Midleton

Ardmore

Skellig

BEARA

Bantry

Bantry Bay

N71

CORK

N71

Cobh

N25

Kinsale

R600

Skibbereen

to Roscoff, France

Rick Steves'
IRELAND
2003

Rick Steves & Pat O'Connor

AVALON
TRAVEL

Other ATP travel guidebooks by Rick Steves
Rick Steves' Best of Europe
Rick Steves' Europe 101: History and Art for the Traveler (with Gene Openshaw)
Rick Steves' Europe Through the Back Door
Rick Steves' Mona Winks: Self-Guided Tours of Europe's Top Museums
   (with Gene Openshaw)
Rick Steves' Postcards from Europe
Rick Steves' France (with Steve Smith)
Rick Steves' Germany, Austria & Switzerland
Rick Steves' Great Britain
Rick Steves' Italy
Rick Steves' Scandinavia
Rick Steves' Spain & Portugal
Rick Steves' Amsterdam, Bruges & Brussels (with Gene Openshaw)
Rick Steves' Florence (with Gene Openshaw)
Rick Steves' London (with Gene Openshaw)
Rick Steves' Paris (with Steve Smith and Gene Openshaw)
Rick Steves' Rome (with Gene Openshaw)
Rick Steves' Venice (with Gene Openshaw)
Rick Steves' Phrase Books for: French, German, Italian, Portuguese, Spanish,
   and French/German/Italian

Thanks to Rozanne Stringer for her writing on the Celts, Celtic Tiger,
St. Brendan, and Irish Art. Thanks, too, to Mike Kelly for his help.

Avalon Travel Publishing, 1400 65th Street, Suite 250, Emeryville, CA 94608

Text © 2003 by Rick Steves
Maps © 2003 by Europe Through the Back Door

Printed in the United States of America by R. R. Donnelley
First printing January 2003

For the latest on Rick's lectures, guidebooks, tours, and public television series,
contact Europe Through the Back Door, Box 2009, Edmonds, WA 98020,
tel. 425/771-8303, fax 425/771-0833, www.ricksteves.com, or e-mail:
rick@ricksteves.com.

ISBN 1-56691-458-2 • ISSN 1538-1587

Europe Through the Back Door Managing Editor: Risa Laib
Europe Through the Back Door Editors: Jill Hodges, Cameron Hewitt
Avalon Travel Publishing Editor: Laura Mazer
Copy Editor: Kate McKinley
Production & Typesetting: Kathleen Sparkes, White Hart Design
Design: Linda Braun
Cover Design: Janine Lehmann
Maps & Graphics: David C. Hoerlein, Rhonda Pelikan, Zoey Platt
Front matter color photos: p. i, Irish children, © Rick Steves;
   p. iv, Kylemore Abbey, County Galway, © Mary Liz Austin
Cover Photo: Jerpoint Cistercian Abbey, County Kilkenny, © Mary Liz Austin

Distributed to the book trade by Publishers Group West, Berkeley, California

CONTENTS

Top Destinations in Ireland

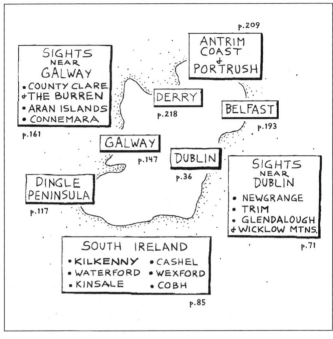

SIGHTS NEAR GALWAY
- COUNTY CLARE & THE BURREN
- ARAN ISLANDS
- CONNEMARA

p.161

ANTRIM COAST & PORTRUSH
p.209

DERRY
p.218

BELFAST
p.193

GALWAY
p.147

DUBLIN
p.36

DINGLE PENINSULA
p.117

SIGHTS NEAR DUBLIN
- NEWGRANGE
- TRIM
- GLENDALOUGH & WICKLOW MTNS.

p.71

SOUTH IRELAND
- KILKENNY
- WATERFORD
- KINSALE
- CASHEL
- WEXFORD
- COBH

p.85

INTRODUCTION

This book breaks Ireland into its top big-city, small-town, and rural destinations. It gives you all the information and opinions necessary to wring the maximum value out of your limited time and money in each of these destinations. If you plan three weeks or less for Ireland and have a normal appetite for information, this lean and mean little book is all you need. If you're a travel-info fiend, this book sorts through all the superlatives and provides a handy rack upon which to hang your supplemental information.

Experiencing Irish culture, people, and natural wonders economically and hassle-free has been my goal for more than 25 years of traveling, tour guiding, and travel writing. With this new edition I pass on to you the lessons I've learned, updated for your trip in 2003.

Rick Steves' Ireland is a personal tour guide in your pocket. Better yet, it's actually two tour guides in your pocket: Rick's cowriter/researcher for this guidebook is Pat O'Connor. Pat is the Ireland specialist and senior Ireland tour guide at Rick Steves' Europe Through the Back Door. Rick has enjoyed Ireland over 20 years of travel, but nobody has a more Irish name than Pat—whose travel passion has long been the Emerald Isle. Together, we will (in the first person singular) keep this book up-to-date and accurate.

The places covered are balanced to include a comfortable mix of exciting big cities and great-to-be-alive-in small towns. Note that this book covers the highlights of the entire island, including Northern Ireland. While you'll find the predictable biggies (such as the Book of Kells, a medieval castle banquet, and the Cliffs of Moher), the book also mixes in a healthy dose of Back Door intimacy (rope-bridge hikes, holy wells, and Gaelic music pubs). I've been selective. On a short trip, visiting both the Ring of Kerry and the Dingle peninsula is redundant; I cover just the best (Dingle). There are plenty of great manorhouse gardens; again, I recommend just the tops (Powerscourt).

The best is, of course, only my opinion. But after more than two busy decades of travel writing, lecturing, and tour guiding, I've developed a sixth sense for what grabs the traveler's imagination. The places featured in this book give anyone the "gift of gab."

This Information Is Accurate and Up-to-Date

Most publishers of guidebooks that cover a country from top to bottom can afford an update only every two or three years, and rarely is the research done in person. Since this book is selective, covering only the top three weeks of sightseeing, I'm able to update it each year. Even with annual updates, prices and key information change. Travel with the current edition of this book; I guarantee it's the most up-to-date information available in print (for the latest, see www.ricksteves.com/update). If you're packing an old book, you'll learn the seriousness of your mistake...in Ireland. Your trip costs about $10 per waking hour. Your time is valuable. This guidebook saves lots of time.

Planning Your Trip

This book is organized by destinations, each one a mini-vacation on its own, filled with exciting sights and homey, affordable places to stay. In each chapter, you'll find the following:

Planning Your Time, a suggested schedule with thoughts on how to best use your limited time.

Orientation, including tourist information, city transportation, and an easy-to-read map designed to make the text clear and your arrival smooth.

Sights, with ratings: ▲▲▲—Don't miss; ▲▲—Try hard to see; ▲—Worthwhile if you can make it; No rating—Worth knowing about.

Sleeping and **Eating,** with addresses and phone numbers of my favorite good-value hotels and restaurants.

Transportation Connections to nearby destinations by train or bus and route tips for drivers.

The chapter **Ireland: Past and Present** gives you an overview of Irish history, a look at contemporary Ireland, and a taste of the Irish language.

The **appendix** has helpful information on telephoning, the climate, and festivals.

Browse through this book, choose the destinations that excite you the most, and link them up. Then have a great trip! You'll travel like a temporary local, getting the absolute most out of every mile, minute, and dollar. You won't waste time on mediocre sights because, unlike others, this guidebook covers only the best. Since your major financial pitfall is lousy, expensive hotels, I've worked hard to assemble the best accommodation values for each stop. And as you travel the route I know and love, I'm happy you'll be meeting some of my favorite Irish people.

Trip Costs

Five components make up your trip costs: airfare, surface transportation, room and board, sightseeing/entertainment, and shopping/miscellany.

Airfare: Don't try to sort through the mess. Find a good travel agent. A round-trip United States–to–Dublin flight costs $500–1,000 (even cheaper in winter), depending on where you fly from and when. If your travels take you beyond Ireland, consider saving time and money in Europe by flying "open-jaw" (into one city and out of another; for instance, into Dublin and out of Paris).

Surface Transportation: For a three-week whirlwind trip of all my recommended Irish destinations, allow $200 per person for public transportation (train tickets and key buses), or $500 per person (based on 2 people sharing) for a three-week car rental, gas, and insurance. Car rental is cheapest if arranged from the United States. Since Ireland's train system has gaps, you'll usually save money by simply buying train and bus tickets as you go, rather than buying a railpass (see "Transportation," below).

Room and Board: You can thrive in Ireland on $75 a day per person for room and board (allow $90 per day for Dublin). A $75-per-day budget allows $10 for lunch, $15 for dinner, and $50 for lodging (based on 2 people splitting a $100 double room that includes breakfast). That's doable, particularly outside Dublin. Students and tightwads can do it on $45 ($25 for a bed, $20 a day for meals and snacks). But budget sleeping and eating require the skills and information covered below (and in greater detail in my book *Rick Steves' Europe Through the Back Door*).

Sightseeing and Entertainment: In big cities, figure $5–8 per major sight (e.g., The Book of Kells at Trinity College-$7), $2 for minor ones (climbing church towers), $10 for guided walks, and $25 for bus tours and splurge experiences (such as the Dunguaire medieval castle banquet). An overall average of $15 a day works for most. Don't skimp here. After all, this category directly powers most of the experiences all the other expenses are designed to make possible.

You'll be tempted to buy the Irish Heritage Card, which gets you into 75 historical monuments, gardens, and parks maintained by Duchas (the Irish Heritage Service) in the Republic of Ireland. Consider buying it if you plan on visiting half a dozen or more included sights (€19, seniors-€13, students-€8, families-€46, covers free entry to all Heritage sights for 1 year, card comes with handy map and list of sights' hours and prices, purchase at Duchas sights or Dublin's tourist information office on Suffolk Street, www.heritageireland.ie). People traveling by car are more likely to get their money's worth out of the card. Otherwise, individual adult entry prices to these sights usually run between €2 and €4.50 each. A typical sightseer with three weeks in Ireland will probably pay to see nearly all 16 of the following sights (covered in this book): Kilmainham Jail-€4.75 (Dublin); Bru na Boinne-€4 (Newgrange & Visitors Centre in Boyne Valley); Hill of Tara-€2 (Boyne Valley); Mellifont Abbey-€2 (Boyne Valley); Trim Castle-€3.25 (Boyne Valley); Glendalough-€2.50 (Wicklow Mountains); Kilkenny Castle-€4.50 (Kilkenny); Rock of Cashel-€4.50 (Cashel);

Reginald's Tower-€2 (Waterford); Charles Fort-€3.20 (Kinsale); Desmond Castle-€2.50 (Kinsale); Muckross House & Farms-€7.75 (near Killarney); Blasket Centre-€3.20 (near Dingle); Dún Aenghus-€1.30 (Inishmore, Aran Islands); and Ennis Friary-€1.20 (Ennis). This totals nearly €50; a pass saves you about €30.

Shopping and Miscellany: Figure $1 per postcard, ice-cream cone or cup of tea and $2.50 per beer. Shopping can vary in cost from nearly nothing to a small fortune. Good budget travelers find that this category has little to do with assembling a trip full of life-long and wonderful memories.

Exchange Rates

I've priced things throughout this book in local currencies. The Republic of Ireland has adopted the euro currency. Northern Ireland, which is part of the United Kingdom, has retained its traditional currency, the British pound sterling.

---

1 euro (€) = about $1.
1 British pound (£1) = about $1.50.

Republic of Ireland: Like dollars, one euro is broken down into 100 cents. You'll find coins ranging from 1 cent to 2 euros, and bills ranging from 5 euros to 500 euros.

Northern Ireland: The British pound sterling (£), also called a "quid," is broken into 100 pence (p). Pence means "cents." You'll find coins ranging from 1p to £2 and bills from £5 to £50.

To roughly convert prices in pounds to dollars, add 50 percent to British prices: £6 is about $9, £3 is about $4.50, and 80p is about $1.20.

Northern Ireland issues its own currency, the Ulster pound, worth the same as an English pound. English and Ulster pounds are technically interchangeable in both regions, although Ulster pounds are "undesirable" in Britain. Banks in either region will convert your Ulster pounds into English pounds at no charge. Don't worry about the coins, which are accepted throughout the United Kingdom.

Prices, Times, and Discounts

The opening hours and telephone numbers listed in this book are accurate as of mid-2002. Ireland is always changing, and I know you'll understand that this guidebook, like any other, starts to yellow even before it's printed. Always pick up a listing of sights and opening times at local tourist information offices as you travel.

You'll be using the 24-hour clock. After 12:00 noon, keep going—13:00, 14:00, and so on. For anything over 12, subtract 12 and add p.m. (14:00 is 2 p.m.).

While discounts (called "concessions" in Ireland) are not listed in this book, many Irish sights are discounted for seniors (loosely defined as anyone retired or willing to call themselves a "senior"), youths (ages 8–18), students, groups of 10 or more, and families.

When to Go

July and August are peak season—my favorite time—with very long days, the best weather, and the busiest schedule of tourist fun. Prices and crowds don't go up as dramatically in Ireland as they do in much of Europe. Still, travel during "shoulder season" (May, early June, Sept, and early Oct) is easier and a bit less expensive. Shoulder-season travelers get minimal crowds, decent weather, the full range of sights and tourist fun spots, and the joy of being able to just grab a room almost whenever and wherever they like—often at a flexible price.

Winter travelers find absolutely no crowds and soft room prices, but shorter sightseeing hours. Some attractions are open only on weekends or are closed entirely in the winter (Nov–Feb). The weather can be cold and dreary, and nightfall draws the shades on sightseeing well before dinnertime. While Ireland's rural charm falls with the leaves, city sightseeing is fine in the winter.

Plan for rain no matter when you go. Just keep going and take full advantage of "bright spells." Conditions can change several times in a day, but rarely is the weather extreme. As the locals say, "There is no bad weather, only inappropriate clothing." Daily averages throughout the year range between 42 and 70 degrees Fahrenheit. Temperatures below 32 or over 80 degrees are cause for headlines (see the climate chart in the appendix). While sunshine may be rare, summer days are very long. Dublin is as far north as Edmonton, Canada, and Portrush is as far north as Ketchikan on the Alaskan panhandle. The summer sun is up from 5:30 until 22:00. It's not uncommon to have a gray day, eat dinner, and enjoy hours of sunshine afterward.

Sightseeing Priorities

Depending on the length of your trip, here are my recommended priorities:

3 days:	Not worth the trouble
5 days:	Dublin, Dingle Peninsula
7 days, add:	Galway and a day in Belfast
9 days, add:	County Clare/Burren
11 days, add:	Northern Ireland's Antrim Coast
15 days, add:	Aran Islands, Wicklow Mountains
19 days, add:	Kinsale, Waterford, Boyne Valley
21 days, add:	Derry, Connemara area

Best Three-Week Trip in Ireland by Car

Day	Plan	Sleep in
1	Fly into Dublin, rent car, Glendalough	Kilkenny
2	Kilkenny with side-trip to Cashel	Kilkenny
3	Waterford	Waterford
4	Explore County Wexford	Waterford
5	Cobh	Kinsale
6	Kinsale	Kinsale
7	Muckross House, Tralee	Dingle
8	Dingle Peninsula loop	Dingle
9	Blaskets, Dingle town, (laundry and rest)	Dingle
10	Cliffs of Moher, Burren, Dunguaire banquet	Galway
11	Galway	Galway
12	Aran Islands	Aran Islands
13	Tour Connemara	Westport
14	Drive to Northern Ireland	Derry
15	Explore Derry, then drive to Portrush	Portrush
16	Explore Antrim Coast	Portrush
17	Belfast	Belfast
18	Drive to Boyne Valley sights, return car in Dublin	Dublin
19	Dublin	Dublin
20	Dublin	Dublin
21	Fly home	

While this three-week itinerary is designed to be done by car, you can do it by train and bus. For three weeks without a car, spend your first three nights in Dublin using buses and taxis. Cut back on the recommended sights with the most frustrating public transportation (Boyne Valley, County Wexford, Connemara). You can book day tours by bus for parts of these areas through local tourist offices. If there are at least two of you traveling together, don't forget that taxis are affordable if the bus schedule doesn't fit your plans (i.e., Cork to Kinsale, Waterford to New Ross, Dublin to Trim).

Whirlwind Three-Week Trip in Ireland

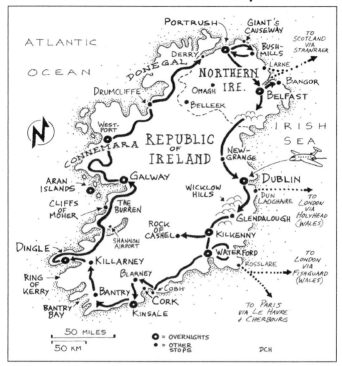

Itinerary Tips

Most people fly into Dublin and remain there for a few days. If you have a car rental set up at the Dublin airport, consider a mellower small-town start in Kilkenny or Trim. Then visit Dublin at the end of your trip after you've turned your car back in at the airport. You'll be more rested and ready to tackle Ireland's greatest city. Dublin traffic has gotten busier over the years, and visitors find city sightseeing easier on foot or by taxi.

To give yourself a little rootedness, minimize one-night stands. It's worth a long drive after dinner to be settled into a town for two nights. B&Bs are also more likely to give a good price to someone staying more than one night.

Red Tape and Taxes

You need a passport, but no visa or shots, to travel in Ireland.

If you're bringing electrical gadgets, pack along a three-prong adapter to plug into Ireland's outlets (which are just like Britain's) rather than the two-prong adapter you'd need for the rest of western Europe.

VAT Refunds for Shoppers: Wrapped into the purchase price of your Irish souvenirs is a Value Added Tax (VAT) that's generally about 18 percent. If you make a purchase at a store that participates in the VAT refund scheme, you're entitled to get most of that tax back. Personally I've never felt that VAT refunds are worth the hassle, especially if you're spending less than about $100, but if you do, here's the scoop.

If you're lucky, the merchant will subtract the tax when you make your purchase (this is more likely to occur if the store ships the goods to your home). Otherwise, you'll need to:

(1) Get the paperwork. Have the merchant completely fill out the necessary refund document, called a "Tax-Free Shopping Cheque." You'll have to present your passport at the store.

(2) Have your cheque(s) stamped at your last stop in the European Union by the customs agent who deals with VAT refunds. It's best to keep your purchases in your carry-on for viewing, but if they're too large or dangerous to carry on, then track down the proper customs agent to inspect them before you check your bag. You're not supposed to use your purchased goods before you leave. If you show up at customs wearing your new sweater, officials might look the other way—or deny you a refund.

(3) To collect your refund, you'll need to return your stamped documents to the retailer or its representative. Many merchants work with a service, such as Global Refund or Cashback (also called Vatback), which have offices at major airports, ports, and border crossings. These services, which extract a 4 percent fee, can refund your money immediately in your currency of choice or credit your card (within two billing cycles). If you have to deal directly with the retailer, mail the store your stamped documents and then wait. It could take months.

Banking

Throughout Ireland, cash machines are the way to go. Bring an ATM or debit card (with a PIN code—numbers only, no letters) to withdraw funds from cash machines as you travel. Bring a couple hundred American dollars as a backup.

You can use a credit or debit card to rent a car or to book rooms and transportation tickets over the phone. In general, Visa and MasterCard are more widely accepted than American Express.

Traveler's checks are a waste of time and money. Banks commonly charge a commission fee of €2.50–5 or even more. If you're relying on traveler's checks, it can pay to shop around if there are a few banks nearby. American Express exchange offices don't charge a commission on their checks or any others. The same goes for Thomas Cook checks at Cook offices. This can save you around 1.5 percent. But don't let this cloud your assessment of their exchange rates.

Whether you use cash machines or banks, save time and money by changing plenty of money at a time. Even in mist-kissed Ireland you should use a money belt (order online at www .ricksteves.com or call 425/771-8303 for a free newsletter/catalog). Thieves target tourists, especially Americans. A money belt provides peace of mind. You can carry lots of cash safely in a money belt—and given the high bank fees, you should.

Bank holidays bring most businesses to a grinding halt on Christmas, December 26, New Year's Day, Good Friday, Easter Monday, and the first Mondays in May, June, and August.

Travel Smart

Your trip to Ireland is like a complex play—easier to follow and really appreciate on a second viewing. While no one does the same trip twice to gain that advantage, reading this book in its entirety before your trip—and rereading it as you travel—accomplishes much the same thing.

Upon arrival in a new town, lay the groundwork for a smooth departure. Visit local tourist-information offices. Buy a phone card and use it for reservations and confirmations. You speak the language—use it! Enjoy the friendliness of the local people. Ask questions. Most locals are eager to point you in their idea of the right direction. Carry a pocket-size notebook to organize your thoughts. Plan ahead for laundry, post-office chores, and picnics. Those who expect to travel smart, do.

Pace yourself. Mix intense and relaxed periods. Every trip (and every traveler) needs at least a few slack days. Assume you will return.

As you read this book, make note of festivals and days when sights are closed. Sundays have pros and cons for travelers, as they do in the United States (special events, limited hours, closed shops and banks, limited public transportation, no rush hours). Saturdays are virtually weekdays. Popular places are even more popular on weekends—especially sunny weekends, which are sufficient cause for an impromptu holiday in this soggy corner of Europe.

Before you go: Consider making the following travel arrangements before your trip or within a few days of arrival.
  • Reserve a room for your first night.
  • If you'll be traveling in late June, July, or August and want to sleep in my lead listings, book your B&Bs (and the Dunguaire medieval banquet) as soon as you're ready to commit to a date.

- Confirm car-rental and pick-up plans with your rental agency (picking up a car on Sat afternoon or Sun may be difficult).

Tourist Information

Virtually every town in Ireland has a tourist-information center (abbreviated "TI" in this book). Take full advantage of this service. Arrive (or telephone) with a list of questions and a proposed sight-seeing plan. Pick up maps, brochures, and walking-tour information. In Dublin, you can pick up everything you'll need for Ireland in one stop at the TI in the old church on Suffolk Street.

For all the help TIs offer, steer clear of their room-finding services (bloated prices, fees, no opinions, and they take a 10 percent cut from your host).

Ireland's national tourist office in the United States—called Tourism Ireland—offers a wealth of information on both the Republic of Ireland and Northern Ireland. Before your trip, request anything you may want, such as city maps and schedules of upcoming festivals.

Tourism Ireland: 345 Park Avenue, 17th floor, New York, NY 10154, tel. 800/223-6470 or 212/418-0800, fax 212/371-9052, www.tourismireland.com. They offer a useful *Ireland Magazine*, as well as a country map, an events calendar, and ideas for golfing, outdoor activities, and historical sights.

Recommended Guidebooks

You may want some supplemental travel guidebooks, especially if you're traveling beyond my recommended destinations. I know it hurts to spend $25–35 on extra books and maps, but when you consider the money they'll save you and the improvements they'll make in your $3,000 vacation, it's money well spent.

While this book offers everything you'll need for the structure of your trip, each place you will visit has plenty of great little guide-books to fill you in on local history. For cultural and sightseeing background in bigger chunks, Michelin and Cadogan guides to Ireland are good. The best budget travel guides to Ireland are the Lonely Planet and Let's Go guidebooks. Lonely Planet's guidebook is more thorough and informative, but it's not updated annually. *Let's Go Ireland* is updated annually and youth-oriented, with good coverage of nightlife, hostels, and cheap transportation deals.

Rick Steves' Books and Videos

Rick Steves' Europe Through the Back Door 2003 gives you budget-travel skills, such as minimizing jet lag, packing light, planning your itinerary, traveling by car or train, finding beds without reservations, changing money, avoiding rip-offs, outsmarting thieves, using cell phones, staying healthy, taking great photographs, and much more. The book also includes chapters on 35 of Rick's favorite Back Doors, two of which are in Ireland.

Rick Steves' Country Guides are a series of eight guidebooks—including this book—covering Rick's favorite continent: Best of Europe; Great Britain; France; Italy; Spain and Portugal; Scandinavia; and Germany, Austria, and Switzerland. All are updated annually and come out in December and January.

Rick Steves' City Guides cover London, Paris, Rome, Venice, Florence, and—new for 2003—*Rick Steves' Amsterdam, Bruges & Brussels.* These practical guides offer in-depth coverage of the sights, hotels, restaurants, and nightlife in these grand cities, along with illustrated tours of their great museums.

Rick Steves' Europe 101: History and Art for the Traveler (cowritten with Gene Openshaw) gives you the story of Europe's people, history, and art. Written for smart people who were sleeping in their history and art classes before they knew they were going to Europe, *101* helps Europe's sights come alive. However, this book has far more coverage of the continent than of Ireland.

Rick Steves' Mona Winks (cowritten with Gene Openshaw), provides fun, easy-to-follow, self-guided tours of Europe's top 25 museums and cultural sites in London, Paris, Amsterdam, Madrid, Rome, Venice, and Florence.

Rick's new public TV series, *Rick Steves' Europe*, keeps churning out shows. Of 82 episodes (the new series plus *Travels in Europe with Rick Steves*), five shows cover Ireland, including three of the newest episodes. These air nationally on public television and the Travel Channel. They're also available as information-packed home videos and DVDs (order online at www.ricksteves.com or call 425/771-8303 for our free newsletter/catalog).

Rick Steves' Postcards from Europe, Rick's autobiographical book, packs more than 25 years of travel anecdotes and insights into the ultimate 2,000-mile European adventure. Through his guidebooks, Rick shares his favorite European discoveries with you. *Postcards* introduces you to his favorite European friends.

All of Rick's books are published by Avalon Travel Publishing (www.travelmatters.com).

Maps

The black-and-white maps in this book, designed and drawn by Dave Hoerlein, are concise and simple. Dave has designed the maps to help you locate recommended places and get to the TI office, where you'll find more in-depth maps of the city or region. The color maps at the front of this book will help you navigate from town to town.

Consider the new Rick Steves' Britain and Ireland Planning Map. Designed for the traveler, it lists sightseeing destinations prominently. For an all-Europe trip, consider the Rick Steves' Europe Planning Map (order either map online at www.ricksteves .com or call 425/771-8303 for our free newsletter/catalog).

Maps to buy in Ireland: Train travelers can do fine with a simple rail map (available as part of the free Intercity Timetable found at Irish train stations) and city maps from TIs. (Get free maps of Dublin and Ireland from the Irish Tourist Board before you go; see "Tourist Information," above.) If you're driving, get a detailed road atlas covering all of Ireland. Ordnance Survey, AA, and Bartholomew editions are available for about €11 in TIs, gas stations, and bookstores. Drivers, hikers, and bikers may want more detailed maps for Dingle, Connemara, County Wexford, the Antrim Coast, and the Boyne Valley (easy to buy locally).

Tours of Ireland

Travel agents can tell you about all the normal tours, but they won't tell you about ours. At Europe Through the Back Door we offer 15-day tours of Ireland featuring the all-stars covered in this book, a roomy bus, and two great guides (departures May–Sept, maximum 24 people, call us at 425/771-8303 or visit www.ricksteves.com).

Transportation in Ireland

By Car or Train?

Cars are best for three or more traveling together (especially families with small kids), those packing heavy, and those scouring the countryside. Ireland's far-flung rural charms are most easily experienced by car.

Trains and buses are best for solo travelers, blitz tourists, and city-to-city travelers. Most rail lines spoke outward from Dublin, so you'll need to mix in bus transportation to bridge the gaps. Ireland has a good train-and-bus system, though departures are not as frequent as the European norm. Travelers who don't want (or can't afford) to drive a rental car find they still enjoy their travels using public transportation.

Deals on Rails, Wheels, and Wings in Ireland

Trains: Ireland's various passes offer a better value than BritRail's pricey "BritRail plus Ireland" pass (see chart on next page). Irish railpasses can be purchased easily and most cheaply in Ireland at major stations (Dublin info tel. 01/836-6222).

If you'd rather buy point-to-point tickets, just buy your tickets in Ireland as you go. To avoid long station lines in Dublin,

Prices listed are for 2002. My free *Rick Steves' Guide to European Railpasses* has the latest on 2003 prices. To get the railpass guide, call us at 425/771-8303 or visit www.ricksteves.com/rail.

BRITRAIL PLUS IRELAND PASS

	1st class	Standard
5 days out of 1 month	$529	$399
10 days out of 1 month	749	569

This pass covers the entire British Isles (England, Wales, Scotland, Northern Ireland and the Republic of Ireland) including a round-trip Stena Line ferry crossing between Wales or Scotland and the Emerald Isle during the pass's validity (okay to leave via one port and return via another). Reserve boat crossings a day or so in advance—sooner for holidays. One child (5-15) travels along free with each pass. Extra kiddies pay half fare; under 5 free.

DEALS ONCE YOU GET TO IRELAND:

These local specials are sold at major train stations in Ireland. €1 = about $1 U.S.

Ireland:

Approximate point-to-point one-way 2nd class fares in $US by rail (solid line), bus (dashed line), and ferry (dotted line). First class costs 50% more. Add up fares for your itinerary to see whether a rail and/or bus pass will save you money.

Pass Name	Version	Area	Duration	Price
Emerald Card	Rail & Bus	Republic & North	Any 8 days in 15	€168
			Any 15 days in 30	€290
Irish Explorer	Rail & Bus	Republic only	Any 8 days in 15	€145
Irish Rover	Rail only	Republic & North	Any 5 days in 15	€122
Irish Explorer	Rail only	Republic only	Any 5 days in 15	€98
Irish Rover	Bus only	Republic & North	Any 3 days in 8	€60
			Any 8 days in 15	€135
			Any 15 days in 30	€195
Irish Rambler	Bus only	Republic only	Any 3 days in 8	€45
			Any 8 days in 15	€100
			Any 15 days in 30	€145

SEALINK FERRIES AND CATAMARANS CONNECTING BRITAIN AND IRELAND

British port to...	Irish port	crossings daily	ferry/cat. hrs	ferry/cat. cost
Holyhead	Dun Laoghaire	3	3.5 / 1.5	$30 / $45
Fishguard	Rosslare	6	3.5 / 1.5	$30 / $40
Stranraer	Belfast	6	3.5 / 1.5	$35 / $40
London (RR + boat)	Dublin	1 direct	8.5	$85 / $90

See also www.seaview.co.uk. Dun Laoghaire is a 30-minute bus or train ride from Dublin. Travelers from London to Dublin may find it worthwhile to catch a quick $80 shuttle flight (see www.cheapflights.com). National Express (Britain's Greyhound) offers great London-Dublin bus+ferry tickets for as low as $30 (restrictions apply).

Public Transportation in Ireland

THIS MAP SHOWS MAJOR RAIL & BUS ROUTES FOR PLACES COVERED IN THIS BOOK. BUSES PARALLEL MOST RAIL LINES.

— RAIL
--- BUS
••• BOAT

GIANT'S CAUSEWAY
PORTRUSH
DERRY
BEL.-POR 8/DAY, 2 HRS
LARNE
TO STRANRAER & TROON (SCOTLAND)
DONEGAL
BELFAST
BANGOR/ CULTRA
SLIGO
DUB-BEL 8/DAY, 2 HRS
DROGHEDA
TO HOLYHEAD (N. WALES)
GAL-DUB 4/DAY, 3 HRS
GALWAY
DUBLIN
ARAN ISLANDS
DUN LAOGHAIRE
WICKLOW
ENNIS
LIME-RICK
DUB-TRA or LIM 4/DAY, 4 HRS
DUB-ROS 3/DAY, 3 HRS.
TRALEE
LIME-RICK JUNCTION
WATER-FORD
TO FISHGUARD (S. WALES)
KILLARNEY
DINGLE
BLARNEY
ROSS-LARE
CORK
RING.
KINSALE
TO ROSCOFF
ROS-TRA 1/DAY, 5 HRS.
TO CHERBOURG (FRANCE)

you can book train tickets in advance in person or by phone with your credit card at the Iarnrod Eireann Travel Centre (35 Lower Abbey Street, tel. 01/703-4070).

Research options in advance by studying Irish train schedules at www.irishrail.ie or listening to a talking timetable at 01/805-4222.

Buses: Buses are about 33 percent slower than trains, but they're also a lot cheaper. Round-trip bus tickets usually cost less than two one-way fares (i.e., Tralee to Dingle costs €8 one-way and €12 round-trip). The Irish distinguish between "buses" (for local runs with lots of stops) and "coaches" (long-distance express runs). On many Irish buses, pop music or sports games are piped throughout the bus; have earplugs handy if you prefer silence.

Buses pick you up when the trains let you down. From Dublin to Dingle without a car, you'll need to take a train to Tralee and then catch a bus from there. From Dublin to Kinsale without a car, you'll need to take a train to Cork and then a bus from there.

If you're traveling up and down Ireland's west coast, buses are best (or a combination of buses and trains); relying on "rail only" here is too time-consuming.

Bus stations are normally at or near train stations. The Bus Eireann Expressway Bus Timetable comes in handy (free, available at some bus stations or online at www.buseireann.ie, bus info tel. 01/836-6111).

A couple of companies offer **backpacker's bus circuits.** These hop-on, hop-off bus circuits take mostly youth hostelers around the country super-cheap and easily with the assumption that they'll be sleeping in hostels along the way. For instance, **Paddy Wagon** cuts Ireland in half and offers three- or six-day "tours" of each half (north and south) that can be combined into one whole tour that connects Dublin, Cork, Killarney, Dingle, Galway, Westport, Donegal, Ballintoy, and Belfast (3 days/€139, 6 days/€269, 17 Westmoreland Street, Dublin, tel. 01/672-6007, www.paddywagontours.com); they also offer Sunday-only one-day tours of Belfast from Dublin (€40). **Tir na nOg** offers similar three- or six-day trips (same rates as Paddy Wagon, connecting Dublin, Kilkenny, Cork, Killarney, Tralee, Galway, Westport, Donegal, Derry, and Belfast; 57 Lower Gardiner Street, Dublin, tel. 01/836-4684, www.tirnanogtours.com).

Youth Deals: Students can use their ISIC (student card) to get discounts on rail, cross-country coaches, and city bus tickets (up to 50 percent), but only if they first purchase a "Travelsave Stamp" for €10 at any major train station in Ireland or at the USIT Now Travel Agency office (19/21 Aston Quay, O'Connell Bridge, Dublin, tel. 01/602-1600).

Children ages 5–15 pay half-price on trains, and wee ones under five go free.

Flights: If you're connecting Ireland with Britain or the Continent, look into cheap flights offered by Ryanair (Irish tel. 01/609-7878, www.ryanair.com), bmi british midland (Irish tel. 01/407-3036, U.S. tel. 800/788-0555, www.flybmi.com), and easyJet (flies in and out of Belfast only, Irish tel. 04894-484-929, British tel. 0870-600-0000, www.easyjet.com). Also consider www.cheapflights.co.uk. Returns can be cheaper than one-way—ask. To get the best prices, it's usually smart to book as soon as you have a date set. Each flight has an allotment of cheap seats; these sell fast, leaving the higher-priced seats for latecomers. (Ryanair is the exception, offering promotional deals throughout the year.)

Car Rental

To see all of Ireland, I prefer the freedom of a rental car. Connemara, the Antrim Coast, County Wexford, and the Boyne Valley are really only worth it if you have wheels.

Touring Ireland by car is cheapest if arranged in advance through your hometown travel agent. The best rates are weekly with unlimited mileage or leasing (possible for rentals over 3 weeks). You can pick up and drop off just about anywhere, anytime. For a trip that covers both Ireland and Britain, you're better off with two separate car rentals. You can drive your rental car from the Republic of Ireland into Northern Ireland, but be aware of drop-off charges (from $75–150) if you drop it off in the North.

If you pick up the car and stay out of big cities, you'll more likely survive your first day on the Irish roads. If you drop the car off early or keep it longer, you'll be credited or charged at a fair, prorated price. Big companies have offices in most cities. (Ask to be picked up at your hotel.) Small local rental companies can be cheaper but aren't as flexible.

The Ford 1.3-liter Escort-category car costs about $50 more per week than the smallest cars but feels better on the motorways and safer on the small roads. Remember, minibuses are a great budget way to go for 5–9 people.

For peace of mind, spring for the CDW insurance (Collision Damage Waiver, about $15–20 per day), which gives a zero (or low) deductible rather than the standard value-of-the-car "deductible." A few "gold" credit cards cover CDW insurance; quiz your credit-card company on the worst-case scenario.

Driving

Your U.S. driver's license is all you need to drive in Ireland. Driving in Ireland is basically wonderful—once you remember to stay on the left and after you've mastered the "roundabouts." But be warned: Every year I get a few cards from traveling readers advising me that, for them, trying to drive in Ireland was a nerve-racking and regrettable mistake. To get a little slack on the roads, drop by a gas station or auto shop and buy a red "L" (new driver with license) sign to put in your window. An Irish Automobile Association membership comes with most rentals. Understand its towing and emergency-road-service benefits.

Gas (petrol) costs over $4 per gallon and is self-serve. Some pumps are unleaded. Seat belts are required by law. Speed limits are 30 miles per hour in town, 70 miles per hour on the motorways (highways), and 50 or 60 miles per hour elsewhere. Be very careful with alcohol . . . the Garda (police) set up random checkpoints, and if you drink more than one pint, you're legally drunk in Ireland.

Study your map before taking off. Know the areas you'll be lacing together since road numbers are inconsistent. Avoid driving in big cities whenever possible. Most have modern ring roads to skirt the congestion. The shortest distance between any two points

Driving in Ireland: Distance and Time

is usually the motorway. Miss a motorway exit and you can lose 30 minutes. An Ordnance Survey Irish road atlas (sold at gas stations and bookstores) is $11 well spent.

Road signs can be confusing, too little, and too late. There are three main kinds of road signs: (1) Those with white lettering on a green background are found on major routes and give distances in kilometers. (2) Signs with black lettering on a white background are older and trickier: Distances shown with a "km" following it are in kilometers, while distances with nothing following it are in miles. (3) Brown signs with white lettering alert drivers to sights, lodging, and tourist offices.

Parking is confusing. One yellow line marked on the pavement means no parking Monday through Saturday during business hours. Double yellow lines mean no parking at any time. Broken yellow lines mean short stops are OK, but you should always look for explicit signs or ask a passerby.

Standard European Road Signs

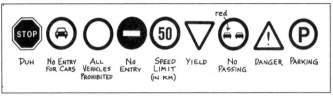

				red				
Duh	No Entry For Cars	All Vehicles Prohibited	No Entry	Speed Limit (in km)	Yield	No Passing	Danger	Parking

Even in small towns, rather than fight for street parking, I just pull into the most central and handy "disk" parking lot I can find. Disks can be bought at nearby shops, and rates are reasonable by U.S. standards. You buy one disk for each hour you want to stay. Scratch off the time you arrived on the disk and put it on your dashboard. I keep a bag of coins in the ashtray for parking meters and parking voucher machines (no change given for large coins).

Set your car up for a fun road trip. Establish a cardboard-box pantry of munchies. Buy a rack of liter boxes of juice for the trunk. Buy some Windex and a roll of paper towels for cleaner sightseeing.

Telephones, Mail, and E-mail

Use the telephone routinely. You can make long-distance calls directly, cheaply, and easily, and there's no language barrier. Call ahead to reserve or reconfirm rooms, check opening hours, and confirm tour times.

To call long distance you'll need the correct area code. You'll find area codes listed throughout this book, or you can get them from directory assistance (dial 11811 in Ireland, 192 in Northern Ireland). For information on telephoning throughout Europe, see the appendix.

The Irish telephone system is great. Easy-to-find public phone booths are either coin- or card-operated. Phones clearly list which coins they'll take, and a display shows how your money supply's doing. Only completely unused coins will be returned, so put in biggies with caution. (If money's left over, rather than hanging up, push the "make another call" button.)

The more convenient phone-card booths are common. You can purchase Telecom Eireann **phone cards** for €4, €7, or €15 at newsstands, TIs, and post offices; insert the card into the phone and dial away.

Insertable phone cards are getting a lot of competition from the cheaper-per-minute **PIN cards**. These cards, which have a scratch-off "personal identification number," allow you to call home at the rate of about five minutes per dollar. The main difference is that an insertable Irish phone card can only be used at a phone-card booth, but PIN cards (which are not inserted into a phone) allow you to dial from virtually any phone, even from your hotel room. To use a PIN card, follow the instructions clearly written on the card (you'll end up dialing a lot of numbers). There are many different brands of PIN cards; simply ask for an "international calling card" (sold at most newsstands, exchange bureaus, and minimarts). Because PIN cards occasionally malfunction, avoid the high denominations. To make numerous calls with a PIN card without having to redial the long access number each time, press the keys (see instructions on card) that allow you to launch directly into your next call. PIN cards work only within the country of purchase, with the exception of some of the Spirit brand cards, usable in both the U.K. and Ireland (confirm before purchase).

Dialing Direct: You'll save money by dialing direct rather than going through an operator. You just need to learn to break the codes. For a listing of **international access codes** and **country codes** and a handy "European Calling Chart," see the appendix.

When calling long distance within the Republic of Ireland, first dial the area code (which starts with 0), then the local number. When dialing internationally, dial the international access code (00 if you're calling from Europe, 011 if you're calling from the U.S. or Canada), the country code of the country you're calling, the area code (without its initial 0 if you're calling Ireland), and the local number. For example, Dublin's area code is 01. To call the recommended Harding Hotel in Dublin from the United States or Canada, dial 011 (international access code), 353 (Ireland's country code), 1 (Dublin's area code without its initial 0), then 679-6500 (the hotel's number). To call the same hotel from Galway, dial 01/679-6500.

To call Northern Ireland from the United States, dial 011, 44 (the U.K. country code), 28 (Northern Ireland's area code without its initial 0), then the local number. To call Northern Ireland from the Republic of Ireland, dial 048, then the local number without any area code at all.

To call my office from anywhere in Ireland, I dial 00 (Europe's international access code), 1 (U.S. country code), 425 (Edmonds' area code), then 771-8303.

U.S. Calling Cards: Since direct-dialing rates have dropped, calling cards (offered by AT&T, MCI, and Sprint) are no longer the good value they used to be. In fact, they're a rip-off. You'll likely pay $3 for the first minute with a $4 connection fee; if you get an answering machine, it'll cost you $7 to say "Sorry I missed you." Simply dialing direct (even from your hotel room) is a much better deal.

Cell Phones: You can buy inexpensive cell phones— about $70 on up—to make local and international calls. The cheapest phones work only in the country where they're sold; the pricier phones work throughout Europe (but it'll cost you about $40 per country to outfit the phone with the necessary chip and prepaid phone time). Because of their expense, cell phones are most economical for travelers staying in one country for two weeks or more. If you're interested, stop by one of the ubiquitous phone-shops or the cell-phone counter in a department store. Confirm with a clerk whether the phone works only in Ireland or through-out Europe. Make sure the clerk shows you how to use the phone—practice making a call to the store or, for fun, to the clerk's personal cell phone. You'll need to pick out a policy; different policies offer, say, better rates for making calls at night or for calling cell phones rather than fixed phones. I get the basic fixed rate: a straight 30 cents per minute to the United States and 15 cents per minute to any fixed or cell phone in the home country at any hour. Receiving calls is generally free. When you run out of calling time, buy more time at a newsstand. Upon arrival in a different country, purchase a new chip (which comes with a new phone number). If you're on a budget, skip cell phones and buy PIN phone cards instead.

Mail: Get stamps at the neighborhood post office, news-stands within fancy hotels, and some minimarts and card shops. To arrange for mail delivery, reserve a few hotels along your route in advance and give their addresses to friends, or use American Express mail services (free to AmEx cardholders and for a minimal fee to anyone else). Allow 10 days for a letter to arrive. Phoning is so easy that I've dispensed with mail stops altogether.

E-mail: More and more hoteliers have e-mail addresses and Web sites (listed in this book). Some family-run pensions can become overwhelmed by the volume of e-mail they receive, so be patient if you don't get an immediate response. Internet service providers (ISPs) can change with alarming frequency, so if your e-mail message to a hotel bounces back, search for the hotel's name in a search engine such as Google (www.google.com) to see if it has a new Web site. If that doesn't work, fax or call the hotel.

Cybercafés and little hole-in-the-wall Internet-access shops (offering a few computers, no food, and cheap prices) are pop-ular in most cities. If the extension .com doesn't work, try .ie for Ireland.

If you're traveling with a lap-top and modem, and you intend to go online from your hotel room, you'll need an Internet service provider that has local phone numbers for each country you'll visit. While an American modem cable plugs into European phone jacks, you may have to tweak your settings to make your computer recognize a pulse instead of the U.S. dial tone or vice versa. Bring a phone jack tester that reverses line polarity as needed.

Sleeping

In the interest of smart use of your time, I favor accommodations (and restaurants) handy to your sightseeing activities. Rather than list hotels scattered throughout a city, I choose two or three favorite neighborhoods and recommend the best accommodation values in each, from $15 bunk beds to fancy-for-my-book $200 doubles. Outside of Dublin you can expect to find good doubles for $60–100, including tax and a cooked breakfast.

I've described my recommended hotels and B&Bs with a standard code. Prices listed are for one-night stays in peak season, include a hearty breakfast (unless otherwise noted), and assume you're booking direct and not through a TI. Prices can soften off-season, for stays of two nights or longer, or for payment in cash (rather than by credit card). Teenagers are generally charged as adults. Little kids sleep almost free.

When establishing prices with a hotelier or B&B owner, confirm whether the charge is per person or per room (if a price is too good to be true, it's probably per person). In this book, room prices are listed per room, not per person.

Many places have three floors of rooms, steep stairs, and no elevator. If you're concerned about stairs, call and ask about ground-floor rooms.

In Ireland, virtually all rooms have sinks. Rooms with a private bathroom (toilet plus shower and/or tub) are called "en suite"; rooms that lack private plumbing are "standard." As more rooms go en suite, the hallway bathroom is shared with fewer standard rooms. If money's tight, ask for standard rooms.

Ireland has a rating system for hotels and B&Bs. These stars and shamrocks are supposed to imply quality, but I find that they mean only that the place sporting symbols is paying dues to the tourist board. Rating systems often have little to do with value.

Bed-and-Breakfasts

Compared to hotels, bed-and-breakfast places give you double the cultural intimacy for half the price. In 2003, you'll generally pay €30–50 (about $30-50) per person for a B&B in Ireland. Prices include a big cooked breakfast. How much coziness, teddies, tea, and biscuits are tossed in varies tremendously.

If you have a reasonable but limited budget, skip hotels. Go the B&B way. If you can use a telephone and speak English, you'll enjoy homey, friendly, clean rooms at a great price by sticking to my listings. Always call first.

If you're traveling beyond my recommended destinations, you'll find B&Bs where you need them. Any town with tourists has a TI that books rooms or can give you a list and point you

Sleep Code

To give maximum information with a minimum of space, I use this code to describe accommodations listed in this book. Prices in this book are listed per room, not per person. Breakfast is included.

S = Single room, or price for one person in a double.

D = Double or twin room. (I specify double- and twin-bed rooms only if they are priced differently, or if a place has only one or the other. When reserving, you should specify.)

T = Three-person room (often a double bed with a single).

Q = Four-person room (adding an extra child's bed to a T is usually cheaper).

b = Private bathroom with toilet and shower or tub.

s = Private shower or tub only. (The toilet is down the hall.)

CC = Accepts credit cards (Visa and MasterCard, rarely American Express).

no CC = Does not accept credit cards; pay in local cash.

According to this code, a couple staying at a "Db-€95, CC" hotel would pay a total of €95 (about $95) per night for a room with a private toilet and shower (or tub). The hotel accepts credit cards or cash.

in the right direction. In the absence of a TI, ask people on the street for help.

"Twin" means two single beds, and "double" means one double bed. If you'll take either one, let them know or you might be needlessly turned away. "Standard" rooms come with just a sink (many better places have standard rooms that they don't even advertise). If you want a room that contains a private bathroom, specify "en suite"; B&B owners sometimes use the term "private bathroom" for a bathroom down the hall that only your room has the key for.

B&Bs range from large guesthouses with 15–20 rooms to small homes renting out a spare bedroom. The philosophy of the management determines the character of a place more than its size and the facilities offered. Avoid places run as a business by absentee owners. My top listings are run by couples who enjoy welcoming the world to their breakfast table.

The B&Bs I've recommended are nearly all stocking-feet comfortable. I look for a place that is friendly (i.e., enjoys Americans); located in a central, safe, quiet neighborhood; clean, with firm beds; a good value; not mentioned in other guidebooks (and therefore filled mostly with Irish travelers); and willing to hold a room until 16:00 or so without a deposit (though more and more places are requiring a deposit or credit-card number). In certain cases, my recommendations don't meet all of these prerequisites. I'm more impressed by a handy location and a fun-loving philosophy than hair dryers and shoeshine machines.

A few tips: B&B proprietors are selective as to whom they invite in for the night. Very young children aren't always welcome (ask). Risky-looking people (2 or more single men are often assumed to be troublemakers) find many places suddenly full. If you'll be staying for more than one night you are "a desirable." In popular weekend getaway spots you're unlikely to find a place to take you for Saturday night only. Sometimes staying several nights earns you a better price—ask about it. If you book through a TI, it takes a 10 percent commission. If you book directly, the B&B gets it all (and you'll have a better chance of getting a discount). If my listings are full, ask for guidance. (Mentioning this book can help.) Owners usually work together and can call up an ally to land you a bed.

B&Bs are not hotels; if you want to ruin your relationship with your hostess, treat her like a hotel clerk. Americans often assume they'll get new towels each day. The Irish don't, and neither will you. Hang them up to dry and reuse. Some B&Bs stock rooms with a hot-water pot, cups, tea bags, and coffee packets (if you prefer decaf, buy a jar at a grocery and dump the contents into a baggie for easy packing). B&Bs have plenty of stairs. Expect good exercise and be happy you packed lightly.

In B&Bs, no two showers are alike. Sometimes you'll encounter "telephone" showers—a hand-held nozzle in a bathtub. Many B&Bs have been retrofitted with plumbing, and water is heated individually for each shower rather than by one central heating system. While the switch is generally left on, in some rooms you'll have a hot-water switch to consider. Any cord hanging from the ceiling is for lights (not emergencies). Once in the shower you'll find a multitude of overly clever mechanisms designed to somehow get the right amount and temperature of water. Good luck.

Cheap Modern Hotels

Hotel chains, offering predictably comfortable accommodations at reasonable prices, are popping up in the center of big cities in Ireland. The biggies are Jurys Inn (call their hotels directly or book online, reservations tel. 01/607-0000, U.S. tel. 800/843-3311,

www.jurys.com), Comfort/Quality Inns (Republic of Ireland tel.
1-800-500-600, Northern Ireland tel. 0800-444-444, U.S. tel.
800/654-6200, www.choicehotels.com), and Travelodge (also has
freeway locations for tired drivers, reservation center in Britain,
tel. 08700-850-950, www.travelodge.co.uk).

These super-convenient hotels offer simple, clean, and
modern rooms for up to four people (2 adults/2 children) for
€100–150, depending on the location. Most rooms have a double
bed, single bed, five-foot trundle bed, private shower, WC, and
TV. Hotels usually have an attached restaurant, good security,
and a 24-hour staffed reception desk. Of course, they're as cozy
as a Motel 6, but they're great for families, and many travelers
love them. You can book over the phone (or online) with a credit
card, then pay when you check in. When you check out, just drop
off the key, Lee.

Making Reservations

It's possible to travel at any time of year without reservations, but
given the high stakes, erratic accommodation values, number of people traveling with this book, and the quality of the gems I've listed,
I highly recommend calling ahead for rooms at least a few days in
advance as you travel. When tourist crowds are down, you might
make a habit of calling your hotel between 9:00 and 10:00 on the day
you plan to arrive, when the hotel knows who'll be checking out and
just which rooms will be available. I've taken great pains to list telephone numbers with long-distance instructions (see "Telephones,
Mail, and E-mail," above; also see the appendix). Get a phone card
and use it to confirm and reconfirm as you travel. A hotel reception-
ist will trust you and hold a room until 16:00 without a deposit,
though some will ask for a credit-card number.

*Honor your reservations or cancel by phone: Trusting travelers to
show up is a huge, stressful issue and a financial risk for small B&B
owners.* I promised the owners of the places I list that you will be
reliable when you make a telephone reservation; please don't let
them (or me) down. If you'll be delayed or won't make it, simply
call in. Americans are notorious for reserving B&Bs long in
advance and never showing up (causing B&B owners to lose
money—and respect for Americans). Being late is no problem
if you are in telephone contact. Calling long distance is cheap and
easy from public phone booths.

While it's generally easy to find a room, a few national holidays
jam things up (especially "bank holiday" Mondays) and merit reservations long in advance. Mark these dates in red on your travel calendar: Good Friday; Easter and Easter Monday (April 20_21 in 2003);
the first Mondays in May, June, and August; Christmas; December

26; and New Year's Day. Monday bank holidays are preceded by busy weekends; book the entire weekend in advance.

If you know exactly which dates you need and really want a particular place, reserve a room before you leave home. To reserve from home, call, e-mail, or fax the hotel. To fax or e-mail, use the form in the appendix (online at www.ricksteves.com /reservation). A two-night stay in August would be "2 nights, 16/8/03 to 18/8/03"—Europeans write the date day/month/year, and hotel jargon uses your day of departure. You'll often receive a letter back requesting one night's deposit. Your credit-card number and expiration date will usually be accepted as a deposit, though you may need to send a signed traveler's check or a bank draft in the local currency. If your credit card is the deposit, you can pay with your card or cash when you arrive; if you don't show up, you'll be billed for one night. Reconfirm your reservations a few days in advance for safety (or you may be bumped—really). Also, don't just assume you can extend. Take the time to consider in advance how long you'll stay.

Hostels

Ireland has hostels of all shapes and sizes. They can be historic castles or depressing huts, serene and comfy or overrun by noisy school groups. Unfortunately, many of the International Youth Hostel Federation (IYHF) hostels have become overpriced, and, in general, I no longer recommend them. The only time I do is if you're on a very tight budget, want to cook your own meals, or are traveling with a group that likes to sleep on bunk beds in big rooms. But many of the informal private hostels are more fun, easy-going, and cheaper. These alternatives to IYHF hostels are more common than ever and allow you to enjoy the benefits of hosteling.

If you're traveling alone, hosteling is the best way to conquer hotel loneliness. Hostels are also a tremendous source of local and budget travel information. And if you hostel selectively, you'll enjoy historical and interesting buildings.

Hostels of Europe (U.S. tel. 519/251-8821, www.hostelserope .com) and the Internet Guide to Hostelling (www.hostels.com) have good listings. Ireland's Independent Holiday Hostels (www .hostels-ireland.com) is a network of 145 independent hostels, requiring no membership and welcoming all ages. All IHH hostels are approved by the Irish Tourist Board.

You'll pay an average of €16 for a bed, €2 for sheets, and €3 for breakfast. Anyone of any age can hostel in Ireland. While there are no membership concerns for private hostels, IYHF hostels require membership. Those without cards simply buy one-night guest memberships for €2.50. You can book online for many hostels.

Eating

Ireland has long been labeled the "land of potatoes," but you'll find modern-day Irish cuisine delicious and varied, from vegetables, meat, and dairy products to fresh and salt-water fish. Try the local specialties wherever you happen to be eating.

The traditional breakfast, the "Irish Fry" (known in the North as the "Ulster Fry"), is a hearty way to start the day—with juice, tea or coffee, cereal, eggs, bacon, sausage, a grilled tomato, sautéed mushrooms, and optional black pudding (made from pigs' blood). Toast is served with butter and marmalade. This meal tides many travelers over until dinner. But there's nothing un-Irish about skipping the "fry"—few locals actually start their day with this heavy traditional breakfast. You can simply skip the heavier fare and enjoy the cereal, juice, toast, and tea.

Many B&Bs don't serve breakfast until 8:00. If you need an early start, ask politely if it's possible. While they may not make you a cooked breakfast, they can usually put out cereal, toast, juice, and coffee.

Picnicking saves time and money. Try boxes of orange juice (pure, by the liter), fresh bread (especially Irish soda bread), tasty Cashel blue cheese, meat, a tube of mustard, local eatin' apples, bananas, small tomatoes, a small tub of yogurt (they're drinkable), rice crackers, gorp or nuts, plain "digestive biscuits" (the chocolate-covered ones melt), and any local specialties. At open-air markets and supermarkets you can get produce in small quantities. Supermarkets often have good deli sections, packaged sandwiches, and sometimes salad bars. I often munch a relaxed "meal on wheels" in a car, train, or bus to save 30 precious minutes for sightseeing.

At classier restaurants, look for "early-bird specials," allowing you to eat well and affordably, but early (around 17:30–19:00, last order by 19:00). At a sit-down place with table service, tip around 10 percent—unless the service charge is already listed on the bill (for details, see "Tipping" sidebar on next page).

Pub Grub and Beer

Pubs are a basic part of the Irish social scene, and whether you're a teetotaler or a beer guzzler, they should be a part of your travel here. Pubs, short for "public houses," serve as the community's living room and gossip center, as well as watering hole. Pub grub gets better every year and is Ireland's best eating value. For around $6–9, you can get a basic budget hot lunch or dinner in friendly surroundings.

Pub menus consist of a hearty assortment of traditional dishes such as Irish stew (mutton with mashed potatoes, onions, carrots, and herbs); soups and chowders; coddle (bacon, pork sausages,

Tipping

Tipping in Ireland isn't as automatic and generous as it is in the United States, but for special service, tips are appreciated, if not expected. As in the United States, the proper amount depends on your resources, tipping philosophy, and the circumstance, but some general guidelines apply.

Restaurants: Tipping is an issue only at restaurants and fancy pubs that have waiters and waitresses. If you order your food at a counter, don't tip.

If the menu states that service is included—generally about 10 percent—there's no need to tip beyond that. If service isn't included, tip about 10 percent by rounding up. You can hand the tip to the waiter together with the amount for the bill.

Taxis: To tip the cabbie, round up. For a typical ride, round up to a maximum of 10 percent (to pay a €4.50 fare, give €5; for a €28 fare, give €30). If the cabbie hauls your bags and zips you to the airport to help you catch your flight, you might want to toss in a little more. But if you feel like you're being driven in circles or otherwise ripped off, skip the tip.

Special Services: Tour guides at public sites might hold out their hands for tips after they give their spiel; if I've already paid for the tour, I don't tip extra, though some tourists do give a euro, particularly for a job well done.

Hotels sometimes bill you for a service charge. I don't tip at hotels (whether or not a service charge has been tacked on), but if you're a tipper, give the porter about a euro for carrying bags and leave a couple euros in your room at the end of your stay for the maid if the room was kept clean.

In general, if someone in the service industry does a super job for you, a tip of a euro or two is appropriate…but not required.

When in doubt, ask. If you're not sure whether (or how much) to tip for a service, ask your hotelier or the TI; they'll fill you in on how it's done on their turf.

potatoes, and onions stewed in layers); fish and chips; and collar and cabbage (boiled bacon coated in breadcrumbs and brown sugar, then baked and served with cabbage). Irish bread nicely rounds out a meal. In coastal areas, a lot of seafood is available, such as mackerel, mussels, and Atlantic salmon. There's seldom table service in Irish pubs. Order drinks and meals at the bar. Pay as you order, and don't tip.

I recommend certain pubs, and your B&B host is usually up-to-date on the best neighborhood pub grub. Ask for advice (but adjust for nepotism and cronyism, which run rampant).

When you say "a beer, please" in an Irish pub, you'll get a pint of Guinness (the black beauty with a blonde head). If you want a small beer, ask for a glass or a half pint. Never rush your bartender when he's pouring a Guinness. It takes time—almost sacred time.

The Irish take great pride in their beer. At pubs, long hand pulls are used to pull the traditional rich-flavored "real ales" up from the cellar. These are the connoisseur's favorites: They're fermented naturally, vary from sweet to bitter, and often include a hoppy or nutty flavor. Experiment with the obscure local micro-brews (the best are at the Porter House in Dublin's Temple Bar). Short hand pulls at the bar mean colder, fizzier, mass-produced, and less-interesting keg beers. Stout is dark and more bitter, like Guinness. If you don't like Guinness, try it in Ireland. It doesn't travel well and is better in its homeland. Murphy's is a very good Guinness-like stout, but a bit smoother and milder. For a cold, refreshing, basic American-style beer, ask for a lager such as Harp. Ale drinkers swear by Smithwick's. Caffrey's is a newcomer that's a satisfying cross between stout and ale. Try the draft cider (sweet or dry)...carefully. Teetotalers can order a soft drink.

Pubs are generally open daily from 11:00 to 23:30 and Sunday from noon to 22:30. Children are served food and soft drinks in pubs (sometimes in a courtyard or the restaurant section), and you must be 18 to order a beer. A cup of darts is free for the asking.

You're a guest on your first night; after that you're a regular. A wise Irishman once said, "It never rains in a pub." The relaxed, informal atmosphere feels like a refuge from daily cares. Women traveling alone need not worry—you'll become part of the pub family in no time. By the way, Irish pubs are usually smoky; don't waste time looking for a smoke-free one.

It's a tradition to buy your table a round and then for each person to reciprocate. If an Irishman buys you a drink, thank him by saying, "*Guh rev mah a gut.*" Offer him a toast in Irish— "*Slahn chuh!*" A good excuse for a conversation is to ask to be taught a few words of Gaelic.

Craic (pron. crack), the art of conversation, is the sport that accompanies drinking in a pub. People are there to talk. If you feel a bit awkward, remind yourself of that. To encourage conver-sation, stand or sit at the bar, not at a table.

Here's a goofy excuse for some *craic:* Ireland—small as it is— has many dialects. People from Cork are famous for talking very fast (and in a squeaky voice)—so fast that some even talk in letters alone. ABCD fish? (Anybody see the fish?) DR no fish. (There are no fish.) DR fish. (There are fish.) CDBDIs? (See the beady eyes?) OIBJ DR fish. (Oh aye, be Jeeze, there are fish.) For a possibly more-appropriate spin, replace the fish with "bird" (girl). This is obscure, but your pub neighbor may understand and enjoy hearing it. If nothing else, you won't seem so intimidating to him anymore.

Traditional Irish Music

Traditional music is alive and popular in pubs throughout Ireland. "Sessions" (musical evenings) may be planned and advertised or impromptu. Traditionally, musicians just congregate and jam. There will generally be a fiddle, a flute or tin whistle, a guitar, a *bodhrán* (goatskin drum), and maybe an accordion. Things usually get going around 21:30 or 22:00. Last call for drinks is around 23:30.

The *bodhrán* is played with a small two-headed club. The performer's hand stretches the skin to change the tone and pitch. The wind and string instruments embellish melody lines with lots of improvised ornamentation. Occasionally the fast-paced music will stop and one person will sing an a cappella "lament." This is the one time when the entire pub will stop to listen as sad lyrics fill the smoke-stained room. Stories—ranging from struggles against English rule to love songs—are always heartfelt. Spend a lament enjoying the faces in the crowd. A *ceilidh* (pron. KAY-lee) is an evening of music and dance...an Irish hoedown.

The music comes in sets of three songs. Whoever happens to be leading determines the next song only as the song the group is playing is about to be finished. If he wants to pass on the decision, it's done with eye contact and a nod.

A session can be magic or lifeless. If the chemistry is right, it's one of the great Irish experiences. The music churns intensely while members of the group casually enjoy exploring each other's musical style. The drummer dodges the fiddler's playful bow with his half-ash cigarette sticking straight from the middle of his mouth. Sipping their pints, they skillfully maintain a faint but steady buzz. The floor on the musicians' platform is stomped paint-free, and bar-maids scurry artfully through the commotion, gathering towers of empty cream-crusted glasses. Make yourself right at home, drumming the table in time with the music. Talk to your neighbor. Locals often have an almost evangelical interest in explaining the music.

Stranger in a Strange Land

We travel all the way to Europe to enjoy differences—to become temporary locals. You'll experience frustrations. There are certain truths that we find God-given and self-evident, such as cold beer,

ice in drinks, sunshine, bottomless cups of coffee, and driving on
the right side of the road. One of the benefits of travel is the eye-
opening realization that there are logical, civil, and even better
alternatives. A willingness to go local ensures that you'll enjoy a
full dose of hospitality.

Back Door Manners

When updating this book, I hear over and over again that my
readers are considerate and fun to have as guests. Thank you for
traveling as temporary locals who are sensitive to the culture.
It's a joy to follow you in my travels.

Send Me a Postcard, Drop Me a Line

If you enjoy a successful trip with the help of this book and would
like to share your discoveries, please fill out the survey at the end
of this book and send it to me at Europe Through the Back Door,
Box 2009, Edmonds, WA 98020. I personally read and value all
feedback. Thanks in advance—it helps a lot.

For our latest travel information, tap into www.ricksteves.com.
To check for any updates for this book, visit www.ricksteves.com
/update. My e-mail address is rick@ricksteves.com. Anyone can
request a free issue of our newsletter (by going online or calling
425/771-8303).

Judging from the happy postcards I receive from travelers,
it's safe to assume you're on your way to a great, affordable
vacation—with the finesse of an independent, experienced
traveler. Thanks, and happy travels!

BACK DOOR TRAVEL PHILOSOPHY
from *Rick Steves' Europe Through the Back Door*

Travel is intensified living—maximum thrills per minute and one of the last great sources of legal adventure. Travel is freedom. It's recess, and we need it.

Experiencing the real Europe requires catching it by surprise, going casual . . . "through the Back Door."

Affording travel is a matter of priorities. (Make do with the old car.) You can travel—simply, safely, and comfortably—anywhere in Europe for $80 a day plus transportation costs. In many ways, spending more money only builds a thicker wall between you and what you came to see. Europe is a cultural carnival, and, time after time, you'll find that its best acts are free and the best seats are the cheap ones.

A tight budget forces you to travel close to the ground, meeting and communicating with the people, not relying on service with a purchased smile. Never sacrifice sleep, nutrition, safety, or cleanliness in the name of budget. Simply enjoy the local-style alternatives to expensive hotels and restaurants.

Extroverts have more fun. If your trip is low on magic moments, kick yourself and make things happen. If you don't enjoy a place, maybe you don't know enough about it. Seek the truth. Recognize tourist traps. Give a culture the benefit of your open mind. See things as different but not better or worse. Any culture has much to share.

Of course, travel, like the world, is a series of hills and valleys. Be fanatically positive and militantly optimistic. If something's not to your liking, change your liking. Travel is addictive. It can make you a happier American as well as a citizen of the world. Our Earth is home to six billion equally important people. It's humbling to travel and find that people don't envy Americans. They like us, but, with all due respect, they wouldn't trade passports.

Globe-trotting destroys ethnocentricity. It helps you understand and appreciate different cultures. Travel changes people. It broadens perspectives and teaches new ways to measure quality of life. Many travelers toss aside their hometown blinders. Their prized souvenirs are the strands of different cultures they decide to knit into their own character. The world is a cultural yarn shop. And Back Door travelers are weaving the ultimate tapestry. Come on, join in!

REPUBLIC OF IRELAND

- The Republic of Ireland is 70,000 square kilometers, or 27,000 square miles (slightly larger than West Virginia).
- Population 3.8 million (54 per square kilometer, increasing slowly, 91 percent Catholic).
- 1 euro (€) = about $1.

Though a relatively small island, Ireland has had a disproportionately large impact on the rest of the world. For hundreds of years, Ireland's greatest export has been its friendly yet feisty people. Geographically isolated in the damp attic of Dark Age Europe, Christian Irish monks tended the flickering flame of literacy, then bravely reintroduced it to the barbaric Continent. Later, pressure from wars and famines at home combined with opportunities abroad compelled many Irish to leave their island and scramble for a better life in far-flung America, Canada, and Australia.

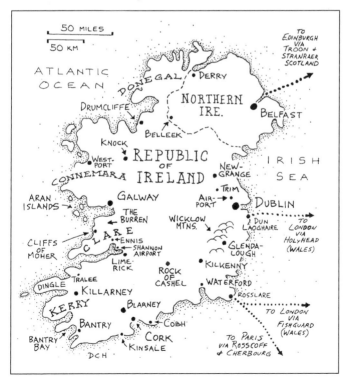

The Republic of Ireland is only 80 years old, but its inhabitants proudly claim their nation to be the only modern independent state to sprout from Celtic roots (the Romans never bothered to come over and organize the wild Irish). Through the persuasive and culturally enlightened approach of early missionaries such as St. Patrick, Ireland may also be the only country to have initially converted to Christianity without bloodshed. The influences of later Viking raiders and Norman soldiers of fortune were absorbed while the 750-year shadow of English occupation was endured.

Just a few decades ago, Ireland was an isolated agricultural economic backwater that had largely missed out on the Industrial Revolution. Membership in the European Union began to turn things around and the Irish government instituted far-sighted tax laws to entice foreign corporations to set up shop in Ireland.

Today the Republic enjoys a renaissance as its Celtic Tiger economy attracts expatriate Irish and new foreign investment. More than 40 percent of the Irish population is under 25 years old, leading many high-tech and pharmaceutical firms to take advantage of this young, well-educated, English-speaking labor force. Microsoft, Intel, Dell, Gateway, Apple, Compaq, and IBM all have factories here (welcome to the "Silicon Bog"). Pfizer makes Viagra in Ringaskiddy, County Cork. And for the first time Ireland has also become a destination for Third World emigrants seeking a better life . . . a switch from the days when Irish fled to start new lives abroad.

The resilient Irish character was born of dark humor, historical reverence, and an optimistic, "we'll get 'em next time" rebel spirit. The Catholic Church still plays a major part in Irish life, though its influence is less apparent these days. RTE (the national radio and TV station) still pauses for 30 seconds at noon and 18:00 to broadcast the chimes of the Angelus bells.

The vast majority of Irish people speak English, but you'll be treated to some Irish Gaelic if you venture to the western Irish fringe.

At first glance, Ireland's landscape seems unspectacular, with few mountains over 3,000 feet and an interior consisting mostly of grazing pastures and peat bogs. But its slowly seductive beauty grows on you. The gentle rainfall, called "soft weather" by the locals, really does create 40 shades of green and quite a few rainbows as well. Ancient moss-covered ring forts crouch in lush valleys, while stone-strewn monastic ruins and lone castle turrets brave the wind on nearby hilltops. Charming fishing villages dot the coast near rugged, wave-battered cliffs. Slow down to contemplate the checkerboard patterns created by the rock walls outlining the many fields. Examine the colorful small-town shop fronts that proudly state the name of the proprietor.

Irish food may be better than you expected. For a hearty traditional meal, try Irish stew (made from lamb, carrots, and potatoes) or bacon and cabbage. A *boxty* is kind of a potato pancake rolled over like a taco and filled with fish, meat, or vegetables. *Champ* is potato mashed with milk and onions. You'll have to try a Guinness in Ireland, although some find the dark stout beer to be an acquired taste. For a change, sample the local ale called Smithwick's or a Bulmers hard apple cider.

DUBLIN

With reminders of its stirring history and rich culture on every corner, Ireland's capital and largest city is a sightseer's delight. Dublin's fair city will have you humming "Cockles and mussels, alive, alive-O."

Founded as a Viking trading settlement in the ninth century, Dublin grew to be a center of wealth and commerce second only to London in the British Empire. Dublin, the seat of English rule in Ireland for 700 years, was the heart of a "civilized" Anglo-Irish area (eastern Ireland) known as "the Pale." Anything "beyond the Pale" was considered uncultured and almost barbaric . . . purely Irish.

The Golden Age of English Dublin was the 18th century. The British Empire was on a roll, and Dublin was right there with it. Largely rebuilt during this Georgian era, Dublin—even with its tattered edges—became an elegant and cultured capital.

Then nationalism and human rights got in the way. The ideas of the French Revolution inspired Irish intellectuals to buck British rule and, after the revolt of 1798, life in Dublin was never quite the same. But the 18th century left a lasting imprint on the city. Georgian (that's British for neoclassical) squares and boulevards gave the city an air of grandness. The National Museum, National Gallery, and many government buildings are in the Georgian section of town. Few buildings (notably Christ Church Cathedral and St. Patrick's Cathedral) survive from before this Georgian period.

In the 19th century, with the closing of the Irish Parliament, the famine, and the beginnings of the struggle for independence, Dublin was treated—and felt—more like a colony than a partner. The tension culminated in the Rising of 1916, independence, and the tragic civil war. With many of its elegant streets left in ruins, Dublin emerged as the capital of the only former colony in Europe.

While bullet-pocked buildings and dramatic statues keep memories of Ireland's recent struggle for independence alive, it's boom time now, and the city is looking to a bright future. Locals are enjoying the "Celtic Tiger" economy—the best in Europe—while visitors enjoy a big-town cultural scene wrapped in a small-town smile.

Planning Your Time

On a three-week trip through Ireland, Dublin deserves three nights and two days. Consider this aggressive sightseeing plan:

Day 1: 10:15–Trinity College guided walk, 11:00–Book of Kells and Old Library, 12:00–Browse Grafton Street, lunch there or picnic on Merrion Square, 13:30–Visit Number Twenty-Nine Georgian House, 15:00–National Museum, 17:00–Return to hotel, rest, have dinner—eat well for less during "early-bird specials," 19:30–Evening walk (musical or literary), 22:00–Irish music in Temple Bar area.

Day 2: 10:00–Dublin Castle tour, 11:00–Historic town walk, 13:00–Lunch, 14:00–O'Connell Street walk, 16:00–Kilmainham Jail, 18:00–Guinness Brewery tour finishing with view of city, Evening–Catch a play, concert, or Comhaltas traditional music in Dun Laoghaire (pron. DUN leary).

Orientation (area code: 01)

Greater Dublin sprawls with over a million people—nearly a third of the country's population. But the center of touristic interest is a tight triangle between O'Connell Bridge, St. Stephen's Green, and Christ Church Cathedral. Within this triangle you'll find Trinity College (Book of Kells), Grafton Street (top pedestrian shopping zone), Temple Bar (trendy nightlife center), Dublin Castle, and the hub of most city tours and buses.

The River Liffey cuts the town in two. Focus on the southern half (where nearly all your sightseeing will take place). Dublin's main drag, O'Connell Street (near Abbey Theater and the outdoor produce market) runs north of the river to the central O'Connell Bridge, then continues as the main city axis—mostly as Grafton Street—to St. Stephen's Green. The only major sights outside your easy-to-walk triangle are the Kilmainham Jail and the Guinness Brewery (both west of the center).

Tourist Information

Dublin's main tourist information office (TI) is a big shop with little to offer other than promotional fliers and long lines (Mon–Sat 9:00–17:30, Sun July–Aug only 10:30–15:00, located in a former church on Suffolk Street, 1 block off Grafton Street,

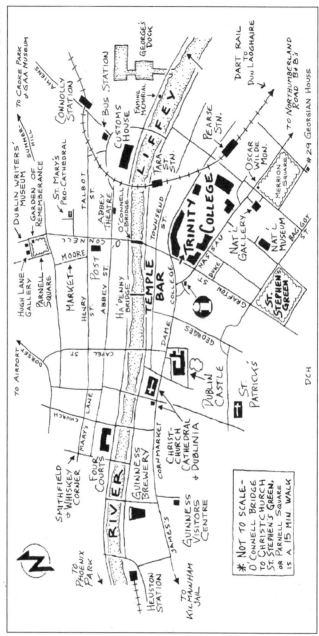

tel. 01/605-7700, www.visitdublin.com). It has an American Express office, car-rental agency, bus-info desk, café, and traditional knick-knacks. But perhaps its greatest value is the chance to peruse the rack opposite the info counter and pick up brochures for destinations throughout Ireland. There's also a TI at the airport (daily 8:00–22:00) and one at the Dun Laoghaire ferry terminal.

While you can buy the TI's lousy map for €0.50, its free newspaper *(The Guide to Dublin)* has the same one on its staple page. The handy *Dublin's Top Visitor Attractions* booklet has a small map and the latest on all of the town's sights—many more than I list here (€3.50, sold at TI bookshop without any wait). For a schedule of happenings in town, check the minimal calendar of events inside *The Guide to Dublin* newspaper (free at TI), or better, buy the informative *In Dublin* at any newsstand (published fortnightly, €2.50).

The excellent *Collins Illustrated Dublin Map* (€8 at TIs and newsstands) is the ultimate city map, listing just about everything of interest, along with helpful opinions.

Arrival in Dublin

By Train: Dublin has two stations. Heuston Station, on the west end of town, serves west and southwest Ireland (a 30-minute walk from O'Connell Bridge; take taxi or bus #90 instead, see below). Connolly Station—which serves the north, northwest, and Rosslare—is closer to the center (a 10-min walk from O'Connell Bridge). Each station has a luggage-check facility and ATMs.

Bus #90 runs along the river, connecting both train stations, the bus station, and the city center (€0.85, 6/hr). When you're leaving Dublin, to reach Heuston Station from the city center, catch bus #90 on the south side of the river; to get to Connolly Station and the Busaras bus station from the city center, catch #90 on the north side of the river.

By Bus: Bus Eireann, Ireland's national bus company, uses the Busaras Central Bus Station next to Connolly Station (10-min walk or short ride on bus #90 to the city center).

By Ferry: Irish Ferries dock at the mouth of the River Liffey (near the town center), while the Stena Line docks at Dun Laoghaire (easy DART train connections into Dublin, at least 3/hr, 20 min).

By Plane: The airport has ATMs, change bureaus, car-rental agencies, baggage check, a café, and a supermarket at the parking lot. Taxis from the airport into Dublin cost about €18, to Dun Laoghaire about €32.

Airport Buses: Consider buying a bus pass that covers the Airlink bus into town (see "Getting Around Dublin," below), but read this first to see if Airlink is best for you. To get to the recommended accommodations in the **city center**, take Airlink bus #748 (not #747) and ask the driver which stop is closest to your hotel (€4.50, €2.50 with Aer Lingus boarding pass, pay driver, 6/hr, 40 min, connects airport with Heuston train station and Busaras bus station, near Connolly train station). For the **St. Stephen's Green** neighborhood, the Aircoach is your best bet (€5, 4/hr, runs 5:30–22:30; pay driver and confirm best stop for your hotel). If you're staying in **Dun Laoghaire,** take Airlink bus #746 direct to Dun Laoghaire.

City Bus: To get from the airport cheaply to downtown Dublin, take the city bus from the airport; buses marked #16A, #41A, #41B, and #41C go to Marlborough Street, a five-minute walk from O'Connell Bridge (€1.50, exact change required, 3/hr, 40 min).

Helpful Hints
Tourist Victim Support Service: This thoughtful service can be helpful if you run into any problems (Mon–Sat 10:00–18:00, Sun 12:00–18:00, tel. 01/478-5295).

U.S. Embassy: It's on 42 Elgin Road in the Ballsbridge neighborhood (Mon–Fri 8:30–12:00 for passport concerns, tel. 01/668-7122 or 01/668-8777, www.usembassy.ie).

Internet Access: There are Internet cafés on nearly every street. The one at the top of Dame Street (facing Kinlay House) is fast and open 24 hours a day.

Laundry: Capricorn Launderette, a block southwest of Jury's Inn Christ Church on Patrick Street, is full-service only. Allow four hours and about €8 (Mon–Fri 7:30–20:00, Sat 9:00–18:00, Sun 10:00–16:00, tel. 01/473-1779). The All-American Launderette offers self- and full-service options (Mon–Sat 8:30–19:00, Sun 10:00–18:00, 40 South Great George's Street, tel. 01/677-2779).

Car Rental: For Dublin car-rental information, see the appendix.

Festivals: St. Patrick's Day is a five-day extravaganza in Dublin (www.stpatricksday.ie). June 16 is Bloomsday, dedicated to the Irish author James Joyce and featuring the Messenger Bike Rally. On rugby weekends (about 4 per year), hotels raise their prices and are packed. Book ahead during festival times and for any weekend.

Getting around Dublin
You'll do most of Dublin on foot. Big green buses are cheap and cover the city thoroughly. Most lines start at the four quays (pron. keys), or piers, nearest O'Connell Bridge. If you're away

from the center, nearly any bus takes you back downtown. Tell the driver where you're going, and he'll ask for €0.75, €1.05, or €1.30, depending on the number of stops. Bring exact change or lose any excess.

Passes: The bus office at 59 Upper O'Connell Street has free "route network" maps and sells city-bus passes. The three-day Rambler costs €9 (covers Airlink airport bus but not DART trains) and the three-day Short Hop pass costs €13.50 (includes DART but not Airlink). Passes are also sold at each TI (bus info tel. 01/873-4222).

DART: Speedy commuter trains connect Dublin with Dun Laoghaire (ferry terminal and recommended B&Bs, at least 3/hr, 20 min, €1.50).

Taxi: Taxis are honest, plentiful, friendly, and good sources of information (under €6 for most downtown rides, €30 per hour for a guided joyride available from most any cab).

Tours of Dublin

While the physical treasures of Dublin are mediocre by European standards, the city has a fine story to tell and people with a natural knack for telling it. It's a good town for walking tours and the competition is fierce. Pamphlets touting creative walks are posted all over town. There are medieval walks, literary walks, 1916 Easter Rising walks, Georgian Dublin walks, and more. The evening walks are great ways to meet other travelers.

▲▲**Historical Walking Tour**—This is your best introductory walk. A group of hardworking history graduates—many of whom claim to have done more than just kiss the Blarney Stone—enliven Dublin's basic historic strip (Trinity College, Old Parliament House, Dublin Castle, and Christ Church Cathedral) with the story of their city, from its Viking origin to the present. Guides speak at length about the roots of Ireland's struggle with Britain. As you listen to your guide's story, you stand in front of buildings that aren't much to see but are lots to talk about (daily May–Sept at 11:00 and 15:00, Oct–April only Fri, Sat, and Sun at 12:00). From May to September, the same group offers more focused tours at noon (1916 Easter Rising "Terrible Beauty" walks on Mon and Fri; juicy slice-of-old-life Dublin "Sex & the City" walks on Sat, Sun, and Wed; and gritty "Architecture & Society" walks on Tue and Thu). All walks last two hours and cost €10 (but get the student discount with this book, depart from front gate of Trinity College, private walks also available, tel. 01/878-0227, www.historicalinsights.ie).

The 1916 Rebellion company offers, as you might guess, **1916 Rebellion Walks** (€10 but get student price with this book, 2 hrs, daily mid-April–Sept Mon–Sat at 11:30, Sun at

13:00, depart from International Bar at 23 Wicklow Street, tel. 01/676-2493, www.1916rising.com).

▲**Dublin Literary Pub Crawl**—Two actors take 30 or so tourists on a walk, stopping at four pubs. Half the time is spent enjoying their entertaining banter, which introduces the novice to the high *craic* (conversation) of Joyce, O'Casey, and Yeats. The two-hour tour is punctuated with 20-minute pub breaks (free time). While the beer lubricates the social fun, it dilutes the content of the evening (€10, April–Oct daily at 19:30, plus Sun at noon; Nov–March Thu–Sun only; can normally just show up but call ahead in July–Aug when it can fill up, meet upstairs in Duke Pub, off Grafton on Duke Street, tel. 01/670-5602, www.dublinpubcrawl.com).

▲▲**Traditional Irish-Music Pub Crawl**—This is similar to the Literary Pub Crawl but features music. You meet upstairs at 19:30 at Gogarty's Pub (Temple Bar area, corner of Fleet and Anglesea) and spend 40 minutes each in the upstairs rooms of three pubs listening to two musicians talk about, play, and sing traditional Irish music. While having only two musicians makes the music a bit thin (Irish music aficionados will tell you you're better off just finding a good session), the evening, though touristy, is not gimmicky. It's an education in traditional Irish music. The musicians demonstrate a few instruments and really enjoy introducing rookies to their art (€10, €1 discount with this book, beer extra, April–Oct nightly; Nov and Feb–March Fri–Sat only, allow 2.5 hrs, expect up to 50 tourists, tel. 01/478-0193).

▲**Hop-on Hop-off Bus Tours**—Two companies (Dublin City Tours and City Sightseeing/Guide Friday) offer hop-on hop-off bus tours of Dublin, doing virtually identical 90-minute circuits, allowing you to hop on and off at your choice of about 16 stops. Buses are mostly topless, with running live commentaries. They go to Guinness Brewery but not to Kilmainham Jail. Buy your ticket on board. Each company's map, free with ticket, details various discounts you'll get on Dublin's sights. Your ticket's valid for the day you purchase it—not for 24 hours (daily, 4/hr from 9:30–17:30, until 18:30 in summer, fewer buses Nov–March with shorter hours 9:30–15:30). **Dublin City Tour** runs the green-and-cream buses (€10, driver narrates, tel. 01/873-4222). **City Sightseeing/Guide Friday** costs a bit more but includes Phoenix Park and comes with a guide and a driver, rather than a driver who guides (€12, black-and-gold buses, tel. 01/676-5377).

▲**Viking Splash Tours**—If you'd like to ride in a WWII amphibious vehicle—driven by a Viking-costumed guide who is as liable to spout history as he is to growl—this is for you. The tour starts with a group roar from the Viking within us all. At first the guide talks as if he were a Viking ("When we came here in 841 . . . "), but soon the patriot emerges as he tags Irish history onto the sights you pass. Near the end of the 75-minute tour (punctuated by occasional group roars at passersby), you don a life jacket for a slow spin up and down a boring canal. Kids who expect a Viking splash may feel they've been trapped in a classroom, but historians will enjoy the talk more than the gimmick (€14, Feb–Nov Tue–Sun 10:00–17:00, sometimes later in summer, closed Mon, about hourly, depart from Bull Alley, beside St. Patrick's Cathedral; ticket office at 64–65 Patrick Street, on gray days boat is covered but still breezy—dress warmly, tel. 01/855-3000, www.vikingsplashtours.com).

Sights—Dublin's Trinity College
▲**Trinity College**—Founded in 1592 by Queen Elizabeth I to establish a Protestant way of thinking about God, Trinity has long been Ireland's most prestigious college. Originally the student body was limited to rich Protestant males. Women were admitted in 1903, and Catholics, though allowed entrance by the school much earlier, were given formal permission to study at Trinity in the 1970s. Today half of Trinity's 12,500 students are women, and 70 percent are culturally Catholic (although only about 20 percent of Irish youth are churchgoing).

▲▲**Trinity College Tour**—Inside the gate of Trinity, students organize and lead 30-minute tours of their campus. You'll get a rundown on the mostly Georgian architecture; a peek at student life, both in the early days and today; and enjoy the company of a witty Irish college kid who talks about the school (late May–Sept daily 10:15–15:30; late Feb and early May usually weekends only, weather permitting; look for small blue kiosk inside gate, the €9 tour fee includes the €7 fee to see the Book of Kells, where the tour leaves you).

▲▲▲**Book of Kells in the Trinity Old Library**—The only Trinity campus interior welcoming tourists—just follow the signs—is the Old Library, with its precious Book of Kells. The first-class *Turning Darkness into Light* exhibit puts the 680-page illuminated manuscript in its historical and cultural context and prepares you for the original book and other precious manuscripts in the treasury. The exhibit is a one-way affair leading to the actual treasury, which shows only four books under glass in one display case. Make a point to spend at least half an hour in the exhibit (before reaching the actual Book of Kells). The video clips showing the exacting care that went into the "monkuscripts" and the ancient art of bookbinding are especially interesting.

Written on vellum (baby calfskin) in the eighth or early ninth century—probably by Irish monks in Iona, Scotland—this

South Dublin

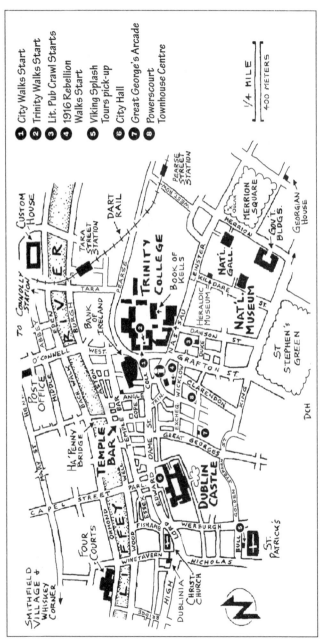

1 City Walks Start
2 Trinity Walks Start
3 Lit. Pub Crawl Starts
4 1916 Rebellion
  Walks Start
5 Viking Splash
  Tours pick-up
6 City Hall
7 Great George's Arcade
8 Powerscourt
  Townhouse Centre

¼ MILE

400 METERS

enthusiastically decorated copy of the four Gospels was taken to the Irish monastery at Kells in A.D. 806 after a series of Viking raids. Arguably the finest piece of art from what is generally called the Dark Ages, the Book of Kells shows that monastic life in this far fringe of Europe was far from dark. It has been bound into four separate volumes. At any given time, two of the four gospels are on display. The crowd around the one glass case with the treasures can be off-putting, but hold your own and get up close. You'll see four richly decorated, 1,200-year-old pages—two text and two decorated cover pages. The library treasury also displays two other books—likely the Book of Armagh (A.D. 807) and the Book of Durrow (A.D. 680)—neither of which can be checked out.

Next, a stairway leads to the 60-meter-long main chamber of the Old Library (from 1732), stacked to its towering ceiling with 200,000 of the library's oldest books. Here you'll find one of a dozen surviving original copies of the Proclamation of the Irish Republic. Patrick Pearse read these words outside the General Post Office on April 24, 1916, starting the Easter Rising that led to Irish independence. Read the entire thing…imagining it was yours. Notice the inclusive opening phrase and the seven signatories (each of whom was executed). Another national icon is nearby—the oldest surviving Irish harp, from the 15th century (€7, at Trinity College Library, year-round Mon–Sat 9:30–17:00, Sun 9:30–16:30, Oct–May Sun 12:00–16:30, tel. 01/608-2308). A long line often snakes out of the building. It's the line to purchase a ticket—not to actually get in. If you take the Trinity College tour or if you buy the combo-ticket at the *Dublin Experience*, you've already bought your Book of Kells ticket and can scoot right past the line and into the exhibit.

▲*Dublin Experience*—This 40-minute fancy slideshow giving a historic introduction to Dublin is one more tourist movie with the sound turned up. It's good—offering a fine sweeping introduction to the story of Ireland—but pricey and riding on the coattails of the Book of Kells. Considering that the combo-ticket gets you this for half-price and gets you past any Kells line, it's not a bad value (€4.50, or half-price with a €10 combo Kells/*Dublin Experience* ticket, June–Sept daily, showings on the hour 10:00–17:00, in modern arts building across from Trinity Old Library).

Sights—Dublin, South of the River Liffey
▲▲**Dublin Castle**—Built on the spot of the first Viking fortress, this castle was the seat of British rule in Ireland for 700 years. Located where the Poddle and Liffey Rivers came together, making a black pool ("*dubh linn*" in Irish), Dublin Castle was the official residence of the viceroy, who implemented the will of the

British royalty. In this stirring setting, in 1922, the Brits handed power over to Michael Collins and the Irish. Today it's used for fancy state and charity functions. The 45-minute tours offer a room-by-room walk through the lavish state apartments of this most English of Irish palaces (€4.25, 4/hr, Mon–Fri 10:00–17:00, Sat–Sun 14:00–17:00, tel. 01/677-7129). The tour finishes with a look at the foundations of the Norman tower and the best remaining chunk of the 13th-century town wall.

Dublin City Hall—The first neoclassical building in this very neoclassical city stands proudly overlooking Dame Street, in front of the gate to Dublin Castle. Built in 1779 as the Royal Exchange, it introduced the neoclassical style (then very popular on the continent) to Ireland. Step inside (it's free) to feel the prosperity and confidence of Dublin in her 18th-century glory days. In 1852 it became the city hall. Under the grand rotunda, a cycle of heroic paintings tell the city's history. Pay your respects to the 18-foot-tall statue of Daniel O'Connell (the great orator and "liberator" who won Catholic emancipation in 1829 from those vile Protestants over in London). The greeter sits like the Maytag repairman at the information desk, eager to give you more information. Downstairs is a simple *Story of the Capital* exhibition—storyboards and video clips of Dublin's history (€4, Mon–Sat 10:00–17:00, Sun 14:00–17:00).

Dublinia—This tries valiantly, but fails, to be a "bridge to Dublin's medieval past." The amateurish look at the medieval town starts with a walk through dim rooms of tableaus, followed by several rooms of medieval exhibits, a scale model of old Dublin, and an interesting room devoted to medieval fairs. Then, after piles of stairs, you get a tower-top view of Dublin's skyline of churches and breweries (€5.75, €7 includes Christ Church Cathedral, saving you €1.75; April–Sept daily 10:00–17:00, Oct–March daily 11:00–16:00, brass rubbing, coffee shop, across from Christ Church Cathedral, tel. 01/679-4611).

Christ Church Cathedral—The first church here, built of wood in about 1040 by King Sitric, dates back to Viking times. The present structure dates from a mix of periods: Norman and Gothic, but mostly Victorian neo-Gothic (1870s restoration work). The unusually large crypt under the cathedral—actually the oldest building in Dublin—contains stocks, statues, and the cathedral's silver (€3 donation to church, €3 extra for crypt silver exhibition, free brochure with self-guided tour, daily 10:00–17:00). Because of Dublin's British past, neither of its top two churches is Catholic. Christ Church Cathedral and the nearby St. Patrick's Cathedral are both Church of Ireland. In Catholic Ireland they feel hollow and are more famous than visit-worthy.

Evensong: At Christ Church, a 45-minute evensong service is sung regularly (less regularly during the summer) several times a week (Wed at 18:00—girls' choir, Thu at 18:00—adult choir, Sat at 17:00—adult choir, and Sun at 15:30—adult choir). The 13th-century St. Patrick's Cathedral, where Jonathan Swift (author of *Gulliver's Travels*) was dean in the 18th century, also offers even-song (Sun at 15:15, Mon–Fri at 17:30, but not Wed July–Aug).

▲▲▲**National Museum**—Showing off the treasures of Ireland from the Stone Age to modern times, this museum is itself a national treasure and wonderfully digestible under one dome. Ireland's Bronze Age gold fills the center. Up four steps, the prehistoric Ireland exhibit rings the gold. In a corner (behind a 2,000-year-old body), you'll find the treasury with the most famous pieces (brooches, chalices, and other examples of Celtic metalwork) and an 18-minute video (played on request), giving an overview of Irish art through the 13th century. The collection's superstar is the gold, enamel, and amber eighth-century Tara Brooch. Jumping way ahead (and to the opposite side of the hall), a special corridor features *The Road to Independence*, with guns, letters, and death masks recalling the fitful birth of the "Terrible Beauty" (1900–1921, with a focus on the 1916 Easter Rising). The best Viking artifacts in town are upstairs with the medieval collection. If you'll be visiting Cong (in Connemara, near Galway), seek out the original Cross of Cong (free entry, Tue–Sat 10:00–17:00, Sun 14:00–17:00, closed Mon, good café, Kildare Street 2, between Trinity College and St. Stephen's Green). Greatest-hits tours are given several times a day (€1.50, 40 min, tel. 01/677-7444 in morning for schedule). For background information, read "Irish Art" in the Ireland: Past and Present chapter.

▲**National Gallery**—Along with a hall featuring the work of top Irish painters, this has Ireland's best collection of European masters. It's impressive—although not nearly as extensive as those in London or Paris (free, Mon–Sat 9:30–17:30, Thu until 20:30, Sun 12:00–17:30, guided tours on weekends, Merrion Square West, tel. 01/661-5133, www.nationalgallery.ie).

▲▲**Grafton Street**—Once filled with noisy traffic, today Grafton Street is Dublin's liveliest pedestrian shopping mall. A five-minute stroll past street musicians takes you from Trinity College up to St. Stephen's Green (and makes you wonder why American merchants are so terrified of a car-free street). Walking by a buxom statue of "sweet" Molly Malone (known by locals as "the tart with the cart"), you'll soon pass two venerable department stores: the Irish Brown Thomas and the English Marks & Spencer. An alley leads to the Powerscourt Townhouse Shopping Centre, which tastefully fills a converted Georgian mansion. The huge, glass-covered St. Stephen's Green Shopping Centre and the peaceful and green Green itself mark the top of Grafton Street.

▲**St. Stephen's Green**—This city park, originally a medieval commons, was enclosed in 1664 and gradually surrounded with fine Georgian buildings. Today it provides 22 acres of grassy refuge for Dubliners. On a sunny afternoon, it's a wonderful world apart from the big city.

▲▲**Number Twenty-Nine Georgian House**—The carefully restored house at Number 29 Lower Fitzwilliam Street gives an intimate glimpse of middle-class Georgian life—which seems pretty high-class. From the sidewalk, descend the stairs to the basement-level entrance (at the corner of Lower Fitzwilliam and Lower Mount Streets). Start with an interesting 12-minute video (you're welcome to bring in a cup of coffee from the café) before joining your guide, who takes you on a fascinating 35-minute walk through this 1790 Dublin home (€3.25, Tue–Sat 10:00–17:00, Sun 14:00–17:00, closed Mon and last half of Dec, tel. 01/702-6165, www.esb.ie).

▲**Merrion Square**—Laid out in 1762, the square is ringed by elegant Georgian houses decorated with fine doors—a Dublin trademark—with elegant knobs and knockers. The park, once the exclusive domain of the residents, is now a delightful public escape. More inviting than St. Stephen's Green, it's ideal for a picnic. If you want to know what "snogging" is, walk through the park on a sunny day. Oscar Wilde, lounging wittily on the corner nearest the town center and surrounded by his clever quotes, provides a fun photo op.

▲**Temple Bar**—This was a Georgian center of craftsmen and merchants. As it fell on hard times in the 19th century, the lower rents attracted students and artists, giving the neighborhood a bohemian flair. With recent government tax incentives and lots of development money, the Temple Bar district has become a thriving cultural (and beer-drinking) hotspot. Today this much-promoted center of trendy shops, cafés, theaters, galleries, pubs with live music, and restaurants feels like the heart of Dublin. Dublin's "Left Bank"—actually on the right bank—fills the cobbled streets between Dame Street and the river. ("Bar" means a walkway along the river.) The central **Meeting House Square** (just off Essex Street) hosts free street theater, a lively organic-produce market (Sat 9:30–15:00), and a book market (Sat 11:00–18:00). The square is surrounded by interesting cultural centers.

For a listing of events and galleries, visit the **Temple Bar Information Centre** (Eustace Street, tel. 01/671-5717, www.temple-bar.ie). Rather than follow particular pub or restaurant recommendations (mine are below, under "Eating"), venture down a few side lanes off the main drag to see what looks good.

The pedestrian-only **Ha' Penny Bridge,** named for the half-pence toll people used to pay to cross it, leads from Temple Bar over the River Liffey to the opposite bank and more sights.

Sights—Dublin, North of the River Liffey

▲▲**O'Connell Bridge**—This bridge spans the River Liffey, which has historically divided the wealthy, cultivated south side from the poorer, cruder north side. While there's plenty of culture north of the river, even today "the north" is considered rougher and less safe. (Currently, the big investment seems to be directed to this area which, in time, is expected to be another fresh and lively prosperity zone.)

From the bridge look upriver (west) as far upstream as you can see. The big concrete building houses the city planning commission. Maddening to locals, this eyesore is in charge of making sure new buildings in the city are built in good taste. It marks (and covers) the place where the Vikings established Dublin in the ninth century.

Across the river stands the Four Courts, today's Supreme Court building, bombed and burned in 1922 during the tragic civil war that followed Irish independence. The closest bridge upstream—the elegant iron Ha' Penny Bridge—leads left into the Temple Bar nightlife district. Just beyond that old-fashioned 19th-century bridge is Dublin's pedestrian Millennium Bridge, inaugurated in 2000. (Note that buses leave from O'Connell Bridge—specifically Aston Quay—for the Guinness Brewery and the Kilmainham Jail.)

Turn 180 degrees and look downstream to see the tall union headquarters—for now the tallest building in the Republic—and lots of cranes. Booming Dublin is developing downstream. The Irish (forever clever tax fiddlers) have subsidized and revitalized this formerly dreary quarter with great success. A short walk downstream along the north bank leads to a powerful series of modern statues memorializing the great famine of 1845–1849.

▲▲**O'Connell Street Stroll**—Dublin's grandest street leads from O'Connell Bridge through the heart of north Dublin. Since the 1740s, it has been a 45-yard-wide promenade. Ever since the first O'Connell Bridge connected it to the Trinity side of town in 1794, it's been Dublin's main drag. (But it was only named O'Connell after independence was won in 1922.) The street, though lined with fast-food and souvenir shops, echoes with history. Take the following stroll:

Statues line O'Connell Street, celebrating great figures in Ireland's fight for independence. At the base of the street stands **Daniel O'Connell** (1775–1847), known as "the Liberator," who

North Dublin

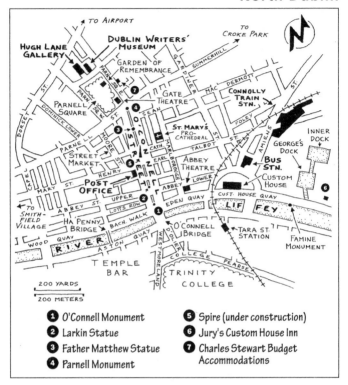

1 O'Connell Monument
2 Larkin Statue
3 Father Matthew Statue
4 Parnell Monument
5 Spire (under construction)
6 Jury's Custom House Inn
7 Charles Stewart Budget Accommodations

founded the Catholic Association and was a strong voice for Irish Catholic rights in the British Parliament.

Looking a block east down Abbey Street you can see the famous **Abbey Theatre**—rebuilt after a fire and now a non-descript modern building. It's still the much-loved home of the Irish National Theatre.

The statue of **James Larkin** honors the founder of the Irish Workers' Union. The one monument that didn't wave an Irish flag—a tall column crowned by a statue of the British hero of Trafalgar, Admiral Nelson—was blown up in 1966...the IRA's contribution to the local celebration of the 50th anniversary of the Easter Rising. This vacant spot will be marked by the 120-yard-tall steel spike called the O'Connell Street Monument (planned for 2003).

The **General Post Office** is not just any P.O. It was from here that Patrick Pearse read the Proclamation of Irish Independence in 1916 and kicked off the Easter Rising. The GPO building itself—a kind of Irish Alamo—was the rebel headquarters and scene of a five-day bloody siege that followed the proclamation. Its facade remains pockmarked with bullet holes. Step inside and trace the battle by studying the well-described cycle of 10 paintings that circle the main hall (open for business and sightseers Mon–Sat 8:00–20:00, Sun 10:00–18:00).

The **Moore Street Market** is nearby. After the GPO, detour left two blocks down people-filled Henry Street and then wander to the right into the busy Moore Street Market (Mon–Sat 8:00–18:00). Many of its merchants have manned the same stall for 30 years. Start a conversation. It's a great workaday scene. You'll see lots of mums with strollers—a reminder that Ireland is Europe's youngest country, with about 40 percent of the population under the age of 25. An immense glass canopy is planned to cover the street market.

Back on O'Connell Street, cross to the meridian and continue your walk. The lampposts display the colorful three-castle city seal. The Latin motto below states, "Happy the city where citizens obey," and the flames rising from the castles symbolize the citizens' zeal to defend Dublin.

St. Mary's Pro-Cathedral, a block east of O'Connell down Cathedral Street, is Dublin's leading Catholic church. But, curiously, it's not a cathedral, even though the pope declared Christ Church one in the 12th century—and later, St. Patrick's. (Stubbornly, the Vatican has chosen to ignore the fact that Christ Church and St. Patrick's haven't been Catholic for centuries.) Completed in 1821, it's done in the style of a Greek temple.

Continuing up O'Connell Street, you'll find a statue of **Father Matthew,** a leader of the temperance movement of the 1830s who, some historians claim, was responsible for enough Irish peasants staying sober to enable Daniel O'Connell to organize them into a political force. (Perhaps understanding this dynamic, the USSR was careful to keep the price of vodka affordable.) The fancy Gresham Hotel is a good place for an elegant tea or beer.

Charles Stewart Parnell stands boldly at the top of O'Connell Street. The names of the four ancient provinces of Ireland and all 32 Irish counties (North *and* South, since this was erected before Independence) ring the statue, honoring the member of Parliament who nearly won Home Rule for Ireland in the late 1800s. (A sex scandal cost him the support of the Church, which let the air out of any chance for a free Ireland.)

Continue straight up Parnell Square East. At the Gate Theater (on the left), Orson Welles and James Mason got their acting starts.

The Garden of Remembrance (top of the square, on left) honors the victims of the 1916 Rising. The park was dedicated by Eamon de Valera in 1966 on the 50th anniversary of the uprising that ultimately led to Irish independence. The bottom of the cross-shaped pool is a mosaic of Celtic weapons, symbolic of how the early Irish would proclaim peace by throwing their weapons into the river. The Irish flag flies above the park: green for Catholics, orange for Protestants, and white for the hope that they can live together in peace. Across the street...

The **Dublin Writers' Museum** fills a splendidly restored Georgian mansion. No country so small has produced such a wealth of literature. As interesting to fans of Irish literature as it is boring to those who aren't, this three-room museum features the lives and works of Dublin's great writers (€4, Mon–Sat 10:00–17:00, Sun 11:00–17:00, June–Aug Mon–Fri until 18:00, helpful audioguide available, 18 Parnell Square North, tel. 01/872-2077). With hometown wits such as Swift, Yeats, Joyce, and Shaw, there is a checklist of residences and memorials to see. Those into James Joyce may want to hike 350 meters east to see the James Joyce Center at 35 North Great George Street (more Joyce memorabilia is in Dun Laoghaire's James Joyce Museum).

Hugh Lane Gallery (next door to the Dublin Writers' Museum) is a fine little gallery in a grand neoclassical building with a bite-size selection of Pre-Raphaelite, French Impressionist, and 19th- and 20th-century Irish paintings (Tue–Thu 9:30–18:00, Fri–Sat 9:30–17:00, Sun 11:00–17:00, closed Mon, tel. 01/874-1903). Sir Hugh went down on the *Lusitania* in 1915; due to an unclear will, his collection is shared by this gallery and the National Gallery in London.

Your walk is over. Here on the north end of town, you'll never be closer to the Gaelic Athletic Association Museum (described below). Otherwise, hop on your skateboard and return to the river.

Sights—Dublin's Smithfield Village

Huge investments may make Smithfield Village—until recently a run-down industrial area—the next Temple Bar. It's worth a look for "Cobblestores" (a redeveloped Duck Lane lined with fancy crafts and gift shops), the Old Jameson Distillery whiskey tour, and a chimney observatory with big Dublin views. The sights are clustered close together, two blocks north of the river behind the Four Courts—the Supreme Court building.

The Old Jameson Distillery—Whiskey fans enjoy visiting the old distillery. You get a 10-minute video, 20-minute tour, and a free shot in the pub. Unfortunately, the "distillery" feels fake and put together for tourism. The Bushmills tour in Northern Ireland

Charles Stewart Parnell (1846–1891)

Parnell, who led the Irish movement for Home Rule, did time in Kilmainham Jail. A Cambridge-educated Protestant and member of Parliament, he had a vision of a modern and free Irish Republic filled mostly with Catholics but not set up as a religious state. Momentum seemed to be on his side. With the British Prime Minister of the time, Gladstone, in favor of a similar form of Home Rule, it looked as if all of Ireland was ripe for independence. Then a sex scandal broke around Parnell and his mistress. The press, egged on by the powerful Catholic bishops (who didn't want a free but secular Irish state), battered away at the scandal until finally Parnell was driven from office. Sadly, after that, Ireland became mired in the Troubles of the 20th century: an awkward independence (1921) featuring a divided island, a bloody civil war, and sectarian violence ever since. It's said Parnell died of a broken heart. Before he did, this great Irish statesman requested to be buried outside of Ireland.

(in a working factory) and the Midleton tour near Cork (in the huge, original factory) are better experiences. If you do take this tour, volunteer energetically when offered the chance to take the "whiskey taste test" at the end (€7, daily 9:30–18:00, last tour at 17:30, Bow Street, tel. 01/807-2355).

The Chimney—Built in 1895 for the distillery, the chimney is now an observatory. Ride the elevator 175 feet up for a Dublin panorama not quite as exciting as the view from the Guinness Brewery's Gravity Bar (overpriced at €6, Mon–Fri 9:30–17:30, Sat–Sun 11:00–17:30, tel. 01/817-3838).

Sights—Outer Dublin

The jail and the Guinness Brewery are the main sights outside of the old center. Combine them in one visit.

▲▲▲**Kilmainham Gaol (Jail)**—Opened in 1796 as the Dublin County Jail and a debtors' prison and considered a model in its day, it was used frequently as a political prison by the British. Many of those who fought for Irish independence were held or executed here, including leaders of the rebellions of 1798, 1803, 1848, 1867, and 1916. National heroes Robert Emmett and Charles Stewart Parnell each did time here. The last prisoner to be held here was Eamon de Valera (later president of Ireland). He was released on July 16, 1924, the day Kilmainham was finally shut down. The buildings, virtually in ruins, were restored in the 1960s. Today it's a shrine to the Nathan Hales of Ireland.

Start your visit with a guided tour (1 hr, 2/hr, includes 25 min in prison chapel for a rebellion-packed video, spend waiting time in museum). It's touching to tour the cells and places of execution while hearing tales of terrible colonialism and heroic patriotism alongside Irish schoolkids who know these names well. The museum is an excellent exhibit on Victorian prison life and Ireland's fight for independence. Don't miss the museum's dimly lit Last Words 1916 hall upstairs, displaying the stirring last letters patriots sent to loved ones hours before facing the firing squad (€4.75, April–Sept daily 9:30–18:00, Oct–March 9:30–17:00, last admission 1 hour before closing; €5 taxi, bus #51b, #78a, or #79 from Aston Quay or Guinness, tel. 01/453-5984). I'd taxi to the jail and then catch the bus from there to Guinness (leaving the prison, take three rights, crossing no streets, to the bus stop and hop bus #51b or #78a).

▲**Guinness Brewery**—A visit to the Guinness Brewery is, for many, a pilgrimage. Arthur Guinness began brewing the famous stout here in 1759. By 1868 it was the biggest brewery in the world. Today the sprawling brewery fills several city blocks. Around the world, Guinness brews more than 10 million pints a day. The home of Ireland's national beer welcomes visitors, for a price, with a sprawling new museum (but there are no tours of the actual working brewery). The museum fills the old fermentation plant, used from 1902 through 1988, vacated, and then opened in 2000 as a huge shrine-like place. Stepping into the middle of the ground floor, look up. A tall beer glass–shaped glass atrium—14 million pints big—leads past four floors of exhibitions and cafés to the skylight. Atop the building, the Gravity Bar provides visitors with a commanding 360-degree view of Dublin—with vistas all the way to the sea—and a free beer. The actual exhibit makes brewing seem more grandiose than it is and treats Arthur like the god of human happiness. Highlights are the cooperage (with old film clips showing the master wood-keg makers plying their now-extinct trade), a display of the brewery's clever ads, and the Gravity Bar, which really is spectacular (€13—including a €4 pint, daily 9:30–17:00, enter on Market Street, bus #78A from Aston Quay near O'Connell Bridge, or bus #123 from Dame Street and O'Connell Street, tel. 01/408-4800). Hop-on, hop-off bus tours stop here.

▲**Gaelic Athletic Association Museum**—The GAA was founded in 1884 as an expression of an Irish cultural awakening. While created to foster the development of Gaelic sports—specifically Irish football and hurling (and to ban English sports such as cricket and rugby)—it played an important part in the fight for independence. This museum, at the newly expanded 97,000-seat Croke

Park Stadium, offers a high-tech, interactive introduction to Ireland's favorite games. Relive the greatest moments in hurling and Irish-football history. Then get involved. Pick up a stick and try hurling, kick a football, and test your speed and balance. A 15-minute film clarifies the connection between sports and Irish politics (€3.75, May–Sept daily 9:30–17:00; Oct–April Mon–Sat 10:00–17:00, Sun 12:00–17:00; on game Sundays the museum is open 12:00–17:00 to new stand ticket-holders only; under the new stand at Croke Park, from O'Connell Street walk 20 min or catch bus #3, #11, #11a, #16, #16a, #16c, or #123; tel. 01/855-8176).

Hurling or Irish Football at Croke Park—Actually seeing a match here, surrounded by incredibly spirited Irish fans, is a fun experience. Hurling is like airborne hockey with no injury time-outs, and Irish football is a rugged form of soccer. Matches are held on most Sunday afternoons outside of winter. Tickets (€15–35) are available at the stadium except during championships.

Greyhound Racing—For an interesting lowbrow look at local life, consider going to the dog races and doing a little gambling (€7, generally Wed, Thu, and Sat at 20:00, Shelbourne Park, tel. 01/668-3502). Greyhounds race on the other days at Harold's Cross Racetrack (Mon, Tue, and Fri at 20:00, tel. 01/497-1081).

Day Trips from Dublin—See the next chapter for information on Newgrange, the Wicklow Mountains, and more.

Shopping

Shops are open roughly Monday to Saturday from 9:00 to 18:00, and until 20:00 on Thursday. They have shorter hours on Sunday (if they're open at all). The best shopping area is Grafton, with its neighboring streets and arcades (such as the fun Great George's Arcade between Great George's and Drury Streets), and nearby shopping centers (Powerscourt and St. Stephen's Green). For antiques, try Francis Street. For a street market, consider Mother Redcaps (all day Fri–Sun, bric-a-brac, antiques, crafts, Back Lane, Christ Church). For produce, noise, and color, visit Moore Street (Mon–Sat 8:00–18:00, near General Post Office). For raw fish, get a whiff of Michan Street (Tue–Sat 7:00–15:00, behind Four Courts building). Saturdays at Temple Bar's Meeting House Square, it's food in the morning (from 9:00) and books in the afternoon (until 18:00). Temple Bar is worth a browse any day for its art, jewelry, new-age paraphernalia, books, music, and gift shops.

Entertainment and Theater in Dublin

Ireland has produced some of the finest writers in both English and Irish, and Dublin houses some of Europe's finest theaters. While Handel's *Messiah* was first performed in Dublin (1742), these days

Dublin is famous for its rock bands (U2, Thin Lizzie, and Sinead O'Connor all got started here).

Abbey Theatre is Ireland's national theater, founded by W. B. Yeats in 1904 to preserve Irish culture during British rule (Lower Street, tel. 01/878-7222, www.abbeytheatre.ie). **Gate Theatre** does foreign plays as well as Irish classics (Cavendish Row, tel. 01/874-4045, www.gate-theatre.ie). **Point Theatre,** once a railway terminus, is now the country's top live-music venue (North Wall quay, tel. 01/836-3633, www.thepoint.ie). At the **National Concert Hall,** the National Symphony Orchestra performs most Friday evenings (Earlsfort Terrace, off St. Stephen's Green, tickets €11–18, tel. 01/475-1666, www.nch.ie). Street theater takes the stage in Temple Bar on summer evenings.

Pub Action: Folk music fills the pubs, and street entertainers are everywhere. For the latest on live theater, music, cultural happenings, restaurant reviews, pubs, and current museum hours, pick up a copy of the twice-monthly *In Dublin* (€2.50, any newsstand).

The Temple Bar area thrives with music—traditional, jazz, and pop. It really is *the* comfortable and fun place for tourists and locals (who come here to watch the tourists). **Gogarty's Pub** (corner of Fleet and Anglesea) has top-notch sessions upstairs nightly from 21:00. Use this as a kick-off for your Temple Bar evening fun.

A 10-minute hike up the river west of Temple Bar takes you to a twosome with a local and less-touristy ambience. **The Brazen Head,** famous as Dublin's oldest pub, is a hit for an early dinner and late live music, with smoky, atmospheric rooms and a courtyard made to order for balmy evenings (on Bridge Street, tel. 01/677-9549). **O'Shea's Merchant Pub,** just across the street, is encrusted in memories and filled with locals taking a break from the grind. They have live traditional music nightly (the front half is a restaurant, the magic is in the back half).

Irish Music in Nearby Dun Laoghaire

For an evening of pure Irish music, song, and dance, check out the **Comhaltas Ceoltoiri Eireann,** an association working to preserve this traditional slice of Irish culture. It got started when Elvis and company threatened to steal the musical heart of the new generation. Judging by the pop status of traditional Irish music these days, Comhaltas accomplished its mission. Their "Seisiun" evening is a stage show mixing traditional music, song, and dance (€10, July–Aug Mon–Thu at 21:00, followed by informal music session at 22:30). Fridays all year long they have a *ceilidh* (pron. KAY-lee) where everyone does set dances (€7 includes friendly pointers, 21:30–00:30). On Wednesdays, Fridays, and Saturdays at 21:30, there are informal sessions by the fireside. All musicians are welcome. Performances are held in Cuturlann na Eireann, near the Seapoint DART stop or a 20-minute walk from Dun Laoghaire, at 32 Belgrave Square, Monkstown (tel. 01/280-0295, www.comhaltas.com). Their bar is free and often filled with music.

Sleeping in Dublin
(€1 = about $1, country code: 353, area code: 01)
Sleep Code: **S** = Single, **D** = Double/Twin, **T** = Triple, **Q** = Quad, **b** = bathroom, **s** = shower only, **CC** = Credit Cards accepted, **no CC** = Credit Cards not accepted. Breakfast is included unless otherwise noted. To locate hotels, see map on page 58.

To help you easily sort through these listings, I've divided the rooms into three categories, based on the price for a standard double room with bath:

Higher Priced—Most rooms more than €130.
Moderately Priced—Most rooms €65–130.
Lower Priced—Most rooms €65 or less.

Dublin is popular and rooms can be tight. Book ahead for weekends any time of year, particularly in summer and during rugby weekends. Prices are often discounted on weeknights (Mon–Thu) and from November through February.

Big and practical places (both cheap and moderate) are most central at Christ Church on the edge of Temple Bar. For classy, older Dublin accommodations, you'll pay more and stay a bit farther out (east of St. Stephen's Green). For a small-town escape with the best budget values, take the convenient DART train (at least 3/hr, 20 min) to nearby Dun Laoghaire (see page 41).

Sleeping near Christ Church
These places face Christ Church Cathedral, a great locale a five-minute walk from the best evening scene at Temple Bar and 10 minutes from the sightseeing center (Trinity College and Grafton Street). Full Irish breakfasts, which cost €9 at the hotels, are half the price at the many small cafés nearby (consider the Applewood café at 1b Werburgh Street, next to Burdoch's Fish & Chips). The cheap hostels in this neighborhood, have some double rooms (see page 59).

MODERATELY PRICED
Harding Hotel is a hardwood, 21st-century, Viking-style place with 53 institutional-yet-hotelesque rooms. The rooms are simpler than Jurys (below), but they're also more intimate (Sb-€60, Db/Tb-€89–96, tell them Rick sent you and get 10 percent off, breakfast-€6–9, CC, Internet access,

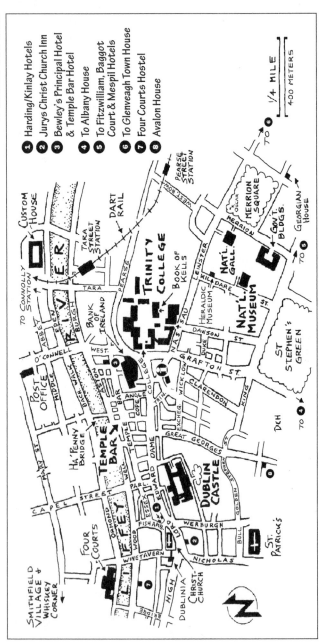

Dublin Hotels

1. Harding/Kinlay Hotels
2. Jurys Christ Church Inn
3. Bewley's Principal Hotel & Temple Bar Hotel
4. To Albany House
5. To Fitzwilliam, Baggot Court & Mespil Hotels
6. To Glenveagh Town House
7. Four Courts Hostel
8. Avalon House

Copper Alley across street from Christ Church, Dublin 2,
tel. 01/679-6500, fax 01/679-6504, ww.hardinghotel.ie,
e-mail: harding.hotel@usitworld.com).

Jurys Christ Church Inn (like its sisters across town, in
Galway, and in Belfast) is central and offers business-class comfort in all of its identical rooms. This no-nonsense, modern,
American-style hotel chain has a winning keep-it-simple-and-
affordable formula. If ye olde is getting old (and you don't mind
big tour groups), there's no better value in town. All 182 rooms
cost the same: €100 for one, two, or three adults or two adults
and two kids (higher weekend rates, breakfast extra). Each room
has a modern bathroom, direct-dial telephone, and TV. Two
floors are strictly non-smoking. Request a room far from the
noisy elevator (book long in advance for weekends, CC, parking
€12/day, Christ Church Place, Dublin 8, tel. 01/454-0000,
fax 01/454-0012, U.S. tel. 800/843-3311, www.jurys.com,
e-mail: info@jurys.com). Another Jurys is near the Connolly
train station (listed below).

LOWER PRICED

Kinlay House, around the corner from Jurys Christ Church Inn,
is the backpackers' equivalent—definitely the place to go for cheap
beds in a central location and an all-ages-welcome atmosphere.
This huge, red-brick, 19th-century Victorian building has 149
metal, prison-style beds in spartan, smoke-free rooms. There are
singles, doubles, and four- to six-bed coed dorms (good for families), as well as a few giant dorms. It fills up most days. Call well
in advance, especially for singles, doubles, and summer weekends
(S-€40–46, D-€50–56, Db-€54–60, dorm beds-€16–24, includes
continental breakfast, CC, kitchen access, launderette-€7.50,
Internet access-€4/hr, left luggage, travel desk, TV lounge, small
lockers, lots of stairs, Christ Church, 2–12 Lord Edward Street,
Dublin 2, tel. 01/679-6644, fax 01/679-7437, www.kinlayhouse.ie,
e-mail: kinlay.dublin@usitworld.com).

Four Courts Hostel is a new 236-bed hostel beautifully
located immediately across the river from the Four Courts, a five-
minute walk from Christ Church and Temple Bar. It's bare and
institutional (as hostels are), but expansive and well-run, with a
focus on security and efficiency (dorm beds from €16–20, bunk
D-€58, bunk Db-€65, includes small breakfast, girls' floor
and boys' floor, elevator, no smoking, Internet access, game
room, laundry service, some parking, left luggage room, 15
Merchant's Quay, Dublin 8, tel. 01/672-5839, fax 01/672-5862,
www.fourcourtshostel.com, e-mail: info@fourcourtshostel.com,
bus #90 from train or bus station).

Sleeping between Trinity College and Temple Bar

HIGHER PRICED

Bewley's Principal Hotel rents 70 decent rooms. For its size, it has an intimate feel, with character (Sb-€115, Db-€139, often mid-week deals, breakfast-€10, CC, non-smoking rooms, request a quiet room off the street, 19-20 Fleet Street, Dublin 2, tel. 01/670-8122, fax 01/670-8103, www.bewleysprincipalhotel.com).

Temple Bar Hotel is a 130-room business-class place, very centrally located midway between Trinity College and the Temple Bar action (Sb-€140, Db-€185, Tb-€250, often discounted, CC, smoke-free rooms, Fleet Street, Temple Bar, Dublin 2, tel. 01/ 677-3333, fax 01/677-3088, e-mail: templeb@iol.ie).

MODERATELY PRICED

Trinity College turns its 800 student-housing rooms on campus into no-frills, affordable accommodations in the city center each summer (mid-June–Sept, S-€47, Sb-€58, D-€94, Db-€116, CC, includes continental breakfast, cooked breakfast €2.50 extra, Trinity College, Dublin 2, tel. 01/608-1177, fax 01/671-1267, www2.tcd.ie/accom, e-mail: reservations@tcd.ie).

Sleeping near St. Stephen's Green

HIGHER PRICED

Albany House's 40 rooms come with classic furniture, high ceilings, Georgian elegance, and some street noise. Request the huge "superior" rooms, which are the same price (Sb-€90, Db-€140, €120 in slow times, Tb-€160, Una promises 10 percent off with this book in 2003, includes breakfast, CC, back rooms are quieter, smoke-free, just 1 block south of St. Stephen's Green at 84 Harcourt Street, Dublin 2, tel. 01/475-1092, fax 01/475-1093, http://indigo.ie/~albany, e-mail: albany@indigo.ie).

The Fitzwilliam has an inviting lounge and rents 13 decent rooms (Sb-€75, Db-€135, CC, 10 percent discount with cash, children under 16 sleep free, 41 Upper Fitzwilliam Street, Dublin 2, tel. 01/662-5155, fax 01/676-7488, e-mail: fitzwilliamguesthouse @eircom.net, Declan Carney).

Baggot Court Accommodations rents 11 similar rooms a block farther away and without a lounge (Sb-€90, Db-€150, Tb-€210, CC, entirely non-smoking, free parking, 92 Lower Baggot Street, Dublin 2, tel. 01/661-2819, fax 01/661-0253, e-mail: baggot@indigo.ie).

downstairs ✓
back d 16 / single   150 euros

LOWER PRICED

Avalon House, near Grafton Street, rents 281 backpacker beds
(S-€30, Sb-€33, D/twin-€56, Db/twin-€60, dorm beds-€15-20,
includes continental breakfast, CC, elevator, Ireland bus tickets,
Internet access, launderette across street, a few minutes off
Grafton Street at 55 Aungier Street, Dublin 2, tel. 01/475-0001,
fax 01/475-0303, www.avalon-house.ie).

Sleeping Away from the Center, East of St. Stephen's Green

HIGHER PRICED

Mespil Hotel is a huge, modern, business-class hotel renting
256 identical three-star rooms (each with a double and single bed,
phone, TV, voice-mail, and modem hookup) at a good price with
all the comforts. This is a cut above Jurys Inn, for a little more
money (Sb, Db, or Tb-€135, breakfast-€12.50, CC, elevator,
non-smoking floor, apartments for weeklong stays, 10-min walk
southeast of St. Stephen's Green or bus #10, Mespil Road, Dublin
4, tel. 01/667-1222, fax 01/667-1244, www.leehotels.ie, e-mail:
mespil@leehotels.ie).

MODERATELY PRICED

Glenveagh Town House rents 13 rooms—Victorian upstairs
and modern downstairs—southeast of the city center, a 15-minute
walk from Trinity College (Sb-€63-70, Db-€100-130, less in
slow times, includes breakfast, CC, car park, 31 Northumberland
Road, Dublin 4, tel. 01/668-4612, fax 01/668-4559, e-mail:
glenveagh@eircom.net). Catch bus #5, #6, #7, #8, or #45, which
lumber down Northumberland Road into downtown Dublin
every 10 minutes.

Sleeping near Connolly Train Station

MODERATELY PRICED

Jurys Inn Custom House, on Custom House Quay, offers the
same value as the Jurys at Christ Church. Bigger (with 234 rooms)
and not quite as well-located (in a boring neighborhood, a 10-min
riverside hike from O'Connell Bridge), this Jurys is more likely to
have rooms available (Db-€100, CC, Dublin 1, tel. 01/607-5000,
fax 01/829-0400, U.S. tel. 800/843-3311, www.jurys.com, e-mail:
info@jurys.com).

Charles Stewart Budget Accommodations is a big, basic
place offering lots of forgettable rooms, many long and narrow
with head-to-toe twins, in a great location for a good price

(S-€32, Sb-€63, D-€76, Db-€89, Tb-€121, Qb-€140, CC, includes cooked breakfast, just beyond top of O'Connell Street at 5 Parnell Square, Dublin 1, tel. 01/878-0350, fax 01/878-1387, e-mail: cstuart@iol.ie).

Sleeping and Eating in nearby Dun Laoghaire
(€1 = about $1, country code: 353, area code: 01, mail: County Dublin)

Dun Laoghaire (pron. DUN leary) is seven miles south of Dublin. This beach resort, with the ferry terminal for Wales and easy connections to downtown Dublin, is a great small-town base for the big city.

While buses run between Dublin and Dun Laoghaire, the DART commuter train is much faster (6/hr in peak times, at least 3/hr otherwise, 20 min, runs Mon–Sat about 6:30–23:15, Sun from 9:00, €1.50 one-way, €2.75 round-trip, Eurail valid but uses day of flexipass; for a longer stay consider the €13.50 Short Hop 3-day bus and rail ticket covering DART and Dublin buses). If you're coming from Dublin, catch a DART train marked "Bray" and get off at the Sandy Cove or Dun Laoghaire stop, depending on which B&B you choose; if you're leaving Dun Laoghaire, catch a train marked "Howth" to get to Dublin—get off at the central Tara Street station.

The Dun Laoghaire harbor was strategic enough to merit a line of Martello Towers (built to defend against an expected Napoleonic invasion). By the mid-19th century, the huge break-waters—reaching like two muscular arms into the Irish Sea—were completed, protecting a huge harbor. Ships sailed regularly from here to Wales (60 miles away), and the first train line in Ireland connected the terminal with Dublin. While still a busy transportation hub, today the nearly mile-long breakwaters are also popular with strollers, bikers, birders, and fishermen. Hike out to the lighthouse at the end of the interesting East Pier.

The **Dun Laoghaire TI** is in the ferry terminal (Mon–Sat 10:00–18:00 year-round, closed Sun). Comhaltas Ceoltoiri Eireann, an association that preserves Irish folk music, offers lively shows in Dun Laoghaire (see "Irish Music in nearby Dun Laoghaire," above). Taxi fare from Dun Laoghaire to central Dublin is about €13, to the airport about €32. With easy free parking and DART access into Dublin, this area is ideal for those with cars (which cost €19 a day to park in Dublin). The Washerette laundry is located in the village of Sandycove (Mon–Sat 8:30–18:00, self- and full-serve, 2 Glasthule, across from church). The Net House Café provides a fast Internet connec-tion 24 hours a day (28 Upper George Street, €3/30 min).

Dun Laoghaire

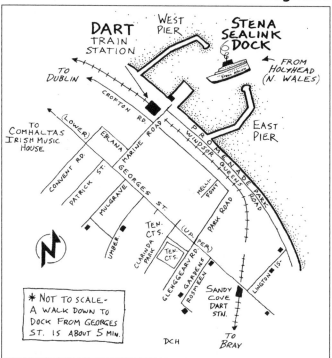

DART TRAIN STATION

WEST PIER

STENA SEALINK DOCK

FROM HOLYHEAD (N. WALES)

TO DUBLIN

CROFTON RD.

TO COMHALTAS IRISH MUSIC HOUSE

(LOWER) EBLANA

CONVENT RD.

PATRICK ST.

MULGRAVE

MARINE ROAD

GEORGES ST.

WINDSOR

PROMENADE QUEENS ROAD

EAST PIER

PARK

MELLI-FONT

PARK ROAD

UMBER

CLARINDA PARK

TEN. CTS.

TEN. CTS.

(UPPER)

GLENGEARY RD.

GARDENS

ROSMEEN

SANDY COVE DART STN.

LINGTON ST.

TO BRAY

DCH

* NOT TO SCALE - A WALK DOWN TO DOCK FROM GEORGES ST. IS ABOUT 5 MIN.

Sleeping near Sandycove DART Station

These listings are within several blocks of the Sandycove DART station and a seven-minute walk to the Dun Laoghaire DART station/ferry landing.

LOWER PRICED

Mrs. Kane's **Seaview B&B** is a modern house with three big, cheery rooms and a welcoming guests' lounge. While a few blocks farther out than the others, it's worth the walk for its bright and friendly feeling (Db-€65 through 2003 with this book, no CC, strictly smoke-free, just above Rosmeen Gardens at 2 Granite Hall, tel. & fax 01/280-9105, e-mail: seaviewbedandbreakfast@hotmail.com).

Windsor Lodge rents four fresh, cheery rooms on a quiet street a block off the harbor and a block from the DART station (Db-€60–64, family deals, no CC, non-smoking, 3 Islington Avenue, Sandycove, Dun Laoghaire, tel. & fax 01/284-6952, e-mail: winlodge@eircom.net, Mary O'Farrell).

Annesgrove B&B has four tidy rooms decorated in beige and brown (S-€40, D-€60, Db-€65, Tb-€90, includes breakfast, no CC, parking, close to park and beach, 28 Rosmeen Gardens, tel. 01/280-9801, Anne D'Alton). **Rosmeen House** is a similar grandfather-clock kind of place renting four smoke-free rooms (S-€40, Db-€65, no CC, 13 Rosmeen Gardens, tel. 01/280-7613, Joan Murphy).

Sleeping near Dun Laoghaire DART Station

Lynden B&B, with a classy 150-year-old interior hiding behind a somber front, rents four big rooms (S-€38, Sb-€43, D-€50, Db-€60, 10 percent discount with this book, no CC, past Mulgrave Street to 2 Mulgrave Terrace, tel. 01/280-6404, e-mail: lynden@iol.ie, Maria Gavin).

Innisfree B&B has a fine lounge and six big, bright, and comfy rooms (D-€48, Db-€52, 10 percent discount with this book, CC, from George Street hike up the plain but quiet Northumberland Avenue to #31, tel. 01/280-5598, fax 01/280-3093, e-mail: djsmyth@club1.ie, Brendan and Mary Smyth).

On the same street, you'll find two places renting four big, well-worn rooms each: **Mrs. Howard's B&B** (S-€34, Sb-€38, D-€52, Db-€58, no CC, TV lounge, 36 Northumberland Avenue, tel. 01/280-3262) and **Mrs. O'Sullivan's Duncree B&B** (D-€52, Db-€58, no CC, family room, no smoking, 16 Northumberland Ave, tel. 01/280-6118).

Eating in Dun Laoghaire

If staying in Dun Laoghaire, I'd definitely eat here and not in Dublin. Glasthule (called simply "the village" locally, just down the street from the Sandycove DART station) has a stunning array of fun, little, hardworking restaurants.

Bistro Vino is the rage lately, with cozy, candlelit, Mediterranean ambience and great food (€12–21 meals, daily 17:00–23:00, nightly €17 early-bird special 17:00–19:00, seafood, pasta, CC, arrive early or have a reservation, 56 Glasthule Road, tel. 01/280-6097).

Duzy's Café fills a classy but garishly painted modern-feeling old room above the Eagle House Pub with happy eaters and French-Irish cuisine. The menu is a joy and their €18.50 early-bird special—three courses with coffee on weeknights until 19:00—is a super value (€19–23 plates, nightly from 18:00, CC, 18 Glasthule Road, tel. 01/230-0210, run by John Dunne and Stephane Couzy).

The big **Eagle House** pub serves hearty €9 pub meals (until 21:00) in a wonderful but smoky atmosphere. This is a great local joint for a late drink. The nearby **Daniel's Restaurant**

and Wine Bar is less atmospheric but also good (€19 meals, closed Mon, 34 Glasthule Road, tel. 01/284-1027).

South Bank Restaurant, a jolly place filled with happy piano music, faces the water and serves fish and European cuisine (€19 main courses, nightly except Mon in winter, 1 Martello Terrace, directly down from Sandycove DART station, reservations smart, tel. 01/280-8788).

Walters Public House and Restaurant is a bright, modern place above a similar pub, offering good food to a dressy crowd (nightly 17:30–23:00, €13–21 meals, 68 Upper George's Street, tel. 01/280-7442).

George's Street, three blocks inland and Dun Laoghaire's main drag, has plenty of eateries and pubs, many with live music. A good bet for families is the kid-friendly **Bits and Pizza** (daily 12:00–24:00, off George's Street at 15 Patrick Street, tel. 01/284-2411).

Eating in Dublin

As Dublin does its boom-time jig, fine and creative eateries are popping up all over town. While you can get decent pub grub for €10 on just about any corner, consider saving pub grub for the countryside. And there's no pressing reason to eat Irish in cosmopolitan Dublin. Dublin's good restaurants are packed from 20:00 on, especially on weekends. Eating early (18:00–19:00) saves time and money (as many better places offer an early-bird special).

Eating Quick and Easy around Grafton Street

Cornucopia is a small, earth-mama-with-class, proudly vegetarian, self-serve place two blocks off Grafton. It's friendly and youthful, with hearty €8 lunches and €9.50 dinner specials (Mon–Sat 8:30–20:00, Sun 12:00–18:00, 19 Wicklow Street, tel. 01/677-7583).

O'Neill's offers dependable €9 carvery lunches in a labyrinth of a pub with a handy location across from the main TI (daily 12:00–15:30, Suffolk Street, tel. 01/679-3656).

Graham O'Sullivan Restaurant and Coffee Shop is a cheap, cheery cafeteria serving soup and sandwiches with a salad bar in unpretentious ambience (Mon–Fri 8:00–18:30, Sat 9:00–17:00, closed Sun, smoke-free upstairs, 12 Duke Street). Two pubs on the same street—**The Duke** and **Davy Burns**—serve pub lunches. (The nearby Cathach Rare Books shop at 10 Duke Street displays a rare edition of *Ulysses* among other treasures in its window).

Bewley's Café is an old-time local favorite offering light meals from €6 and full meals from €10. Sit on the ground floor among Harry Clarke windows and Art Deco lamps or upstairs in the bright atrium decorated by local art students (self-service daily 7:30–23:00, CC, 78 Grafton Street, tel. 01/635-5470).

Dublin Restaurants

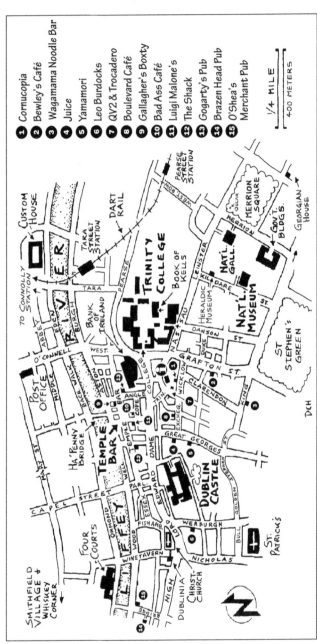

1. Cornucopia
2. Bewley's Café
3. Wagamama Noodle Bar
4. Juice
5. Yamamori
6. Leo Burdocks
7. QV2 & Trocadero
8. Boulevard Café
9. Gallagher's Boxty
10. Bad Ass Café
11. Luigi Malone's
12. The Shack
13. Gogarty's Pub
14. Brazen Head Pub
15. O'Shea's Merchant Pub

¼ MILE

400 METERS

Wagamama Noodle Bar, like its popular sisters in London, is a pan-Asian slurpathon with great and healthy noodle and rice dishes (€9–13) served by walkie-talkie-toting waiters at long communal tables (daily 12:00–23:00, CC, non-smoking, no reservations, often a line, South King Street, underneath St. Stephen's Green Shopping Centre, tel. 01/478-2152).

South Great Georges Street is lined with hardworking little eateries. **Juice** keeps vegetarians happy (daily 12:00–23:00, 73 South Great Georges Street, tel. 01/475-7856).

Yamamori is a plain, bright, and modern Japanese place serving seas of sushi and noodles (€9 lunches daily 12:30–17:30, dinners €11–16, 17:30–23:00, CC, 71 South Great Georges Street, tel. 01/475-5001).

Supermarkets: Marks & Spencer department store (on Grafton Street) has a fancy grocery store in the basement with fine take-away sandwiches and salads (Mon–Fri 9:00–19:00, Thu until 21:00, Sat 9:00–19:00, Sun 11:00–18:30). Locals prefer **Dunne's** department store for its lower prices (same hours, grocery in basement, in St. Stephen's Green Shopping Centre).

Eating Fast and Cheap near Christ Church
Many of Dublin's **late-night grocery stores** (such as the Spar off the top of Dame Street on Parliament Street) sell cheap salads, microwaved meat pies, and made-to-order sandwiches. A €5 picnic dinner back at the hotel might be a good option after a busy day of sightseeing.

Leo Burdocks Fish & Chips is popular with locals (take-out only, daily 12:00–24:00, 2 Werburgh Street, off Christ Church Square).

Dining at Classy Restaurants and Cafés
These three restaurants are located within a block of each other, just south of Temple Bar and Dame Street, near the main TI.

QV2 Restaurant serves "international with an Irish twist"— great cooking at reasonable prices with a happy-colors-and-candlelight atmosphere (€35 meals, Mon–Sat 12:00–15:00 & 18:00–23:00, closed Sun, non-smoking section, CC, 14 St. Andrew Street, tel. 01/677-3363, run by John Count McCormack— grandson of the famous tenor). They offer a quick lunch special (€11–15) and the same lunch menu for early birds ordering before 19:30.

Trocadero, across the street, serves beefy European cuisine to locals interested in a slow, romantic meal. The dressy red-velvet interior is draped with photos of local actors. Come early or make a reservation. This place is a favorite with Dublin's theatergoers

(€26 meals, Mon–Sat 17:00–24:00, closed Sun, non-smoking section, CC, 3 St. Andrew Street, tel. 01/677-5545). The three-course early-bird special at €18 is a fine value (17:00–19:00, leave by 20:00).

Boulevard Café is a mod, local, likeable, trendy place serving Mediterranean cuisine, heavy on the Italian. They serve salads, pasta, and sandwiches for around €7, three-course lunch specials for €11.50 (Mon–Sat 12:00–16:00), and dinner plates for €13–15.50 (daily 17:30–24:00, CC, 27 Exchequer Street, smart to reserve for dinner, tel. 01/679-2131).

Eating at Temple Bar

Gallagher's Boxty House is touristy and traditional, a good, basic value with creaky floorboards and old Dublin ambience. Its specialty is boxties—the generally bland-tasting Irish potato pancake filled and rolled with various meats, veggies, and sauces. The "Gaelic Boxty" is liveliest (€13–15, also serves stews and corned beef, daily 12:00–23:30, non-smoking section, CC, 20 Temple Bar, tel. 01/677-2762). Popular Gallagher's takes same-day reservations only; to reserve for dinner, stop by between 12:00 and 15:00.

Bad Ass Café is a grunge diner serving cowboy/Mex/veggie/pizzas to old and new hippies. No need to dress up (€6.50 lunch and €16.50 3-course dinner deals, kids' specials, daily 11:30–24:00, CC, Crown Alley, just off Meeting House Square, tel. 01/671-2596).

Luigi Malone's, with its fun atmosphere and varied menu of pizza, ribs, pasta, sandwiches, and fajitas, is just the place to take your high school date (€10–20, daily 12:00–23:00, CC, corner of Cecila and Fownes Streets, tel. 01/679-2723).

The Shack, while a bit pricey and touristy, has a reputation for good quality and serves traditional Irish, chicken, seafood, and steak dishes (€15–26 entrées, CC, daily 11:00–23:00, across from Dublin Castle on Dame Street, tel. 01/670-9785). A second location is in the center of Temple Bar (24 East Essex Street, tel. 01/679-0043).

Transportation Connections—Dublin

By bus to: Belfast (7/day, 3 hrs), **Trim** (10/day, 1 hr), **Ennis** (11/day, 4.5 hrs), **Galway** (15/day, 3.5 hrs), **Limerick** (13/day, 3.5 hrs), **Tralee** (6/day, 6 hrs), **Dingle** (4/day, 8 hrs, €21.50, transfer at Tralee). Bus info: tel. 01/836-6111.

By train from Heuston Station to: Tralee (6/day, 4 hrs, talking timetable tel. 01/805-4266), **Ennis** (2/day, 4 hrs), **Galway** (5/day, 3 hrs, talking timetable tel. 01/805-4222).

By train from Connolly Station to: Rosslare (3/day, 3 hrs), Portrush (6/day, 5 hrs, €34 one-way, €47 round-trip, transfer in Belfast or Portadown), **Belfast** (8/day, 2 hrs, talking timetable tel. 01/836-3333). The **Dublin–Belfast train** connects the two Irish capitals in two hours at 90 mph on one continuous, welded rail (€29 one-way, €43 round-trip; round-trip the same day only €29 except Fri and Sun; from the border to Belfast one-way €18, €25 round-trip). Train info: tel. 01/836-6222. North Ireland train info: tel. 048/9089-9400.

Dublin Airport: The airport is well connected to the city center seven miles away (airport info: tel. 01/814-1111; also see "Arrival in Dublin," above). For list of airlines, see below.

Transportation Connections— Ireland and Britain

Dublin and London: The journey by boat plus train or bus takes 7–12 hours, all day, or all night (bus: 4/day, €25–42, British tel. 08705-143-219, www.eurolines.co.uk; train: 4/day, €61–118, Dublin train info: tel. 01/836-6222).

If you're going directly to London, flying is your best bet. Check **Ryanair** first (€82 round-trip, 90 min, Irish tel. 01/609-7878, www.ryanair.com). Other options include **British Airways** (Irish tel. 01/814-5201 or toll-free tel. in Ireland 1-800-626-747, in U.S. 800/247-9297, www.britishairways.com), **Aer Lingus** (tel. 01/886-8888, www.aerlingus.ie), and **bmi british midland** (Irish tel. 01/407-3036, U.S. tel. 800/788-0555, www.flybmi.com). To get the lowest fares, ask about round-trip ticket prices and book months in advance (though Ryanair offers deals nearly all of the time).

Dublin and Holyhead: Irish Ferries sails between Dublin and Holyhead in North Wales (dock is a mile east of O'Connell Bridge, 5/day: 2 slow, 3 fast; slow boats: 3.25 hrs, €30 one-way walk-on fare; fast boats: 1.75 hrs, €40; Dublin tel. 01/638-3333, Holyhead tel. 08705-329-129, www.irishferries.com).

Dublin and Liverpool: Norse Merchant Ferries sails most mornings (Tue–Sat) and every evening year-round from Dublin Harbor (8 hrs, €35–40 one-way by day, €40–45 one-way overnight, cabins €55–65 extra, car transport €120 for day crossing or €180 by night crossing, Dublin tel. 01/819-2999, British tel. 0870-800-4321, www.norsemerchant.com).

Dun Laoghaire and Holyhead: Stena Line sails between Dun Laoghaire (near Dublin) and Holyhead in North Wales (3/day, 2 hrs on HSS *Catamaran,* €36–42 one-way walk-on fare, €4 extra if paying with CC, reserve by phone—they book up long in advance on summer weekends, Dun Laoghaire tel. 01/204-7777, recorded info tel. 01/204-7799, can book online at www.stenaline.ie).

Ferry Connections—Ireland and France

Irish Ferries connect Ireland (Rosslare) with France (Cherbourg and Roscoff) every other day (less Jan–March). While Cherbourg has the quickest connection to Paris, your overall time between Ireland and Paris is about the same (20–25 hrs) regardless of which port is used on the day you sail. One-way fares vary from €60 to €120. Eurailers go half-price. In both directions, departures are generally between 16:00 and 20:00 and arrive late the next morning. While passengers can nearly always get on, reservations are wise in summer and easy by phone. If you anticipate a crowded departure, you can reserve a seat for €10. Doubles (or singles) start at €50. The easiest way to get a bed (except during summer) is from the information desk upon boarding. The cafeteria serves bad food at reasonable prices. Upon arrival in France, buses and taxis connect you to your Paris-bound train (Irish Ferries: Dublin tel. 01/661-0511, recorded info tel. 01/661-0715, Paris tel. 01 44 94 20 40, www.irishferries.com, e-mail: info@irishferries.com, European Ferry Guide: www.youra.com/ferry/intlferries.html).

SIGHTS NEAR DUBLIN

These sights are separated into regions: north of Dublin (Newgrange and Valley of the Boyne) and south of Dublin (Glendalough and Wicklow Mountains).

NORTH OF DUBLIN: NEWGRANGE AND THE HISTORIC VALLEY OF THE BOYNE

The peaceful, green Boyne Valley, just 50 km (30 miles) north of Dublin, has an impressive concentration of historical and spiritual sights. You'll find enigmatic burial mounds at Newgrange, older than the Egyptian pyramids; the Hill of Tara (seat of the high kings of Celtic Ireland), where St. Patrick preached his most per-suasive sermon; the first Vatican-endorsed monastery in Ireland; and several of Ireland's finest high crosses. You'll also see Trim's 13th-century castle—Ireland's biggest—built by invading Normans. You'll also find the site of the historic Battle of the Boyne (1690), in which the Protestants turned the tide against the Catholics and locked in British rule of the Irish.

Planning Your Time

Of these sights, only Newgrange is worth ▲▲▲ (and deserves a good 3 hours). The others, while relatively meager physically, are powerfully evocative to anyone interested in Irish history and culture. Without a car, I'd simply do Newgrange using public transportation from Dublin.

The region is a joy by car because all of the described sights are within a 30-minute drive of each other. You could do the entire region in a day if you ate your Weetabix. While sights are on tiny roads, they're well marked with brown, tourist-friendly road signs

Boyne Valley Area

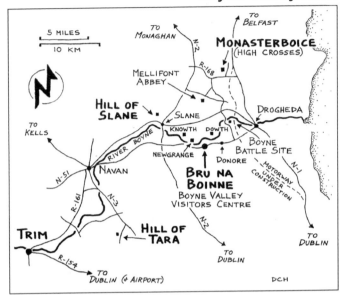

and you can manage with your all-Ireland Michelin map. (Note that the Newgrange sights are signposted Bru na Boinne; following Newgrange signs takes you in the wrong direction.)

As you plan your Ireland itinerary, keep in mind that if you're flying in or out of Dublin and you want to avoid the intensity and expense of big-city Dublin, you could use Trim as an overnight base (45-min drive from airport) and tour these sights from there.

Tours of the Boyne Valley

If you don't have a car, consider a tour of Boyne Valley sights.

Mary Gibbon's Tours visit both Newgrange (including inside the tomb) and the Hill of Tara in a six-hour trip (€35, €29 if you flash this book, 10:40 pickup at Dublin TI on Suffolk Street, 10:50 pickup at Royal Dublin Hotel on O'Connell Street, home by 17:30, book ahead, tel. 01/283-9973, fax 01/260-1456).

Over the Top Tours cover everything but Newgrange and Trim. Leaving Dublin at 9:00 and returning by 18:00, they stop and explain the Hill of Tara, the Hill of Slane (free time for lunch), Loughcrew (prehistoric tombs, less famous than Newgrange), Battle of the Boyne site, and the monasteries of Monasterboice and Mellifont Abbey (€25, daily, departing from Dublin TI on Suffolk Street, 14-seat minibus, reservations required, leave CC, tel. 1-800-424-252, Dublin tel. 01/838-6128, www.overthetoptours.com).

NEWGRANGE (Bru na Boinne)

The famous archaeological site commonly referred to as Newgrange (one of the tombs) is more properly known as Bru na Boinne—"dwelling place of the Boyne." The well-organized site centers on a state-of-the-art museum. Visitors are given appointments for shuttle buses that ferry small groups five minutes away to one of two 5,000-year-old passage tombs, where a guide gives a 30-minute tour. Newgrange is more famous and allows you inside. Knowth (rhymes with south) was opened more recently and is more extensive, but you can't go inside the tomb. At the turnstile you'll buy a ticket to one or both sights and be given bus departure times (if you plan to see both sights, note that buses depart 90 min apart). Newgrange sells out first and comes with a longer wait. If you opt for Knowth, be sure to see the museum's replica of the Newgrange passage entrance (where a short tour and winter-solstice-light-show demo often occur upon request); the replica is connected to the video room. Each site is different enough and worthwhile, but for many, seeing just one is adequate. For information on the prehistoric art, see "Irish Art" in the Ireland: Past and Present chapter.

Newgrange is one single mound, the most restored of the Bru na Boinne sites. Dating from 3200 B.C., it's 500 years older than the pyramids at Giza. While we know nothing of these people, this most certainly was a sacred spot dealing with some kind of sun-god ritual. During your tour you'll squeeze down a narrow passageway to a cross-shaped central chamber under a 20-foot-high igloo-type stone dome. Bones and ashes were placed here under 200,000 tons of stone and dirt to wait for a special moment. As the sun rose on the shortest day of the year (winter solstice, Dec 21), a ray of light would creep slowly down the 60-foot-long passageway. For 17 minutes it would light the center of the sacred chamber. Perhaps this was the moment when the souls of the dead would be transported to the afterlife via that mysterious ray of life-giving and life-taking light.

Knowth (the second Bru na Boinne site) is a necropolis of several grassy mounds around one 85-yard-wide grand tomb. The big mound, covering 1.5 acres, has two passages aligned so that on the spring and fall equinox rays from the rising and setting sun shine down the passageways to the center chamber. Neither of the passages is open to public, but you get a glimpse down one when you visit a room cut into the mound to expose the interior construction layers. The Knowth site thrived from 3000 to 2000 B.C., was the domain of fairies and myths for the next 2,000 years, and became an Iron Age fortress in the early centuries after Christ. Around A.D. 1000 it was an all-Ireland political center, and later a Norman fortress was built atop the mound. You'll see plenty of mysteriously carved stones and new-feeling grassy mounds that you can look down on from atop the grand tomb.

Allow an hour for the excellent museum and an hour for each of the tombs you visit. The museum in the Visitors Centre is included in the following prices: Newgrange-€5, Knowth-€3.80, both tombs-€8.80 (May–Sept daily 9:00–18:30 or 19:00, slightly shorter hours off-season, Newgrange open year-round, Knowth open May–Oct only, tel. 041/988-0300).

Visits are limited, and on busy summer days those arriving in the afternoon may not get a spot (no reservations possible). In peak season, try to arrive by 9:30 for no wait. Generally, upon arrival you'll get a bus departure time for one or both of the passage-tomb sites (the last shuttle bus leaves 1.75 hours before closing). Spend your wait in the museum, watching the great seven-minute video, and munching lunch in the cheery cafeteria. You can't drive directly to the actual passage tombs.

Transportation Connections: To reach the Visitors Centre from Dublin by **car,** drive north on N1 to Drogheda, where signs direct you to the Bru na Boinne Visitors Centre. Or take a Bus Eireann **bus** from Dublin (€11 round-trip, pay driver, buses depart Dublin at 9:00, 10:00, 11:00, 12:00, 13:30, and 14:30 from stop opposite Wynn's Hotel on Lower Abbey Street, just around corner from Busaras central bus station, 90-min trip, transfer in Drogheda, confirm schedule at station and confirm transfer point with driver, tel. 01/836-6111).

More Sights—Valley of the Boyne

▲**Hill of Tara**—This was the most important center of political and religious power in pre-Christian Ireland. While aerial views show plenty of mysterious circles and lines, wandering with the sheep among the well-worn ditches and hills leaves you with more to feel than to actually see. Visits are made meaningful by an excellent 20-minute video presentation and the caring 20-minute guided walk that follows (always available upon request and entirely worthwhile).

You'll see the Mound of Hostages—a Bronze Age passage grave (c. 2500 B.C.), a couple of ancient sacred stones, a war memorial, and vast views over the Emerald Isle. While ancient Ireland was a pig-pile of minor chieftain-kings scrambling for power, the high king of Tara was king of the mountain. It was at this ancient stockade that St. Patrick directly challenged the power of the high king. When confronted by the pagan high king, Patrick convincingly explained the Holy Trinity using a shamrock: three petals with one stem. He won the right to preach Christianity throughout Ireland, and the country had a new national symbol.

This now-desolate hill was also the scene of great modern events. In 1798, passionate young Irish rebels chose Tara for a defensible position but were routed by better-organized (and more sober) British troops. (The cunning British commander had earlier in the day sent three cartloads of whiskey along the nearby road knowing the rebels would intercept it.) In 1843, the great orator and champion of Irish liberty Daniel O'Connell gathered more than 500,000 Irish peasants on this hill for his greatest "monster meeting"—a peaceful show of force demanding the repeal of the Act of Union with Britain.

Stand on the Hill of Tara. Think of the history it's seen, and survey Ireland. It's understandable why this "meeting place of heroes" continues to hold a powerful place in the Irish psyche (€2 includes video and 20-min walk, May–Oct daily 10:00–18:00; last tour 17:15, local guide Jean Thornton brings the lumpy mounds to life; tel. 046/25903).

Mellifont Abbey—This Cistercian abbey (the first in Ireland) was established by French monks who came to the country in 1142 to get the Irish monks more in line with Rome. (Even the abbey's architecture was unusual, marking the first time in Ireland that a formal European-style monastic layout was used.) Cistercians lived isolated rural lives; lay monks worked the land, allowing the more educated monks to devote all their energy to prayer. After Henry VIII dissolved the abbey in 1539, centuries of locals used it as a handy quarry. Consequently, little survives beyond the octagonal lavabo, where the monks would ceremonially wash their hands before entering the refectory to eat. The lavabo gives a sense of the grandeur that once was. The excellent tours, available upon request and included in your admission, give meaning to the site (€2, May–Oct daily 10:00–18:00, free off-season but no tours, tel. 041/982-6459).

Monasterboice—Today this ruined monastery is visit-worthy for its round tower and its ornately carved high crosses—two of the best such crosses in Ireland. In the Dark Ages, these crosses, illustrated from top to bottom with Bible stories, gave monks a teaching tool as they preached to the illiterate masses.

The 18-foot-tall Cross of Murdock (Muiredach's Cross, A.D. 923, named after an abbot) is considered the best high cross in Ireland. The circle—which characterizes the Irish high cross— could represent the perfection of God. Or, to help ease pagans into Christianity, it could represent the sun, which was worshiped in pre-Christian Celtic society. Whatever its symbolic purpose, its real function was to support the crossbeam.

Face the cross (with the round tower in the background), and study the carved sandstone. The center panel shows the Last Judgment, with Christ under a dove symbolizing the Holy Spirit. Those going to heaven are on Christ's right and the damned are being ushered away by devils on His left. Working down you'll see the Archangel Michael weighing souls as the Devil tugs demonically at the scales; the adoration of the three—or four— Magi; Moses striking the rock; scenes from the life of David; and finally Adam, Eve, and the apple next to Cain slaying Abel. Imagine these carvings with their original colorful paint jobs.

Find the even taller cross nearest the tower. It seems the top section was broken off and buried while the bottom part remained standing, enduring the Irish weather.

The door to the round tower was originally 15–20 feet above the ground (so monks under attack could simply pull up their ladder). But after centuries of burials the altitude has risen.

Monasterboice, basically an old graveyard, is always open and free.

Battle of the Boyne Site—One of Europe's great non-sights, this is simply the pastoral riverside site of the pivotal battle in which the Protestant British broke Catholic resistance, establishing protestant rule over all Ireland and Britain. Drop into the information center next to the small parking lot and ask for a guided tour (free, June–Sept daily 9:30–17:30, tel. 041/988-4343). The attendant will generally take you on a 30-minute historic stroll around the Oldbridge Estate on the south bank of the river.

It was here in 1690 that Protestant King William III, with his English and Dutch army, defeated his father-in-law, Catholic King James II, and his Irish and French army. King William's forces, on the north side of the Boyne, managed to cross the river and by the end of the day, James was fleeing south in full retreat. He soon departed Ireland but his forces fought on until their final defeat two years later. James the second (called "James da Turd" by those who scorn his lack of courage and leadership) never returned and died a bitter ex-monarch in France. King William of Orange's victory, on the other hand, is still celebrated in Northern Ireland every July 12th, Orange Day, with controversial marches by Unionist "Orangemen."

TRIM

The sleepy work-a-day town of Trim, straddling the Boyne River, is marked by the towering ruins of Trim Castle. Trim feels littered with mighty ruins that seem to say, "This little town was big-time 700 years ago." The tall "Yellow Steeple" (over the river from the castle) is all that remains of the 14th-century

Augustinian Abbey of St. Mary. A pleasant half-mile walk back toward Dublin takes you to the sprawling ruins of Saints Peter and Paul Cathedral (from 1206), once the largest Gothic church in Ireland. Across the old Norman bridge from the cathedral are the 13th-century ruins of the Hospital of St. John the Baptist.

Trim's main square is a traffic roundabout, and everything's within a block or two. Most of the shops and eateries are on or near Market Street: bank, post office, supermarket, and launderette (Mon–Sat 9:00–18:00, Watergate Street, tel. 046/37176).

The TI is at 5 Emmett Street. Drop in for a free map and take a moment to ask them about Mel Gibson's visit and the filming of *Braveheart* (June–Sept Mon–Sat 10:00–13:00 & 14:00–17:30, closed Sun, Mill Street, tel. 046/37111).

If you're flying in or out of Dublin's airport and don't want to deal with big-city Dublin, Trim is perfect—an easy 45-minute, 50 km (30 miles) drive away. You can rent a car at the airport and make Trim your first overnight base (getting used to driving on the other side of the road in easy country traffic), or spend your last night here before returning your car to the airport. Either way, you don't need or want your car in Dublin (where parking is expensive and sightseeing is best on foot, by bus, or taxi).

Sights—Trim

▲▲**Trim Castle**—This is the biggest Norman castle in Ireland. Its mighty keep towers above a very ruined outer wall in a grassy riverside park at the edge of the sleepy town. The current castle was completed in the 1220s and served as a powerful Norman statement to the restless Irish natives. It remains an impressive sight—so impressive it was used in the 1994 filming of *Braveheart*.

The best-preserved walls ring the castle's southern perimeter and sport a barbican gate that contained two drawbridges. Notice at the base of the castle walls the clever angled "batter" wall—used by defenders who hurled down stones that banked off at great velocity into the attacking army.

The massive 70-foot-high central keep has 20 sides. Offering no place for invaders to hide, it was tough to attack. You can go inside only with the included tour (2/hr, 30 min). In a mostly hollow shell, you'll climb a series of tightly winding original staircases and modern high catwalks, learn about life in the castle, and end at the top with great views of the walls and countryside (€1.30 for castle grounds, €3.25 for entrance to keep and required tour, roughly May–Oct daily 10:00–18:00, last admission 17:15, tour spots are limited so call in peak season to save frustration of arriving to find nothing available, tel. 046/38619). Make time to take a 15-minute walk outside circling the castle walls, stopping at the

Trim

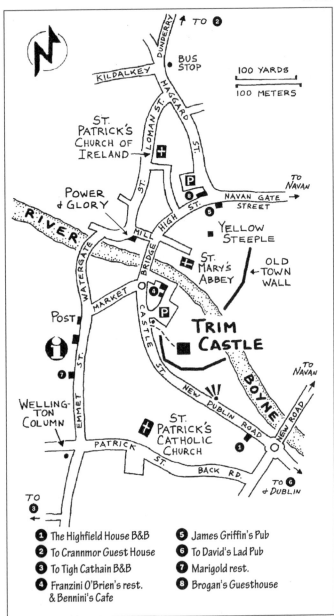

❶	The Highfield House B&B	❺	James Griffin's Pub
❷	To Crannmor Guest House	❻	To David's Lad Pub
❸	To Tigh Cathain B&B	❼	Marigold rest.
❹	Franzini O'Brien's rest. & Bennini's Cafe	❽	Brogan's Guesthouse

informative plaques that show the castle from each viewpoint during its gory glory days. Night strollers are treated to views of the castle hauntingly lit in blue-green hues.

The Power & Glory—This is a grade-schoolish 30-minute slide-show overview of the personalities and history of the castle, followed by an exhibit on life here in Norman times (€3.25, Fri–Sat and Mon–Wed 10:00–17:00, Sun 12:00–17:30, 3 blocks from castle, Mill Street, tel. 046/37227). You can get a half-price ticket for this show at the castle (and the show helps pass the time if you need to wait for your castle tour).

Sleeping in and near Trim
(€1 = about $1, country code: 353, area code: 046)

Sleep Code: **S** = Single, **D** = Double/Twin, **T** = Triple, **Q** = Quad, **b** = bathroom, **s** = shower only, **CC** = Credit Cards accepted, **no CC** = Credit Cards not accepted. Breakfast is included unless otherwise noted. To locate hotels, see map on page 78.

To help you easily sort through these listings, I've divided the rooms into two categories, based on the price for a standard double room with bath:

Moderately Priced—Most rooms more than €65.
Lower Priced—Most rooms €65 or less.

MODERATELY PRICED

Brogan's Guesthouse offers 15 rooms divided between its rustic original front guesthouse and its modern annex out back (Sb-€40–48, Db-€64–76, Tb-€96–114, CC, High Street, tel. 046/31237, fax 046/37648, e-mail: broganh@iol.ie, Adrian and Geraldine Hilliard).

LOWER PRICED

Highfield House B&B, across the street from the castle and a five-minute walk from town, is a stately 170-year-old former maternity hospital with high ceilings, hardwood floors, and seven spacious rooms (Sb-€40, Db-€64, Tb-€90, CC, family-friendly, overlooks roundabout where Dublin Road hits Trim, just before castle at Maudlins Road, tel. 046/36386, fax 046/38182, www.highfieldguesthouse.com, e-mail: highfieldhouseaccom@eircom.net, Geraldine Duignan).

About a mile outside of Trim in the quiet countryside are these two B&Bs (phone ahead for driving directions): North of town, Mrs. O'Regan decorates **Crannmór Guest House** with cheery color schemes (Sb-€38–44, Db-€64, Tb-€90, CC, Dunderry Road, tel. 046/31635, fax 046/38087, www.crannmor.com, e-mail: cranmor@eircom.net). Southwest of town, Mrs. Keane's **Tigh Cathain B&B** has a comfy, rural feel (Db-€60–66, no CC,

Longwood Road, tel. & fax 046/31996, www.tighcathaintrimcom, e-mail: mariekeane@esatclear.ie).

Eating in Trim

A country market town, Trim offers basic meat-and-potatoes lunch and dinner options. Don't waste time searching for gourmet food. The restaurants and cafés along Market Street are friendly, whole-some, and unpretentious (soup-and-sandwich delis close at 18:00).

Your best cafeteria-style lunch bet is **Bennini's Café,** hidden beside the parking lot to the left of Trim Castle's entry gate (daily 9:00–18:00, French's Lane, tel. 046/31002).

Franzini O'Brien's, next door, is the only place in town with a fun dinner menu and enough business to make that work. They serve pasta, steak, fish, and fajitas in a modern candlelit ambience, with nothing Irish but the waiters (€11–25, Tue–Sun 18:00–22:00, closed Mon, CC, French's Lane, tel. 046/31002, fax 046/31118).

If you feel like Chinese food, the **Marigold** fits the bill (Mon–Sat 17:30–24:00, Sun 16:00–24:00, CC, Emmet Street, tel. 046/38788).

For good old-fashioned cooking, ask about **Dunderry Lodge,** a 10-minute drive from town (tel. 046/31671).

For an unvarnished pub experience, check out Trim's two best watering holes. **James Griffin's** (on High Street) is full of local characters, with Mr. Lenihan, who has run the place for 55 years, presiding. **David's Lad** is ideal if you like your beer experience unfiltered (closed Wed, at old Norman Bridge by cathedral ruins, 20-min walk out of town but worth it).

Transportation Connections—Trim

Trim has no train station; the nearest train station is in Drogheda on the coast, but there are no bus connections to Trim from there.

Buses from Trim to **Dublin** (8/day, 1 hr) pick up next to the castle entry on Castle Street and in front of Talbot's News Shop on Haggard Street.

SOUTH OF DUBLIN: GLENDALOUGH AND THE WICKLOW MOUNTAINS

The Wicklow Mountains, while only 10 miles south of Dublin, feel remote—enough so to have provided a handy refuge for oppo-nents to English rule. Rebels who took part in the 1798 Irish up-rising hid out here for years. When the frustrated British built a military road in 1800 to help flush out the rebels, the area became more accessible. Now the R115, this same road takes you through the Wicklow area to Glendalough at its south end. While the valley

Sights South of Dublin

is the darling of the Dublin day-trip tour organizers, it doesn't live up to the hype. But two blockbuster sights—Glendalough and the gardens of Powerscourt—make a visit worth considering.

Getting Around

By car or tour, it's easy. If you lack wheels, take a tour. It's not worth the trouble on public transport.

By car: It's a delight. Take the freeway south from Dublin to Enniskerry, the gateway to the Wicklow Mountains. Signs direct you to the gardens and on to Glendalough. From Glendalough, if you're heading west, you can leave the valley (and pick up the highway to the west) over the famous but dull mountain pass called the Wicklow Gap.

By Tour: Wild Wicklow Tours covers the region with an entertaining guide packing every minute with information and fun *craic* (conversation). With a gang of 29 packed into tight but comfortable mountain-gripping buses, the guide kicks into gear from the first pickup in Dublin. Tours cover Dublin's embassy row, Dun Laoghaire, the Bay of Dublin with the mansions of Ireland's rich and famous, the windy Military Road over scenic Sally Gap, and the Glendalough monasteries (€28, €25 for students—show this book and pay the student price, daily year-round, 9:10 pickup at Dublin TI on Suffolk Street, 10:00 pickup at Dun Laoghaire TI, stop for lunch at a pub—cost not included, home by 17:30, Dun Laoghaire-ites can use the bus to get into Dublin for the evening, tel. 01/280-1899, www.wildcoachtours.com). Wild Wicklow also offers half-day tours: Wild Castle (€20, 9:30–13:30) and Wild Powerscourt (€20, 13:30–18:00). Each covers a few top sights in Dublin and include the general scenic Wicklow drives (see their brochure or Web site for details).

Other tour companies run day trips through the Wicklow Mountains from Dublin. **Mary Gibbon's Tours** visit both Glendalough and the Powerscourt gardens in a six-hour trip (€35, €29 with this book, 10:40 pickup at Dublin TI on Suffolk Street, 10:50 pickup at Royal Dublin Hotel on O'Connell Street, home by 17:30, call ahead to reserve, especially in high season, tel. 01/283-9973, fax 01/260-1456). **Over the Top Tours** bypasses mansions and gardens to focus on Wicklow scenery. Stops include Glendalough, the Glenmacnass waterfall, and Blessington lakes (€23, 9:45 pickup at TI on Suffolk Street, return by 17:30, 14 seat minibus, reservations required, leave CC, tel. 1-800-424-252, Dublin tel. 01/838-6128, www.overthetoptours.com).

Sights—Wicklow Mountains

▲▲**Gardens of Powerscourt**—While the mansion's interior, only partially restored after a 1974 fire, isn't much, its meticulously-kept aristocratic gardens are Ireland's best. The house was commissioned in the 1730s by Richard Wingfield, first viscount of Powerscourt. The gardens, created during the Victorian era (1858–1875), are called "the grand finale of Europe's formal gardening tradition . . . probably the last garden of its size and quality ever to be created." I'll buy that.

Upon entry you'll get a flier laying out 40-minute and 60-minute walks. The "60-minute" walk takes 30 minutes at a slow amble. With the impressive summit of the Great Sugar Loaf Mountain as a backdrop and a fine Japanese garden, an Italian garden, and a goofy pet cemetery along the way, this garden provides the scenic greenery I hoped to find in the rest of the

Wicklow area. The lush movie *Barry Lyndon* was filmed in this well-watered aristocratic fantasy.

The gardens of Powerscourt, a mile above the village of Enniskerry, cover several thousand acres within the 16,000-acre estate. The dreamy driveway alone is a mile long (€6 March–Oct, €4 Nov–Feb, daily 9:30–17:30, great cafeteria, tel. 01/204-6000). Skip the associated waterfall (€3.50, 4 miles away).

▲▲**Military Road over Sally Gap**—This is only for those with a car. From the gardens of Powerscourt and Enniskerry, go to Glencree, where you drive the tiny military road over Sally Gap and through the best scenery of the Wicklow Mountains. Look for the German military cemetery, built for U-boat sailors who washed ashore in World War II. Near Sally Gap, notice the peat bogs and the freshly cut peat bricks drying in the wind. Many locals are nostalgic for the "good old days," when homes were peat-fire heated. At the Sally Gap junction, turn left, where a road winds through the vast Guinness estate. Look down on the glacial lake (Lough Tay) and the Guinness mansion (famous for jet-set parties). Nicknamed "Guinness Lake," the water looks like Ireland's favorite dark-brown stout, and the sand of the beach actually looks like the head of a Guinness beer. From here the road winds scenically down into the village of Roundwood and on to Glendalough.

▲▲**Glendalough**—The steep wooded slopes of Glendalough (pron. GLEN-da-lock; valley of the two lakes), at the south end of Wicklow's military road, hides Ireland's most impressive monastic settlement. Founded by St. Kevin in the sixth century, the monastery flourished (despite repeated Viking raids) throughout the "Age of Saints and Scholars" until the English destroyed it in 1398. While it was finally abandoned during the Dissolution of the Monasteries in 1539, pilgrims kept coming, especially on St. Kevin's Day, June 3. (This might have something to do with the fact that a pope said seven visits to Glendalough had the same indulgence value as one visit to Rome.) While much restoration was done in the 1870s, most of the buildings date from the 8th through 12th centuries.

The valley sights are split between the two lakes. The lower lake has the Visitors Centre and the best buildings. The upper lake has scant ruins and feels like a state park, with a grassy lakeside picnic area, school groups, and fine walks.

General Glendalough plan: Park free at the Visitors Centre. Visit the center, wander the ruins (free) around the Round Tower, walk the traffic-free Green Road one mile to the upper lake, and then walk back to your car. (You can drive to the upper lake—parking €2.) If you're rushed, skip the upper lake. Summer tour-bus crowds are terrible all day on weekends and 11:00–14:00 on weekdays.

Glendalough Visitors Centre: Start your visit here (€2.75, mid-March–mid-Oct daily 9:30–18:00, last admission 17:15, closes earlier off-season, tel. 0404/45325). The 20-minute video provides a good thumbnail background on monastic society in medieval Ireland. While the video is more general than specific to Glendalough, the adjacent museum room features this particular monastic settlement. The model in the center of the room re-creates the fortified village of the year 1050 (although there were no black-and-white Frisian cows in Ireland back then—they would have been red). A browse here shows the contribution these monks made to intellectual life in Dark Age Europe (such as illuminated manuscripts and Irish minuscule, a more compact alphabet developed in the seventh century).

From the center, a short and scenic walk along the Green Road takes you to the Round Tower.

The Monastic Village: Easily the best ruins of Glendalough gather around the famous 110-foot-tall Round Tower. Towers like this (usually 60–110 feet tall) were standard features in such settlements, functioning as beacons for pilgrims, bell towers, storage lofts, and places of final refuge during Viking raids. They had a high door with a pull-up ladder. Several ruined churches (8th–12th centuries) and a sea of grave markers complete this evocative scene. Markers give short descriptions of the ruined buildings.

In an Ireland without cities, these monastic communities were mainstays of civilization. They were remote outposts where ascetics (with a taste for scenic settings) gathered to commune with God. In the 12th century, with the arrival of grander monastic orders such as the Franciscans and the Dominicans and with the growth of cities, these monastic communities were eclipsed. Today Ireland is dotted with the reminders of this age: illuminated manuscripts, simple churches, carved crosses, and about 100 round towers.

Upper Lake: The Green Road continues one mile farther up the valley to the upper lake. The oldest ruins—scant and hard to find—lie near this lake. If you want a scenic Wicklow walk, begin here.

SOUTH IRELAND

If you're driving from Dublin, on Ireland's east coast, to Dingle, on Ireland's west coast, the best two stops to break the long journey are Kilkenny, often called Ireland's finest medieval town, and the Rock of Cashel, a thought-provoking early Christian site crowning the Tipperary Plain. With a few extra days, there are several worthwhile stops (described in this chapter) along the south coast.

The typical tour-bus route includes the Waterford Crystal factory tour, Blarney Castle, Ring of Kerry, Killarney, and Muckross House—all places where most tourists wear name-tags. A major mistake many tourists make is allowing places into their Irish itineraries simply because they are famous (in a song or as part of a relative's big-bus-tour memory). Spend the night in Killarney and you'll understand what I mean. The town is a sprawling line of green Holiday Inns littered with pushy shoppers looking for three-leaf clovers. On my last visit to Blarney Castle, heading back to the tour-bus parking place, a woman behind me asked her friend, "What is the Blarney Stone, anyway?" Her friend said, "It's what you kiss when you come to Ireland."

This chapter is organized with Kilkenny and Cashel first (the basic stops for the one-day Dublin–Dingle drive), followed by the more thorough south-coast route. Along that route, the best overnight stops are Waterford and Kinsale. From Waterford, you can cover the sights of the southeast. From Kinsale, you can wade through the maritime history of Cobh.

The chapter ends with County Kerry and Ireland's southwest region, where you'll find the popular scenic peninsulas and the impressive Victorian Muckross House.

South Ireland

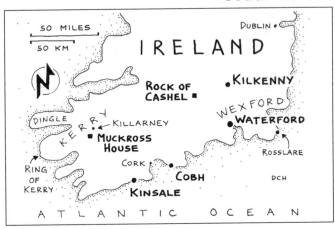

KILKENNY

Famous as "Ireland's loveliest inland city," Kilkenny gives you a feel for salt-of-the-earth Ireland. Its castle and cathedral stand like historic bookends on either side of a higgledy-piggledy High Street of colorful shops and medieval facades. While a small town today (fewer than 20,000 residents), Kilkenny has a big history. It used to be an important center—occasionally even the capital of Ireland in the Middle Ages.

Kilkenny is a good overnight for drivers wanting to break the journey from Dublin to Dingle (necessary if you want to spend more time in the Wicklow area and at the Rock of Cashel). A night in Kilkenny comes with plenty of traditional folk music in the pubs (hike over the river and up John Street).

Tourist Information: The TI, a block off the bridge, offers hour-long guided town walks (€5, 6/day, first one at 9:15, TI open Mon–Sat 9:00–18:00, Sun 11:00–13:00 & 14:00–17:00, Rose Inn Street, tel. 056/51500). Pat Tynan is a good local guide (cellular 087/265-1745, fax 056/63955, www.tynantours.com).

Arrival in Kilkenny: The train/bus station is four blocks from John's Bridge, which marks the center of town. Drivers can park in the disk lot next to the castle (buy disks at local shops, €0.80 each, buy 1 for each hour you want to stay, scratch off your arrival time and leave it on your dash). Or park in the multistory parking garage on Ormonde Street (€1/hr or just get the handy €12 5-day pass if overnighting).

Laundry: Use Hennessy's on Parliament Street (Mon–Sat 8:30–18:00, closed Sun).

Kilkenny

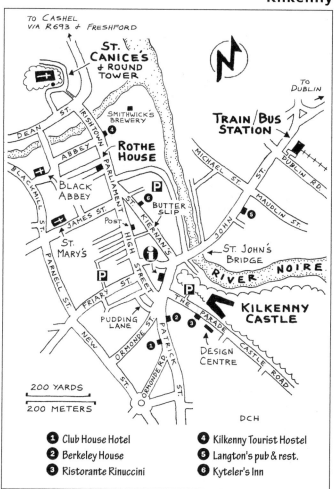

1 Club House Hotel

2 Berkeley House

3 Ristorante Rinuccini

4 Kilkenny Tourist Hostel

5 Langton's pub & rest.

6 Kyteler's Inn

Sights—Kilkenny

▲**Kilkenny Castle**—Dominating the town, this castle is a stony reminder that the Anglo-Norman Butler family controlled the town for 500 years. Tours start with a 12-minute video explaining how the wooden fort built here by Strongbow in 1172 evolved into a 17th-century château. Now restored to its later Victorian splendor, the highlight is the beautiful family portrait gallery putting you face to face with the wealthy Butler-family ghosts

(€4.50, June–Aug 9:30–19:00, April–May 10:30–17:00, Sept–March 10:30–13:00 & 14:00–17:00, tel. 056/21450).

The Kilkenny Design Centre, across the street from the castle, is full of local crafts and offers handy cafeteria lunches upstairs.
St. Canice's Cathedral—This 13th-century cathedral is early-English Gothic, rich with stained glass, medieval carvings, and floors paved in history (daily 10:00–13:00 & 14:00–18:00, tel. 056/64971). The 100-foot-tall round tower, built as part of a long-gone pre-Norman church, recalls the need for a watchtower and refuge. The fun ladder-climb to the top for €2 affords a grand view of the countryside (Easter–Sept Mon–Sat 9:00–13:00 & 14:00–18:00, Sun 14:00–18:00; Oct–Easter Mon–Sat 10:00–13:00 & 14:00–16:00, Sun 14:00–16:00).
Rothe House—This well-preserved Tudor merchant's house expanded around interior courtyards as the family grew. The museum and 15-minute video give a glimpse of life here in Elizabethan times (€3, April–Sept Mon–Sat 10:30–17:00, Sun 15:00–17:00, Oct–March Mon–Sat 13:00–17:00, closed Sun, Parliament Street, tel. 056/22893).

Sleeping in Kilkenny
(€1 = about $1, country code: 353, area code: 056)
Sleep Code: **S** = Single, **D** = Double/Twin, **T** = Triple, **Q** = Quad, **b** = bathroom, **s** = shower only, **CC** = Credit Cards accepted, **no CC** = Credit Cards not accepted.

To help you easily sort through these listings, I've divided the rooms into three categories, based on the price for a standard double room with bath:
Higher Priced—Most rooms more than €130.
Moderately Priced—Most rooms €65–130.
Lower Priced—Most rooms €65 or less.

HIGHER PRICED
Club House Hotel is perfectly central. Originally a gentleman's sporting club, it comes with old-time Georgian elegance; a palatial, well-antlered breakfast room; and 35 large, comfy bedrooms (Sb-€85, Db-€140, 10 percent discount with this book, CC, Patrick Street, tel. 056/21994, fax 056/71920, e-mail: clubhse@iol.ie).

MODERATELY PRICED
Berkeley House, across the street from Club House Hotel, is smaller, less expensive, and comfortable (10 rooms, Db-€70–100, CC, 5 Lower Patrick Street, tel. 056/64848, fax 056/64829, e-mail: berkeleyhouse@eircom.net).
Ristorante Rinuccini, directly opposite the castle, has

seven fine rooms off the street above the restaurant (Db-€120, cheaper off-season, CC, 1 The Parade, tel. 056/61575, fax 056/51288, www.rinuccini.com).

LOWER PRICED
Kilkenny Tourist Hostel, filling a fine Georgian townhouse in the town center, offers cheap beds, a friendly family room, a well-equipped members' kitchen, and a wealth of local information (dorm bed-€13, D-€33, Q-€60, no CC, 2 blocks from cathedral at 35 Parliament Street, tel. 056/63541, fax 056/23397, e-mail: kilkennyhostel@eircom.net).

Eating in Kilkenny

Langton's serves quality Irish dishes (daily 12:30–15:00 & 18:00–22:00, 69 John Street, tel. 056/65133), while **Ristorante Rinuccini** provides your Italian fix (daily 12:00–14:30 & 18:00–22:30, 1 The Parade, tel. 056/61575). For basic pub grub in a fun atmosphere, visit the cellar under **Kyteler's Inn** and ask about their witch (27 St. Kieran's Street, tel. 056/21064). Try a pint of Smithwick's in its hometown.

ROCK OF CASHEL

Rising high above the fertile Plain of Tipperary, the Rock of Cashel is one of Ireland's most historic and evocative sites. Seat of the ancient kings of Munster (about A.D. 400–1100), this is the site where St. Patrick baptized King Aengus in about A.D. 450. In about 1100, Cashel was taken over by the Church and became an ecclesiastical center of the region. On this 200-foot-high outcropping of limestone you'll find a round tower, an early Christian cross, a delightful Romanesque chapel, and a ruined Gothic cathedral, all surrounded by my favorite Celtic-cross graveyard. Begin your visit with the 15-minute video (shown every 30 min) and the tiny museum, which contains St. Patrick's 12th-century high cross (€4.50, mid-June–mid-Sept daily 9:00–19:30, last entry 18:45, closes earlier off-season, tel. 062/61437).

Picture the Rock of Cashel with just its 12th-century round tower (nearly 100 feet tall) and the small Romanesque Cormac's Chapel. The chapel was built in about 1130 by the king and bishop of Cashel, Cormac MacCarthy. Study its misty old carvings and the remarkable frescoes in the interior.

Outside the chapel, notice the replica of St. Patrick's high cross (you just saw the original cross in the museum). Wander through the ruined 13th-century Gothic cathedral. Then tiptoe through the tombstones. Look out over the Plain of Tipperary. Called the Golden Vale, it boasts a rich soil that makes it Ireland's most prosperous farmland. A path leads to the ruined 13th-century Cistercian Hore Abbey in the fields below (free, always open and peaceful). The rock is beautifully illuminated at night.

Bru Boru Cultural Centre—This new center, nestled below the Rock of Cashel parking lot next to the statue of the three blissed-out dancers, adds to your understanding of the Rock in its wider historical and cultural context. The highlight of the Sounds of History museum downstairs is the exhibit showing the Rock's gradual evolution from ancient ring fort to grand church ruins—projected down onto a large disc that visitors gather around.

Those headed for Dingle's great traditional music scene will enjoy the surprisingly good 15-minute film introduction to Irish traditional music in the small museum theater (€5, June–Sept daily 9:00–20:30; Oct–May Mon–Fri 9:00–17:00, closed Sat–Sun, cafeteria, tel. 062/61122). If you overnight in Cashel, consider taking in a performance of the Bru Boru musical dance troupe in the Centre's large upstairs theater (€13, mid-June–mid-Sept Tue–Sat 21:00).

Town of Cashel—The huggable town at the base of the Rock affords a good break on the long drive from Dublin to Dingle (TI open mid-May–mid-Sept Mon–Sat 9:15–18:00, Sun July–Sept only, closed mid-Sept–mid-May, tel. 062/61333). The Heritage Centre (across hall from TI) handles TI services off-season and presents a modest eight-minute audio explanation of Cashel's history around a walled town model.

Sleeping in Cashel
(€1 = about $1, country code: 353, area code: 062)

LOWER PRICED

Dominic Street, a five-minute walk below the rock, offers a couple of homey options. **Rockville House,** with six fine rooms, is close to the rock (Db-€50, tel. 062/61760). **Abbey House,** a bit farther toward town, has five comfortable rooms (Sb-€38, D-€51, Db-€58, CC, tel. & fax 062/61104, e-mail: teachnamainstreach@eircom.net).

O'Brien's Holiday Lodge is a fun hostel behind the rock near Hore Abbey (dorm beds-€15, Db-€45, camping spots-€7, laundry service-€10/load, Dundrum Road R505, tel. 062/61003, fax 062/62797, e-mail: obriensholidayhostel@eircom.net).

Eating in Cashel

Grab a soup-and-sandwich lunch at tiny **Granny's Kitchen** (next to parking lot at base of rock), at the **Bru Boru Centre's** cafeteria (below parking lot), or at snug **King Cormac's** (a block away at base of road up to rock).

For lunch or dinner, **Pasta Milano's** neon-orange glow is easy to spot above a famine work project wall (€12–15 meals, daily 12:00–23:00, Ladyswell Street, tel. 062/62729).

For a splurge dinner, consider the classy **Chez Hans** (Tue–Sat 18:00–22:00, closed Sun–Mon, €21–27 early-bird menu before 19:30, otherwise €25–37 entrées, in an old church a block below the rock, tel. 062/61177).

WATERFORD

The oldest city in Ireland, Waterford was once more important than Dublin. Today, while tourists associate the town's name with its famous crystal, locals are quick to remind you that the crystal is named after the town and not vice versa. Waterford is a plain, gray, workaday town. Pubs outnumber cafés, kids beg on street corners, and when radio stations offer dinner at McDonald's as a prize, people actually call in. It's a dose of real Ireland, which was until recently the poorest country in Western Europe.

Planning Your Time

A day is more than enough time for Waterford. Visit the crystal factory on the south edge of town on your way in or out—to avoid the midday crowds (the TI there has a free visitor's guide with a town map). In Waterford, the best "sight" is the historic walk (11:45 or 13:45), followed by the Museum of Treasures and Reginald's Tower. Parking is easy in one of the harborfront pay lots. To feel the pulse of Waterford, hang out on the town's pedestrian square and stroll through its big modern shopping mall.

Orientation (area code: 051)

Waterford's main drag runs along its ugly harbor (with the bus station and parking lots). All sights and recommended accommodations (except the Waterford Crystal factory tour) are within a five-minute walk of here. Both museums and the TI are on the harborfront. The stubby Victorian clock tower marks the middle of the harbor as well as the pedestrian Barronstrand Street that runs a block to the town square.

Tourist Information: The TI is on Merchant's Quay (June–Aug daily 9:00–18:00; Sept–May Mon–Sat until 17:00, closed Sun, tel. 051/875-823). As with all Irish TIs, it's basically a shop with a counter where clerks tell you about places that they endorse (i.e., get money from).

If you're visiting all three sights (Museum of Treasures, Reginald's Tower, and Waterford Crystal), you can save €4 on admissions by buying a €10 City Pass Ticket (sold at each sight).

Laundry: Launderettes are at 61 Mayor's Walk (Mon–Sat

Waterford History

The Vikings first came in 850 and established Waterford as their base for piracy. Since the spot is located at the gateway to the largest natural navigation system within Ireland, Viking ships could sail 50 miles into Ireland from here. Ireland had no towns at this time, only scattered monastic settlements and small gatherings of clans—perfect for rape, pillage, and plunder. Later, the Vikings decided to "go legal" and do their profiteering from an established trading base they named Vandrafjord ("safe harbor"...eventually Waterford). This became Ireland's first permanent town. It was from this base that the Norsemen invaded England.

In the 12th century, a deposed Irish king invited the Normans over from England, hoping to use their muscle to regain his land from a rival clan. The great warrior knight Strongbow came and never left, and that was the beginning of Ireland's long and troublesome relationship with the English.

8:30–18:30, Sun 11:00–18:00, tel. 051/858-905) and 129 The Quay (Mon–Sat 8:00–18:30, closed Sun, tel. 051/844-100).

Sights—Waterford

▲▲**Waterford Historic Walking Tour**—Jack Burtchaell and his partners lead informative hour-long historic town walks that meet at the Waterford Museum of Treasures (behind TI) every day at 11:45 and 13:45 (just show up and pay €5 at the end, mid-March–mid-Oct only, tel. 051/873711). The tour—really the most enjoyable thing to do in Waterford—is an entertaining walk from the TI to Reginald's Tower, giving you a good handle on the story of Waterford.

Cathedral of the Holy Trinity—In 1793, the English king granted Ireland the Irish Relief Act, which, among other things, allowed the Irish to build churches and worship publicly. With Catholic France (30 million) threatening Britain (8 million) on one side and Ireland (6 million) stirring things up on the other, the king needed to take action to lessen Irish resentment.

Granted this new freedom, the Irish built this interesting cathedral in 1796. It's Ireland's first Catholic post-Reformation church and its only Baroque church. The building was funded by wealthy Irish wine merchants from Cadiz, Spain. Among its treasures are 10 Waterford Crystal chandeliers (free, daily 8:00–19:00).

The cathedral faces **Barronstrand Street,** which leads from

Waterford

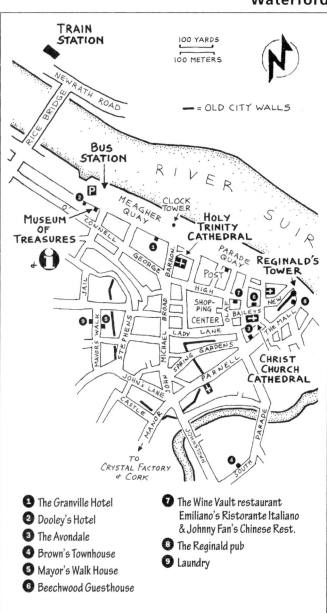

1. The Granville Hotel
2. Dooley's Hotel
3. The Avondale
4. Brown's Townhouse
5. Mayor's Walk House
6. Beechwood Guesthouse
7. The Wine Vault restaurant
   Emiliano's Ristorante Italiano
   & Johnny Fan's Chinese Rest.
8. The Reginald pub
9. Laundry

Thomas Francis Meagher (1823–1867)

Waterford's favorite son had a short but busy life. Born to a conservative Waterford mayor, Meagher joined Daniel O'Connell's nonviolent movement to repeal the Act of Union with Britain. Impatient with the slow-moving peace process, he joined the radical Young Irelander movement and became an inspiring speaker. He went to France in 1848 and came back with the first Irish tricolor flag—a gift from the French—representing the Catholics (green), the Protestants (orange), and peaceful coexistence between them (white). Involved in a failed uprising, Meagher was sentenced to be hanged, drawn, and quartered (one of the last to be given this sentence under British laws), but he managed to get his sentence commuted to life in prison in Tasmania. Meagher escaped Tasmania in 1852 and sailed to America, where he studied law and eventually became a lawyer. After he made a trip to Nicaragua to study the feasibility of building a canal across the isthmus, the American Civil War broke out. Meagher was made a general and raised a regiment of Irish immigrants that he led famously into battle for the Union. After the war, he became the first governor of the Montana territory. Then 44-year-old Thomas Francis Meagher fell off a riverboat and drowned.

the clock tower on the harborfront to the pedestrian-friendly **town square.** The street separates the medieval town (on your left when the river is behind you) from the 18th-century city (on your right). A river once flowed here—part of the town's natural defenses just outside the old wall. The huge **shopping center** that dominates the old town was built right on top of the Viking town. In fact, the center is built over a church dating from 1150 that you can see at the bottom of the escalator next to the kiddie rides.

▲**Reginald's Tower**—This oldest part of the oldest town in Ireland is named after Regnall, the first Viking leader of Waterford, who built a tower here in A.D. 914 and later founded Jorvik (York, England). The tower you see today dates from 1003 and is supposedly Ireland's oldest intact building and its first made of mortar. It was the most important corner of the town wall. Inside you'll see a display of medieval coins, old city models, a few Viking artifacts, and a short video (€2 includes guided tour any time upon request—ask for the 1-hour version, which adds a historic walk around the block, June–Sept 9:30–18:30, Oct–May 10:00–17:00, tel. 051/304220).

▲▲**Waterford Museum of Treasures**—This museum presents, with the help of handheld audioguides, a good sweep through the history of Ireland as seen from Waterford. It's housed, along with the TI, in an old stone grain warehouse where the original Waterford Crystal works stood (€6, daily June–Aug 9:30–19:00, April–May and Sept 9:30–18:00, Oct–March 10:00–17:00, tel. 051/30-4500).

Christ Church Cathedral—This 18th-century neoclassical Protestant cathedral is the fourth church to stand here (see the exposed Gothic column under glass 6 feet below today's floor level). The macabre tomb of a 15th-century mayor comes with a famous epitaph: "I am what you will be, I was what you are, pray for me." To emphasize the point, he requested that his body be dug up one year after his death and his partially decomposed remains be used to model his likeness, now seen on the tomb's lid . . . complete with worms and frogs (free and generally open 10:00–17:00).

▲▲**Waterford Crystal Factory**—With a tradition dating back to 1783, Waterford is the largest and one of the most respected glassworks in the world. Its fine hour-long tours take visitors through the entire production process and offer a close-up look at many of the plant's 1,600 employees hard at work.

While you ride a bus to one end of the factory, your guide orients you. Then you see a huge furnace—which has been burning nonstop for 30 years—where the dipping, blowing, and shaping take place. (It's powered by natural gas, piped in 90 miles from Kinsale.) Next you see the etching. Workers, after a five-year apprenticeship, make the art of crystal blowing and cutting look easy. Each glass piece goes through more than 30 sets of hands before it's ready for sale. Waterford proudly sells no seconds. Due to tiny blemishes detected by quality control, about a third of the pieces are smashed and remelted. (Workers are paid by the successful piece.) The tour finishes with an opportunity to actually meet a cutter, see his diamond-bladed wheel in action, and ask questions. Then you land in the glittering salesroom—with its bulbous Dale Chihuly chandelier as a centerpiece—surrounded by hard-to-pack but easy-to-ship temptations. Before leaving, go upstairs above the gift shop to see the copies of famous sports trophies (they make back-ups of their most important commissions . . . just in case).

Tours are liveliest weekdays before 15:30. Except for a skeleton crew working for the benefit of the tours, the factory is pretty quiet after 16:00 and on weekends. There are no tours from 13:00 to 14:00 on weekends (when those same skeletons are eating). Minimize crowds by coming early and avoiding the afternoon rush. There is a handy TI in the reception area.

The factory is conveniently located on the N-25 Cork road

about two miles south of the city center (€6, March–Oct daily 9:00–16:00, last tours leave at 16:00 sharp, but the shop stays open until 18:00; Nov–Feb Mon–Fri 9:00–15:15; if arriving late call to confirm tour time, tel. 051/332-500, www.waterfordvisitorcentre .com). There are easy city bus connections from the waterfront.

Sleeping in Waterford
(€1 = about $1, country code: 353, area code: 051)
Waterford is a working-class town. Cheap accommodations are fairly rough. Fancy accommodations are venerable old places facing the water.

HIGHER PRICED
The Granville Hotel is Waterford's top, most historic hotel, grandly overlooking the center of the harborfront. The place is plush, from its Old World lounges to its extravagant rooms (Db-€150–190, ask about "corporate discounts," CC, Meagher Quay, tel. 051/305-555, fax 051/305-566, www.granville-hotel.ie, e-mail: stay@granville-hotel.ie).

Dooley's Hotel, a business-class place on the harbor, is less expensive and more modern, with big motel-style rooms (Db-€152, often discounted as low as Db-€89, CC, Merchant's Quay, tel. 051/873-531, fax 051/870-262, e-mail: hotel@dooleys-hotel.ie).

MODERATELY PRICED
The Avondale faces a noisy street a block inland from Reginald's Tower and rents eight comfortable rooms (Sb-€45–50, Db-€70, Qb-130, CC, 2 Parnell Street, tel. 051/852-267, www.staywithus .net, e-mail: info@staywithus.net, Margaret & John Fogarty).

Brown's Townhouse is a charming, Victorian-style, six-room place where guests share one big, homey breakfast table. It's on a quiet residential street a 10-minute walk from the city center (Sb-€60, Db-€70–90, CC, 29 South Parade, tel. 051/ 870-594, fax 051/871-923, www.brownstownhouse.com, e-mail: info@brownstownhouse.com, Les & Barbara Brown).

LOWER PRICED
Mayor's Walk House is a well-worn, grandmotherly place that takes you right back to the 1950s. Kay and John Ryder rent four economical yet comfortable rooms (S-€25, D-€44, T-€66, no CC, 12 Mayor's Walk, tel. & fax 051/855-427).

Beechwood Guesthouse, sitting quietly next to Christ Church Cathedral, has cozy little rooms in a great location (S-€30, D-€48, no CC, no smoking, 7 Cathedral Square, tel. 051/876-677, e-mail: bjoeryan@eircom.net, Mary Ryan).

Eating in Waterford

For something livelier than tired pub grub, consider three good restaurants (wine bar, Italian, and Chinese) that share a tiny street behind Reginald's Tower. All are small, popular, and serve an early-bird special (2 or 3 courses for around €20 before 19:00). **The Wine Vault**—a wine shop by day—offers decent European cuisine and seafood with a good selection of wines from its 18th-century cellar (Mon–Sat 12:30–14:30 & 17:30–22:30, closed Sun, High Street, tel. 051/853-444); you're welcome to climb into the wine cellar below the restaurant.

Emiliano's Ristorante Italiano (Tue–Sun 17:00–22:30, closed Mon, 21 High Street, tel. 051/820-333) and **Johnny Fan's Chinese Cuisine and Seafood** (Mon–Sat 12:30–14:15 & 17:30–23:30, Sun 13:00–15:00 & 18:00–23:00, tel. 051/879-535) are both next door and lively with locals.

Pub Grub: Waterford's staple food seems to be pub grub. Several typical pubs serve dinner in the city center. **The Reginald,** directly behind Reginald's Tower, is one of the most popular (daily 12:00–15:30 & 19:00–21:30, 2 The Mall, tel. 051/855-087). For your musical entertainment, just wander around, read the notices, and follow your ears. You'll find plenty of live action on George Street, Barronstrand Street, and Broad Street.

Transportation Connections—Waterford

By train to: Dublin (4/day, 3 hrs), **Kilkenny** (4/day, 45 min), **Rosslare** (2/day, 1.5 hrs).

By bus to: Cork (13/day, 2.25 hrs), **Kilkenny** (3/day, 1 hr), **Rosslare** (4/day, 1.25 hrs), **Wexford** (8/day, 1 hr).

COUNTY WEXFORD

The southeast corner of Ireland is peppered with pretty views and historic sites, easily accessible to drivers as a day trip from Waterford. While most of the sights are mediocre, four or five (each within an hour's drive of Waterford) are worth considering.

The dramatic Hook Head Lighthouse—capping an intriguing and remote peninsula—comes with lots of history and a great tour. The Kennedy Homestead is a pilgrimage for Kennedy fans. The *Dunbrody* Famine Ship in New Ross gives a sense of what 50 days on a coffin ship with dreams of "Americay" must have been like. The Irish National Heritage Park in Wexford is a Stone-Age Knott's Berry Farm. And the National 1798 Visitors Centre at Enniscorthy explains the roots of the Irish struggle for liberty. New Ross, Enniscorthy, and Wexford are each less than 30 minutes apart, connected by fast highways. The Kennedy Homestead is a 10-minute drive from New Ross, and the lighthouse is a 45-minute trip to the end of the Hook Peninsula. All are easy to find. Connecting Dublin with Waterford, you could visit most of these sights in a best–of–County Wexford day. On a quick trip, the sights are not worth the trouble by public transit. If you'll be spending the night, Enniscorthy and New Ross are rough little workaday towns (with decent hotels and B&Bs) providing a good glimpse of Ireland.

Sights—County Wexford

If you plan on visiting more than one of the following Wexford sights (except the Kennedy Homestead), take advantage of the "Heritage Wexford" discount coupons, which offer 20 percent off each sight (given out at the first sight you visit).

▲**The Hook Head Lighthouse**—This is the oldest operating lighthouse in Northern Europe. According to legend, St. Dubhan arrived in the sixth century and discovered the bodies of ship-wrecked sailors. Dismayed, he and his followers began tending a fire on the headland to warn future mariners. What you see today is essentially 12th-century, built by the Normans (who first landed 5 miles up the east coast at Baginbun Head in 1169). They established Waterford Harbor as a commercial beachhead to the rich Irish countryside that they intended to conquer. This beacon assured them safe access.

Today's lighthouse is 110 feet tall and looks modern on the outside (it was automated in 1996 and its light can be seen 23 miles out to sea). But it's 800 years old, built on a plan inspired by the lighthouse of Alexandria in Egypt—one of the seven wonders of the ancient world.

A working lighthouse, it may be toured only with a guide or escort. Fine 30-minute tours leave about hourly. Inside, with its black-stained, ribbed, vaulted ceilings and stout, 10-foot-thick walls, you can almost feel the presence of the Benedictine monks who tended a coal-burning beacon at the top for the Normans. Climbing 115 steps through four levels rewards you with a breezy, salt-air view from the top (€4.75, March–Oct daily 9:30–17:30, last tour usually at 17:00, call to check tour times before driving out, tel. 051/397-055). There's a decent cafeteria and a shop with fliers explaining other sights on the peninsula. Kids-at-heart can't resist climbing out on the rugged rocky tip of the windy Hook Head.

When Oliver Cromwell arrived here to secure the English claim to this area, he considered his two options and declared he'd take strategic Waterford "by Hook or by Crooke." Hook is the long peninsula with the lighthouse. Crooke is a now-gone little village on the other side (just south of Passage East).

Southeast Ireland: County Wexford

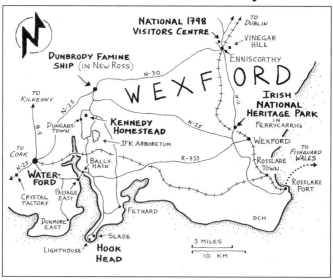

▲**Kennedy Homestead**—Patrick Kennedy, JFK's great-grandfather, left Ireland in 1858. Distant relatives have turned his property into a little museum/shrine for Kennedy pilgrims. Physically, it's not much: A barn and a wing of the modern house survive from 1858. JFK dropped in by helicopter in June of 1963, a few months before he was assassinated. You'll view two short videos: five minutes of Kennedy's actual visit to the farm and a 16-minute newsreel tracing the events of his 1963 trip through Ireland (both fascinating if you like Kennedy stuff). Then Patrick Grennan, a distant Kennedy relative himself whose grandmother hosted the tea here for JFK, gives you a 15-minute tour. Finally you're free to peruse the barn, lined with Kennedy-in-Ireland memorabilia and detailing the history of the Kennedy dynasty. While it's just a private home, anyone into the Kennedys will find it fascinating and worth driving the treacherous narrow lane to see (€4, June–Aug daily 10:00–18:00, May and Sept 11:30–16:30, by appointment after hours, in slow times, and Oct–April—no big deal as it's their home, tel. 051/388-264, 4 miles south of New Ross near Dunganstown—look for sign off of R733, long 1-lane road, www.kennedyhomestead.com).

Don't confuse the Kennedy Homestead with the nearby JFK Arboretum. The arboretum (with legitimate government signposts) is lovely if you like trees and plants. It's a huge park with 4,500 species of trees and a grand six-county view—but no Kennedy history.

▲▲*Dunbrody* **Famine Ship**—Permanently moored in the tiny port of New Ross, this was built as a reminder of the countless hungry Irish who sailed to America on ships like this. The *Dunbrody* is a full-scale reconstruction of a 19th-century three-masted barque built in Quebec in 1845. It's typical of the trading vessels that sailed empty to America to pick up goods, but during the famine ,found they could make a little money on the westward voyage. Extended families camped out for 50 days on bunk beds no bigger than a king-size mattress. Typically, boats like this would arrive in America with only 50 percent of their original human cargo—hence the nickname "coffin ships." After a 10-minute video about the building of the ship, you'll follow an excellent guide through the ship and encounter a couple of grumpy passengers who tell vivid tales about life aboard (€6, 30-min tours go 2/hr, April–Oct daily 9:00–18:00, last tour 17:15, Nov–March daily 10:00–17:00; easy parking and free on Sun, but during work hours you'll need to buy a €0.50-per-hour disk from the TI desk at the ship's reception, tel. 051/425-239, www.dunbrody.com). Root-seekers are welcome to peruse their computerized file of one million names of immigrants who sailed from 1846 through 1865.

▲**Irish National Heritage Park**—This 35-acre wooded park, which contains an 1857 tower commemorating local boys killed in the Crimean War, features re-creations of buildings from each era of Irish history. Ireland's countless ancient sights are generally unrecognizable ruins—hard to re-create in your mind. This park hopes to help out. You'll find buildings and settlements illustrating life in Ireland from the Stone Age through the 12th-century Norman Age. As a bonus, you'll see animal skin–clad characters doing their prehistoric thing—gnawing on meat, weaving, making arrowheads, and so on. Your visit begins with a 12-minute video followed by a 90-minute tour. At 13 stops, your guide explains the various civilizations; the highlight is a monastic settlement from the age when Europe was dark and Ireland was "the island of saints and scholars." While you can wander around on your own, the place is a bit childish (there's nothing actually old here) and only worthwhile if you take the included tour (€7, daily 9:30–18:30, until 17:30 in winter, last entry 90 min before closing, tours go 2/hr, tel. 053/20733). It's clearly signposted on the west end of Wexford—you'll hit it before entering town on the N11 Enniscorthy road.

National 1798 Visitors Centre—Located in Enniscorthy, this museum creatively tells the story of the rise of revolutionary

thinking in Ireland, which led to the ill-fated rebellion of 1798.
Enniscorthy was the crucial Irish battleground of a populist revolution (inspired by the American and French Revolutions) that
witnessed the bloodiest days of the doomed 1798 uprising. The
material is fascinating to anyone interested in struggles for liberty,
but there's little here more than video clips of reenactments and
storyboards on the walls (€6, April-Oct Mon–Sat 9:30–18:00, Sun
11:00–18:00, shorter hours Nov–March, last entry 1 hour before
closing, tel. 054/37596). Enniscorthy is 12 miles north of Wexford
town. The Visitors Centre is the town's major sight and therefore
well signposted.

Leaving the center, look east across the Slaney River that
divides Enniscorthy and you'll see a hill with a stumpy tower on it.
This is Vinegar Hill. The tower is the old windmill that once flew
the green rebel flag. Drive to the top for the views that the exposed
rebels had of the surrounding British forces as they desperately
tried to hold the high ground with no shelter from the merciless
British artillery fire.

KINSALE

While nearby Cork is the biggest town in south Ireland, Kinsale
(15 miles south) is actually more historic, certainly cuter, and a
delight to visit. Thanks to the naturally sheltered bay barbed by
a massive 17th-century star fort, you can submerge yourself in
maritime history from the Spanish Armada to Robinson Crusoe
to the *Lusitania*. Apart from all the history, Kinsale has a laid-back
Sausalito feel with a touch of wine-sipping class.

Planning Your Time

Kinsale is worth two nights and a day. The town's two tiny museums open at 10:00 and will occupy you until the 11:15 town walking tour. After lunch at the Fishy Fishy Café, head out to Charles
Fort for great bay views and insights into British military life in
colonial Ireland. On the way back, stop for a pint at the Bulman
Bar. Finish the day with a gourmet dinner and live music in a pub.
Those on the blitz tour can give Kinsale five hours—see the fort,
wander the town, and have a nice meal—before driving on.

Orientation (area code: 021)

Kinsale, because of its great natural harbor, is older and more
historic than Cobh (Cork's harbor town). While the town is prettier than the actual harbor, the harbor was its reason for being.
Kinsale's long and skinny old-town center is part modern marina
and part pedestrian-friendly medieval town—an easy 15-minute
stroll from end to end.

Kinsale History

Kinsale's remarkable harbor has made this an important port since prehistoric times. The bay's 10-foot tide provided a natural shuttle service for Stone Age hunter-gatherers: They could ride it at two miles per hour twice a day the eight miles up and down the River Bandon. In the Bronze Age, when people discovered that it takes tin and copper to make bronze, tin came from Cornwall and copper came from this part of Ireland. Therefore, from 500 B.C. to A.D. 500, Kinsale was a rich trading center. The result: Lots of Stonehenge-type monuments are nearby (the best is Drombeg Stone Circle, a 1-hour drive west). Kinsale's importance peaked during the 16th, 17th, and 18th centuries—when sailing ships ruled the waves, turning countries into global powers. Kinsale was Ireland's most perfect natural harbor and the gateway to both Spain and France—potentially providing a base for either of these two powers in cutting off English shipping. Because of this, two pivotal battles were fought here in the 17th century: in 1601 against the Spanish, and in 1690 against the French. Two great forts were built to combat these threats from the Continent. England couldn't rule the waves without ruling Kinsale.

To understand the small town of Kinsale, you need to understand the big picture: Around 1500, the pope gave the world to Spain and Portugal. With the Reformation breaking Rome's lock on Europe, maritime powers such as England were ignoring the pope's grant. This was important because trade with the New World and Asia brought huge wealth in spices (necessary for curing meat), gold, and silver. England threatened Spain's New World piñata, and Ireland was Catholic. Spain had an economic and a religious reason to defend the pope and Catholicism. The showdown between Spain and England for mastery of the seas (and control of all that trade) was in Ireland. The excuse: to rescue the dear Catholics of Ireland from the treachery of Protestant England (as if democracy and not oil were the rationale for the Gulf War).

The medieval walled town's economy rested on the stocking of ships. The old walls—which followed what is now O'Connell Street and Main Street—defined the original town. The windy Main Street traces the original coastline. Walking this you'll see tiny lanes leading to today's harbor. These originated as piers—just wide enough to roll a barrel down to an awaiting ship. The wall detoured inland to protect the St. Multose Church, which dates from Norman times (back when worshipers sharpened their

So, the Irish disaster unfolds. The powerful Ulster chieftains Hugh O'Neill and Red Hugh O'Donnell and their clans had been on a roll in their battle against the English. With Spanish aid, they figured they could actually drive the English out of Ireland. In 1601, the Spanish Armada dropped off 5,000 soldiers, who established a beachhead in Kinsale. After the ships left, the Spaniards were pinned down in Kinsale by the English commander (who, breaking with the martial etiquette, actually fought in the winter). Virtually the entire Irish fighting force left the North and marched through a harsh winter to the south coast, thinking they could liberate their Spanish allies and thus win freedom from England.

The numbers seemed reasonable (10,000 Englishmen versus 5,000 Spaniards as 5,000 Irish clansmen approached). The Irish attacked on Christmas Eve in 1601. But, holding the high ground around fortified and Spanish-occupied Kinsale, a relatively small force of English troops could keep the Spaniards hemmed in, leaving the bulk of the English force to outnumber and rout the fighting Irish. The Irish resistance was broken and its leaders fled to Europe (the "flight of the Earls"). England made peace with Spain and began the "plantation" of mostly Scottish Protestants in Ireland (the seeds of today's Troubles in Ulster). England ruled the waves and it ruled Ireland. The lesson: Kinsale is key. England eventually built two huge, star-shaped fortresses to ensure control of the narrow waterway, a strategy it would further develop in later fortifications built at Gibraltar and Singapore.

Kinsale's maritime history continues. Daniel Defoe used the real-life experience of Scottish privateer Alexander Selkirk, who departed from Kinsale in 1703 and was later marooned alone on a desert island, as the basis for his book *Robinson Crusoe*. And it was also just 10 miles off shore from Old Kinsale Head that the passenger liner *Lusitania* was torpedoed by a German submarine in 1915, killing 1,200 and sparking America's entry into World War I.

swords on the doorway of the church—check it out). What seems like part of the old center was actually built later on land reclaimed from the harbor. The town is a kind of quarry with shale hills ideal for a ready supply of fill. Today Kinsale is a wealthy resort of 2,000 residents.

Tourist Information: The TI is central as can be, at the head of the harbor across from the bus stop (July–Aug Mon–Sat 9:00–19:00, Sun 10:00–17:00, March–June and Sept–Nov Mon–Sat

9:30–17:30, closed Sun, shorter hours Dec–Feb, tel. 021/477-2234). It has a free town map and brochures outlining a world of activities in the vicinity.

Arrival in Kinsale: Since Kinsale doesn't have a train station, you'll arrive by bus (the stop is at Esso gas station on Pier Road at south end of town) or by car. Park your car and enjoy the town on foot. While the town's windy medieval lanes are narrow and congested, parking is fairly easy. There's a big lot at the head of the harbor behind the TI (€1.50/hr, €8/day, overnight 18:00–9:00 €5 extra) and a big, safe, and free parking lot just above St. Multose church at the top of town, a three-minute walk from most recommended hotels and restaurants. Street-side parking requires a disk (purchase at any newsstand, €0.50/hr, max 2 hours during the day). The outlying streets, a five-minute stroll from all the action, have wide-open parking.

Helpful Hints

Banking: The two banks in town are Allied Irish Bank on Pearse Street and Bank of Ireland on Emmett Street (both Mon 10:00–17:00, Tue–Fri 10:00–16:00, closed Sat–Sun).

Post Office: It's on Pearse Street (Mon–Sat 9:00–17:30).

Internet Access: Finishing Services calls itself an "E-mail & Internet Bureau" (€6/hr, Mon–Fri 9:00–19:00, Sat–Sun 9:30–16:00, Main Street, tel. 021/477-3571). Curtain Electrical is an appliance store with an e-mail terminal (€2.50/15 min, €4.10/30 min, Mon–Sat 9:00–18:00, Pearse Street). Note that both places close before dinner.

Laundry: Kinsale Launderette will wash and dry in half a day (€8/load, no self-service, Mon–Sat 9:30–6:30, Main Street, tel. 021/477-2205).

Bike Rental: The Hire Shop rents bikes, power tools, and fishing gear (18 Main Street, tel. 021/477-4884.)

Taxi: Kinsale Cabs has regular cab service and minibuses available (Market Square, tel. 021/477-2642).

Tours of Kinsale

▲▲**Don Herlihy's Historic Town Walk**—To understand the important role Kinsale played in Irish, English, and Spanish history, join Don Herlihy on a fascinating 90-minute walking tour (€5, daily April–Oct at 11:15 from the TI, also available for private hire, tel. 021/477-2873). Don is a joy to listen to as he creatively brings to life Kinsale's place in history and makes the stony sights of Kinsale more than just buildings. Don collects for the tour at the end, giving anyone disappointed in his talk an easy escape midway through. Don's walk is Kinsale's best single attraction.

Ghost Walk Tour—This is not just any ghost tour—it's more comedy than horror. Two actors weave funny stunts and stories into a loose history of the town, offering a thoroughly entertaining hour (€8, Mon and Wed–Fri at 21:00, leaves from Tap Tavern, cellular 086-855-5043 or 087-948-0910). This tour doesn't overlap with Don Herlihy's more serious historic town walk (above).

Sights—Kinsale

▲▲**Charles Fort**—Kinsale is protected by what was Britain's biggest star-shaped fort—a state-of-the-art defense when artillery made the traditional castle obsolete (€3.20, mid-March–Oct daily 10:00–18:00, last entry 17:15, Nov–mid-March only Sat–Sun 10:00–17:00, last entry 16:15, 2 miles south of town, Summer Cove, tel. 021/477-2263). The British occupied it until Irish independence in 1922. Its interior buildings were torched in 1923 by anti-treaty IRA forces to keep it from being used by Free State troops during the Irish Civil War. Guided 45-minute tours (depart on the hour, confirm at entry) engross you in the harsh daily life of the 18th-century British soldier. Before or after your tour, peruse the exhibits in the barracks and walk the walls.

For a coffee, beer, or meal nearby, stop by the Bulman Bar (see "Eating in Kinsale," below) in Summercove, where the road runs low near the water on the way back to town. And to actually see how easily the forts could bottle up this key harbor, stop for the grand harbor view at the high point on the road back into town (above Scilly, just uphill from the Spaniard pub).

James Fort—Older, overgrown, and filling a peaceful park, James Fort is Kinsale's other star fort, guarding the bay opposite Charles Fort. Built in the years just after the famous 1601 battle, this fort is more ruined, less interesting, and less visited than Charles Fort. Its satellite blockhouse sat below the fort at the waters' edge opposite Summercove and controlled a strong chain that could be raised to block ships from reaching Kinsale's docks.

Easily accessible by car or bike, it's two miles south of town along Pier Road on the west shore of the bay (cross new bridge and turn left; you'll dead-end at Castle Park Marina, where you can park or leave your bike). To reach the fort by foot from Kinsale, walk to the Trident Hotel Marina on the south edge of town, take a ferry (seasonal, ask TI if ferry operating, €1.50, 1/hr, 5 min) over to Castle Park Marina, and climb five minutes up the hill behind the Dock pub.

▲**Desmond Castle**—This 15th-century fortified Norman customs house has had a long and varied history. It was the Spanish armory during their 1601 occupation of Kinsale. Nicknamed "Frenchman's Prison," it served as a British prison and once

Kinsale

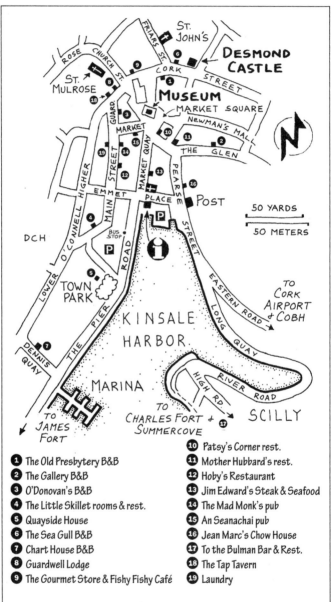

1 The Old Presbytery B&B
2 The Gallery B&B
3 O'Donovan's B&B
4 The Little Skillet rooms & rest.
5 Quayside House
6 The Sea Gull B&B
7 Chart House B&B
8 Guardwell Lodge
9 The Gourmet Store & Fishy Fishy Café
10 Patsy's Corner rest.
11 Mother Hubbard's rest.
12 Hoby's Restaurant
13 Jim Edward's Steak & Seafood
14 The Mad Monk's pub
15 An Seanachai pub
16 Jean Marc's Chow House
17 To the Bulman Bar & Rest.
18 The Tap Tavern
19 Laundry

housed 600 prisoners of the Napoleonic Wars (not to mention earlier American Revolutionary War prisoners captured at sea— who were treated as rebels, not prisoners, and chained to the outside of the building as a warning to any rebellion-minded Irish). In the late 1840s, it was a famine-relief center. Today the evocative little ruin comes with a scant display of its colorful history and a modest one-room Museum of Wine highlighting Ireland's little-known connection to the international wine trade. In the Middle Ages, Kinsale was renowned for its top-quality wooden casks. Developing strong trade links with Bordeaux, local merchants traded their dependable empty casks for casks full of wine (€2.50, mid-April–Oct daily 10:00–18:00, last entry 17:15, 20-min tours often given on the hour, tel. 021/477-4855).

▲**Kinsale Regional Museum**—In the center of the old town, traffic circles the old town market, which later became a courthouse and is now the Regional Museum. Drop by at least to read the fun 1788 tax code for all Kinsale commercial transactions (outside at the front door). The modest museum is worth a quick visit for its fun mishmash of domestic and maritime bygones and for the perspective it gives on the controversial *Lusitania* tragedy (€2.50, Wed–Sat 10:30–17:30, Sun 14:00–17:30, closed Mon–Tue, Market Square, tel. 021/477-7930).

Kinsale had maritime jurisdiction over the waters 10 miles offshore where the luxury liner was torpedoed in 1915. Hearings were held here in the courthouse shortly afterward to investigate the causes of the disaster and to paint the German Hun as a bloodthirsty villain. Claims by Germany that the *Lusitania* was illegally carrying munitions seem to have been borne out by the huge explosion and rapid sinking of the vessel. This event is important because it helped propel America into World War I. But perhaps even more interesting, in the side room, is the boot of the 8-foot 3-inch Kinsale giant, who lived here in the late 1700s.

Sleeping in Kinsale
(€1 = about $1, country code: 353, area code: 021)
Kinsale is a popular place in summer for yachters and golfers (who don't flinch at paying $200 for 18 holes out on the exotic Old Head of Kinsale Golf Course). It's wise to book ahead. I've listed peak-season prices. These places include breakfast and are all within a five-minute walk of the town center.

HIGHER PRICED
The Old Presbytery is a fine, quiet house a block outside of the commercial district, with a goofy floor plan but fine rooms. Well-listed in most guidebooks, it has lots of American guests (10 rooms,

Db-€80–140 depending on size of room, family Qb-€160, 2 self-catering Qb suites-€155 with minimum 3-night stay, CC, private car park, 43 Cork Street, tel. 021/477-2027, fax 021/477-2166, www.oldpres.com, e-mail: info@oldpres.com). The breakfasts are a delight, and Noreen McEvoy runs the place with a passion for excellence.

Chart House B&B is a luxurious Georgian home renting a tidy little single and three grand and sumptuous doubles. It's a block off the harbor at the marina end of the old town. This smoke-free, quiet, and well-run place is top-end in every respect—high ceilings, chandeliers, and a plush living room (Sb-€40–52, Db-€90–152 depending on size and season, CC, 6 Dennis Quay, tel. 021/477-4568, fax 021/477-7907, www.charthouse-kinsale .com, e-mail: charthouse@eircom.net).

MODERATELY PRICED
The Gallery, a bright and funky five-room place with stylish decor, is run by Tom and Carole O'Hare. He's a classical pianist and she's an artist, and the place is run with a fresh informality—you can have ice cream for breakfast (Db-€80–100, family quad, CC, private car park, The Glen, tel. 021/477-4558, www.gallerybnb.com, e-mail: carole@gallerybnb.com).

Quayside House is a grand, blocky building overlooking a small park and the bay along Pier Road. Mary Cotter rents six rooms and offers a warm welcome (Db-€104, €52 in winter, Qb-€120, CC, Pier Road, tel. 021/477-2188, fax 021/477-2664, www.euroka.com/quayside, e-mail: quaysidehouse@eircom.net).

LOWER PRICED
O'Donovan's B&B is six rooms in a 400-year-old building made cheery, homey, and welcoming by Eileen and Michael O'Donovan. Right in the charming medieval center, it's handy but a bit noisy on Fridays and Saturdays (D-€54, Db-€60, CC, non-smoking, Guardwell Street, tel. 021/477-2428, e-mail: odonovans_bb@iolfree.ie).

The Little Skillet is all charm and no grease with one quaint room above a wonderful (and equally quaint) restaurant. Narrow stairways lead into a teddy-on-the-beddy world of exposed ceiling timbers. Anne Ennos runs it with a twinkle in her eye (Db-€60, CC, Main Street, tel. 021/477-4202, www.thelittleskillet.com, e-mail: littleskillet@irelandwide.com).

The Sea Gull, perched up the hill right next to Desmond Castle, offers six well-worn rooms run by Mrs. Mary O'Neill, who also runs the Tap Tavern down the hill (S-€35, Db-€60–64, Tb-€85, 10 percent discount with this book, no CC, Cork Street, tel. 021/477-2240, e-mail: marytap@iol.ie).

Guardwell Lodge is a big, boxy, new building at the top of the old center, with 64 rooms connected by a prison-like series of stairways and catwalks in its inner courtyard. While almost a hostel, it has no hostel-type regulations or restrictions. Its stark but modern and comfortable rooms (each with a fine new bathroom) are far and away the best budget beds in this ritzy town. You'll just have to take a walk to get any local character (€15 beds in 4-bed dorms, Sb-€26, Db-€50, Tb-€63, CC, 10 percent discount with this book, no breakfast, all bedding provided, fully equipped self-catering kitchen, TV lounge, request a quiet room on the church side, on Guardwell Street, tel. 021/477-4686, fax 021/477-4684, www.guardwelllodge.com, e-mail: info@guardwelllodge.com).

Eating in Kinsale

As Ireland's self-proclaimed gourmet capital, Kinsale manages to merge friendly old-fashioned Irish hospitality with quality restaurant options. Local competition is fierce, and restaurants offer creative and tempting menus. You don't have to have a big budget or a cultured palate to enjoy the range of choices available—everything from simple chowder-and-sandwich lunches to memorable fish-and-steak dinner feasts.

Lunch

The Gourmet Store & Fishy Fishy Café is *the* place for a good lunch. It's like eating in a fish market surrounded by the day's catch and a pristine stainless-steel kitchen. Marie and her white-aproned staff hustle wonderful steaming piles of beautifully presented seafood to eager customers (€15–18 specials, lunch only, daily 12:00–16:00, closed Sun off-season, across from church on Guardwell Street, tel. 021/477-4453). Look at the lobster tank and ponder this: A couple of years ago, a soft-hearted, fat-walleted Buddhist tourist bought up the entire day's supply of live lobster (worth over €600) and set them free in the bay. They've refilled the tank since.

For cheap and cheery, try the cramped Patsy's Corner or local breakfast hangout, Mother Hubbard's. Both are near the Market Square and serve sandwiches, baguettes, or salads with coffee for under €6.50.

For a picnic, gather supplies at the Super Valu supermarket (Mon–Sat 8:30–21:00, Sun 10:00–21:00, Pearse Street).

Good Dinners in the Old Center

The Little Skillet feels intimate, with tasty food and a romantic, rough-stone-and-big-fireplace atmosphere. Over the last 11 years, Richard and Anne Ennos have developed a loyal following, serving all the old-time Irish favorites with traditional Irish music, fresh and seasonal veggies, and absolutely no French fries. You can drop in just for a glass of wine and dessert in the upstairs wine bar. Diners can wait at the bar across the street and are welcome to bring in their own pint (dinners €15–19, daily 18:00–22:30, CC, Main Street, tel. 021/477-4202).

Hoby's Restaurant, another well-established favorite, offers modern cuisine in a quiet, candlelit room. It's popular with people from Cork coming down for a special night out (3-course €21 dinners, daily 18:00–22:00, CC, Main Street, tel. 021/477-2200).

At **Jim Edward's Steak & Seafood,** one kitchen keeps eaters happy in both the bar and the restaurant. Choose between a noisy maritime ambience in the restaurant (€17–25 meals) or dark and mellow in the bar (€9–15 meals). While cheaper and less gourmet than other Kinsale eateries, it offers decent steaks, seafood, and vegetables (bar 12:00–22:00, restaurant 18:00–22:00, CC, Market Quay, tel. 021/477-2541).

Several candlelit wine-bar restaurants vie for your attention along the gently curving Main Street. **Max's Wine Bar** has a respected French chef. **Vintage** looks like, feels like, and is the most expensive place in town.

Pubs with decent kitchens abound, serving casual dinners (€8–13) in a smoky and funky atmosphere. Many follow dinner with live music. Consider **The Mad Monk's** (daily 11:30–23:30, Main Street, tel. 021/477-4602) and **An Seanachai** (daily 11:00–23:30, Market Street, tel. 021/477-4472).

For a break from Irish cooking, **Jean Marc's Chow House** serves up good Asian meals (€13–18 dinners, daily 19:00–22:00, Sept–May closed Tue, Pearse Street, tel. 021/477-7117).

Fine Food near Charles Fort
The Bulman Bar and Restaurant has a top-notch chef who serves seafood with seasonal produce and some dishes with an Asian twist. His mussels are especially tasty; on a balmy day or evening, diners take a bucket and a beer out to the seawall. This is the only real way to eat on the water in Kinsale (daily 12:30–21:30, €9 meals in bar, €20 meals upstairs in fancy restaurant, 200 yards toward Kinsale from Charles Fort in hamlet of Summercove, tel. 021/477-2131, run by Oliver Flynn). The pub, strewn with fun decor and sporting a big fireplace, is also good for a coffee or beer after your visit to the fort.

Live Pub Music
Kinsale's pubs are packed with atmosphere and live music. Rather than target a certain place, simply walk the area between

Guardwell, Pearse Street, and the Market Square. Pop into each pub that has live music and then settle into your favorite. Several of the pubs wind deep into buildings. On a Thursday night, I found six places with live music thriving at 23:00 along this proposed loop. **An Seanachai** (pron. SHAN-ah-key) means "storyteller" in Gaelic, but it's now known for its music (Main Street). **The Tap Tavern** is serious about traditional music (just below St. Multose Church).

Transportation Connections—Kinsale

Like many worthwhile corners of Ireland, Kinsale is not accessible by train. The closest train station is in Cork, 15 miles north. But buses run frequently between Kinsale (stop is at Esso gas station on Pier Road, south end of town) and Cork's train station (11/day, 45 min, €5 one-way, €7 round-trip).

By bus from Cork to: Dublin (6/day), **Galway** (12/day), **Tralee** (8/day), and **Kilkenny** (9/day). Bus info: tel. 021/450-8188.

COBH

If your ancestry is Irish, chances are this was the last Irish soil your ancestors had under their feet. Cobh (pron. cove) was the major port of Irish emigration in the 19th century. Of the six million Irish who have emigrated to America, Canada, and Australia since 1815, nearly half left from Cobh.

The first steam-powered ship to make a transatlantic crossing departed from Cobh in 1838—cutting the journey time from 50 days to 18.

When Queen Victoria came to Ireland for the first time in 1849, Cobh was the first Irish ground she set foot on. Giddy, the town renamed itself "Queenstown" in her honor. It was still going by that name in 1912 when the *Titanic* stopped here before heading out on its maiden (and only) voyage. To celebrate their new independence from British royalty in 1922, locals changed the name back to its original Irish name—Cobh.

Cobh sits on a large island in Cork harbor. The town's inviting waterfront is colorful yet salty, with a playful promenade. The butcher's advertisement reads, "always pleased to meet you and always with meat to please you." Stroll past the shops along the water. Ponder the *Lusitania* memorial on Casement Square and the modest *Titanic* memorial nearby on Pearse Square. A hike up the hill to the towering neo-Gothic St. Colman's Cathedral rewards you with a fine view of the port.

Tourist Information: The TI is in the Old Yacht Club on the harbor (Mon–Fri 9:30–17:30, Sat–Sun 11:30–17:30, tel. 021/813-301, www.cobhharbourchamber.ie).

Sights—Cobh

▲**The Queenstown Story**—Cobh's major sightseeing attraction, filling its harborside Victorian train station, is an earnest
attempt to make the city's emigration and maritime history
interesting. The topics—the famine, Irish emigration, Australia-
bound prison ships, the sinking of the *Lusitania*, and the ill-
fated voyage of the *Titanic*—are fascinating enough to make
this museum a worthwhile stop. But the museum itself, while
kid-friendly, is weak on actual historical artifacts. It reminds
me of a big, interesting history picture book with the pages
expanded and tacked on the wall (€5, daily 10:00–18:00, last
entry 17:00, tel. 021/481-3591).

Those with Irish roots to trace are welcome to use the Heritage
Centre's genealogy search service (www.cobhheritage.com, e-mail:
cobhher@indigo.ie).

Sleeping in Cobh
(€1 = about $1, country code: 353, area code: 021)
The following listings are all centrally located near the harbor,
less than a five-minute walk from The Queenstown Story.

Consider the higher-priced **Waters Edge Hotel** (Sb-€70–
90, Db-€110–160, Tb-€130–180, Yacht Club Quay, tel. 021/
481-5566, www.watersedgehotel.ie, info@watersedgehotel.ie);
the moderately priced **Commodore Hotel** (Sb-€60–70,
Db-€95–110, Tb-€150–163, Westbourne Place, tel. 021/
481-1277); and two lower-priced choices: **Ard na Laoi**
(Db-€64, Westbourne Place, tel. 021/481-2742) and **Westbourne House B&B** (cheapest, with no frills, S-€20, D-€40,
Westbourne Place, tel. 021/481-1391).

Transportation Connections—Cobh
By car: Driving to Cobh from Cork or Waterford, leave the
N25 about eight miles east of Cork, following the little R624
over a bridge, onto the Great Island, and directly into Cobh.

Kinsale to Cobh is 25 miles, takes an hour, and involves
catching a small ferry. Leave Kinsale north on the R600 toward
Cork. Just south of Cork and its airport, go east on R613. You
will be following little car-ferry signs but they ultimately take
you to the wrong ferry (Ringaskiddy—to France). After you hit
the N28, take R610 to Monkstown and then Glenbrook where
a (poorly signposted) shuttle ferry takes you to the Great Island
(5 min, €3 ride). Once on the island, turn right and drive a mile
or two into Cobh. In Cobh, follow the Heritage Centre signs
to The Queenstown Story, where you'll find easy parking right
at the museum.

Sights—Between Waterford and Killarney

These stops, easiest for drivers, run roughly from east to west.
Ardmore—This funky little beach resort, with a famous ruined church and round tower, is a handy stop midway between Cork and Waterford (just west of Youghal, 3 miles south of N25). A couple of buses run daily from Ardmore to Cork and to Waterford.

This humble little port town is just a line of pastel houses that appear frightened by the sea. Its beach claims (very modestly) to be "the most swimmable in Ireland." The beachside **TI,** housed in an alien spacecraft, has a flier laying out a historic walk (June–Aug Mon–Sat 11:00–13:00 & 14:00–17:00, Sun 15:00–17:00, closed Sept–May, tel. 024/94444).

The town's historic claim to fame: Christianity came to Ireland here first (thanks to St. Declan, who arrived in A.D. 416—35 years before St. Patrick). As if to proclaim that feat with an 800-year-old exclamation mark, one of Ireland's finest examples of a round tower stands perfectly intact, 97 feet above an evocative graveyard and a ruined church (noted for the faint remains of some early Christian carvings on its west facade). You can't get into the tower—the entrance is 14 feet off the ground. That's intentional: In times of attack, monks would flee here with their books, treasures, and relics, and pull up the ladder.

Sleeping in Ardmore: Consider the moderately priced **Round Tower Hotel** in town (Sb-€50, Db-€90, tel. 024/94494) and the lower-priced **Bryon Lodge B&B** just outside of town (Sb-€35, Db-€62, Tb-€70, tel. 024/94157). The cheap **Ardmore Beach Hostel** is a basic stone building located where Main Street hits the Atlantic (€14 beds in 5-bed dorms, €35 family rooms, tel. 024/94166; if no one's home, go next door to Paddy Mac's Pub).

▲**Midleton Distillery**—Sometime during your Ireland trip, even if you're a teetotaler, you'll want to tour a whiskey distillery. Of the three major distillery tours—Jameson in Dublin, Bushmills in North Ireland, and Midleton 12 miles east of Cork in Midleton—the Midleton experience is the most interesting. After a 10-minute video, you'll walk with a guide through a great old 18th-century plant on a 45-minute tour; see waterwheel-powered crankshafts and a 31,000-gallon copper still—the largest of its kind in the world; and learn the story of whiskey. Predictably, you finish in a tasting room and enjoy a free not-so-wee glass. The finale is a Scotch/Irish Whiskey taste test. Your guide will take two volunteers for this. Don't be shy—raise your hand like an eager little student and enjoy an opportunity to taste the different brands (tour-€6.25, daily 10:00–18:00 year-round, 2/hr in summer, 3/day in winter, cafeteria, about a mile off N25—the main Cork–Waterford road—easy parking, drive right into distillery lot, tel. 021/461-3594).

Southwest Ireland

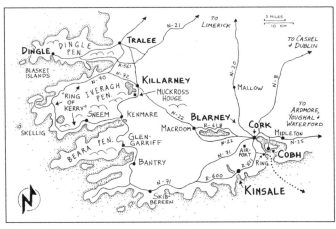

Kinsale and Cobh—See listings above.

Blarney Stone and Castle—The 15th-century Blarney Castle is five miles northwest of Cork (the major city of southern Ireland). The town of Blarney is of no importance, and the castle is an empty hulk (with no attempt made to make it meaningful or interesting). It's only famous as the place of tourist pilgrimage, where busloads line up to kiss a stone on its top rampart and get "the gift of gab." The best thing about this lame sight is the opportunity to watch a cranky man lower lemming tourists over the edge, belly up and head back, to kiss the stone while his partner snaps a photo—which will be waiting for you to purchase back at the parking lot. After a day of tour groups mindlessly climbing up here to perform this ritual, the stone is literally slathered with spit and lipstick. The basis of all this goes back to the late 16th century, when Queen Elizabeth I wished the Irish clan chiefs to recognize the crown, rather than the clan chiefs, as the legitimate title-holder of all lands. One of those chiefs was Cormac MacCarthy, Lord of Blarney Castle. He was smart enough never to disagree with the Queen—instead, he would cleverly avoid acquiescing to her demands by sending a never-ending stream of lengthy and deceptive excuses, disguised with liberal doses of flattery. In her frustration, the Queen declared his endless words nothing but "blarney." Walking back, you'll cross a stream littered with American pennies—as if the good-luck fairy can change them into euros (€5.50, daily 9:00–18:00, later in peak season, shorter hours in winter, free parking lot, helpful TI, tel. 021/438-5252).

Macroom—This colorful, inviting market town is a handy stop between Cork and Killarney. The ghostly gateway of its ruined castle (once owned by the father of the William Penn who founded Pennsylvania) overlooks its entertaining main square, where you'll find plenty of parking. This makes for an excellent coffee or lunch stop midway between Cork and Killarney. The Café Next Door, adjacent to the Castle Hotel, serves a good fast lunch.

Muckross House

Perhaps the best Victorian stately home you'll see in Ireland, Muckross House (built in 1843) is magnificently set at the edge of Killarney National Park.

This regular stop on the tour-bus circuit includes several sights in one: the mansion, a set of traditional farms showing rural life in the 1930s, a fine garden idyllically set on a lake, and an information center for the national park. The Victorian period was the 19th-century boom time, when the sun never set on the British Empire and the Industrial Revolution (born in England) was chugging the world into the modern age. Of course, Ireland was a colony back then, with big-shot English landlords. (The English gentry lived very well, while a third of Ireland's population starved in the famine of 1845–1849. Read the Muckross House lord's defense on page 43 of the fine souvenir book.)

Muckross House feels lived in because it still is—with fine Victorian furniture cluttered around the fireplace under Waterford Crystal chandeliers and lots of antlers. You'll see Queen Victoria's bedroom (ground floor since she was afraid of house fires, used during her 1861 visit). Be certain to take the included 45-minute guided tour that gives the house meaning; the tours—included with admission—leave regularly throughout the day (€5 for house, €7.50 covers house and old farms, daily 9:00–18:00, July–Aug until 19:00, farms open summer only, tel. 064/31440).

The house exit takes you through an information center for Killarney National Park with a relaxing 15-minute video on "Ireland's premier national park" (shown upon request, free, lots of geology, flora, and fauna).

The **Muckross Traditional Farms,** designed to give the Muckross stop a little heft, consists of six different farmhouses showing off life in the 1930s. Several farms come with a person ready to feed you a little home-baked bread and reminisce about the old days. If you've yet to see an open-air folk museum, this might be worthwhile—otherwise it's pretty lightweight. The farms are strung along a mile-long road with an old bus shuttling those who don't want to hike (4/hr, included).

Muckross House is conveniently placed for a break on the long ride from Cork or Cashel to Dingle. Beware of the horse-and-buggy bandits: As you approach from Killarney, you'll think the Muckross House parking lot is a small lot two miles before the actual parking lot. This is used by horse-and-buggy guys to hoodwink tourists into thinking they have to hike there or buy their overpriced services. Giddy-up on by and you'll find a big, safe, and free lot right at the mansion. From Killarney, follow signs to Kenmare, three miles south of town. The bright, modern cafeteria (with indoor/outdoor seating) faces the garden. The adjacent crafts shop shows weaving and pottery in action. The garden is a hit with gardeners, and a €1.50 guide booklet makes the nature trails interesting.

Scenic Peninsulas of the Southwest

There are several scenic and remote peninsulas in the southwest. The tour-bus route around the **Iveragh Peninsula** is so standard that its tourist name, "the Ring of Kerry," is how most refer to the peninsula. To manage the congestion, buses have all agreed to do it "anticlockwise" in a virtual convoy. The Ring of Kerry is undeniably scenic (but I prefer—and cover—the next peninsula north, Dingle, which most agree is as scenic, of more historic interest, and far less touristy). If you decide to drive the Iveragh Peninsula, go with the tour-bus flow. (Bus drivers giggle demonically when they talk of the frazzled tourist who ends up going clockwise.) The **Beara Peninsula** is perhaps even more remote than Dingle, with fine little time-warp villages and great scenery. The tidy resort town of Kenmare is a popular base for exploring either this or the adjacent Ring of Kerry. If you're driving from Cork to Dingle, the main road—while less memorable—is much faster and safer.

DINGLE PENINSULA

Dingle Peninsula, the westernmost tip of Ireland, offers just the right mix of far-and-away beauty, ancient archaeological wonders, and isolated walks or bike rides—all within convenient reach of its main town. Dingle town is just large enough to have all the necessary tourist services and a steady nocturnal beat of Irish folk music.

While the big tour buses clog the neighboring Ring of Kerry before heading east to slobber all over the Blarney Stone, Dingle—although crowded in summer—still feels like the fish and the farm really matter. Forty fishing boats sail from Dingle, tractor tracks dirty its main drag, and a faint whiff of peat fills its nighttime streets.

For 20 years, my Irish dreams have been set here on this sparse but lush peninsula where locals are fond of saying, "The next parish is Boston." There's a feeling of closeness to the land on Dingle. When I asked a local if he was born here, he thought for a second and said, "No, it was about six miles down the road." When I told him where I was from, a faraway smile filled his eyes, and he looked out to sea and sighed, "Ah, the shores of Americay." I asked his friend if he'd lived here all his life. He said, "Not yet."

Dingle feels so traditionally Irish because it's a Gaeltacht, a region where the government subsidizes the survival of the Irish language and culture. While English is always there, the signs, menus, and songs come in Gaelic. Children carry hurling sticks to class, and even the local preschool brags "ALL Gaelic."

Of the peninsula's 10,000 residents, 1,500 live in Dingle town. Its few streets, lined with ramshackle but gaily painted shops and pubs, run up from a rain-stung harbor always busy with fishing boats and yachts. Traditionally, the buildings were drab gray or whitewashed. Thirty years ago Ireland's "tidy town" competition prompted everyone to paint their buildings in playful pastels.

Dingle Peninsula Sights

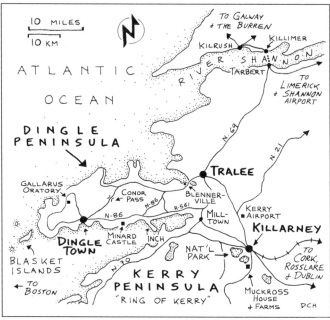

It's a peaceful town. The courthouse (1832) is open one hour a month. The judge does his best to wrap up business within a half hour. During the day you'll see teenagers—already working on ruddy beer-glow cheeks—roll kegs the streets and into the pubs in preparation for another night of music and *craic* (fun conversation and atmosphere).

Planning Your Time

For the shortest visit, give Dingle two nights and a day. It takes 6–8 hours to get there from Dublin, Galway, or the boat dock in Rosslare. I like two nights because you feel more like a local on your second evening in the pubs. You'll need the better part of a day to explore the 30-mile loop around the peninsula by bike, car, or tour bus (see "Circular Tour" on page 133). To do any serious walking or relaxing, you'll need two or three days. It's not uncommon to find Americans slowing way, way down in Dingle town.

Orientation (area code: 066)

Dingle—extremely comfortable on foot—hangs on a medieval grid of streets between the harborfront (where the Tralee bus stops)

Dingle History

The wet sod of Dingle is soaked with medieval history. In the darkest depths of the Dark Ages, peace-loving, bookish monks fled the chaos of the Continent and its barbarian raids. They sailed to the drizzly fringe of the known world—places like Dingle. These monks kept literacy alive in Europe. Charlemagne, who ruled much of Europe in the year 800, imported Irish monks to be his scribes.

It was from this peninsula that the semi-mythical explorer/monk, St. Brendan, is said to have set sail in the sixth century in search of a legendary western paradise. Some think he beat Columbus to North America by nearly a thousand years.

Dingle (An Daingean in Gaelic) was a busy seaport in the late Middle Ages. Dingle and Tralee (covered later in chapter) were the only walled towns in Kerry. Castles stood at the low and high ends of Dingle's Main Street, protecting the Normans from the angry and dispossessed Irish outside. Dingle was a gateway to northern Spain—a three-day sail due south. Many 14th- and 15th-century pilgrims left from Dingle for the revered Spanish church, Santiago de Compostela, thought to house the bones of St. James.

In Dingle's medieval heyday, locals traded cowhides for wine. When Dingle's position as a trading center waned, the town faded in importance. In the 19th century it was a linen-weaving center. Until 1970 fishing dominated, and the only visitors were scholars and students of old Irish ways. In 1970, the movie *Ryan's Daughter* introduced the world to Dingle. The trickle of Dingle fans has grown to a flood as word of its musical, historical, gastronomical, and scenic charms—not to mention its friendly dolphin—has spread.

and Main Street (3 blocks inland). Nothing in town is more than a five-minute walk away. Street numbers are used only when more than one place is run by a family of the same name. Most locals know most locals, and people on the street are fine sources of information. Remember, locals love their soda bread, and tourism provides the butter. You'll find a warm and sincere welcome.

Tourist Information: The TI is a privately owned, for-profit business—little more than a glorified shop with a green staff who are disinclined to really know the town (July–Aug daily 9:00–19:00, June & Sept–Oct 9:30–17:30, Nov–May 10:00–17:00, closed Sun & Tue;

The Voyage of St. Brendan

It has long been part of Irish lore that St. Brendan the Navigator (A.D. 484–577) and 12 followers sailed from the southwest of Ireland to the "Land of Promise" (what is now North America) in a currach—a wood-frame boat covered with ox hide and tar. According to a 10th-century monk who poetically wrote of the journey, St. Brendan and his crew encountered a paradise of birds, were attacked by a whale, and suffered the smoke of a smelly island in the north before finally reaching their Land of Promise.

The legend and its precisely described locations still fascinate modern readers. A British scholar of navigation, Tim Severin, re-created the entire journey from 1976 to 1977. He and his crew set out from Brendan Creek in County Kerry in a currach. The prevailing winds blew them to the Hebrides, the Faeroe Islands, Iceland, and finally to Newfoundland. While this didn't successfully prove that St. Brendan sailed to North America, it did prove that he could have.

St. Brendan fans have been heartened by an intriguing archaeological find in Connecticut. Called the "Gungywamp," the site includes a double circle of stones and a beehive-like chamber built in the same manner as the stone *clochans* huts on the Dingle Peninsula. The Gungywamp beehive chamber has been carbon-dated to approximately A.D. 600. Outside the chamber, a stone slab is inscribed with a cross that resembles the unique style of the Irish cross.

According to his 10th-century biographer, "St. Brendan sailed from the Land of Promise home to Ireland. And from that time on, Brendan acted as if he did not belong to this world at all. His mind and his joy were in the delight of heaven."

on Strand Street by the water, tel. 066/915-1188). For more knowledgeable help, drop by the Mountain Man shop (on Strand Street, see "Dingle Activities," below) or talk to your B&B host.

Helpful Hints

Before You Go: The local Web site (www.dingle-peninsula.ie) lists festivals and events. And www.celticwave.com is a good bet for music and arts listings. Look up old issues of *National Geographic* (April 1976 and Sept 1994).

Crowds: Crowds trample Dingle's charm throughout July

and August. The absolute craziest are the Dingle Races (2nd weekend in Aug), Dingle Regatta (3rd weekend in Aug), and the Blessing of the Boats (end of Aug, beginning of Sept). The first Mondays in May, June, and August are bank holidays, giving Ireland's workers three-day weekends—and ample time to fill up Dingle. The town's metabolism (prices, schedules, activities) rises and falls with the tourist crowds—October through April is sleepy.

Banking: Two banks in town, both on Main Street, offer the same rates (Mon 10:00–17:00, Tue–Fri 10:00–16:00, closed Sat–Sun) and have cash machines. The TI happily changes cash and traveler's checks at mediocre rates. Expect to use cash (rather than credit cards) to pay for most peninsula activities.

Post Office: It's on Main Street near Benners Hotel (Mon–Fri 9:00–17:30, Sat 9:00–13:00, closed Sun).

Laundry: The launderette is full-service only—drop off a load before 10:00 and pick up late that afternoon (tiny load-€7, regular load-€10, Mon–Sat 9:00–17:30, closed Sun; Nov–April open only Mon, Wed, Fri 9:00–17:00, on Green Street down alley opposite church, tel. 066/915-1837).

Internet Access: Dingle Internet Café is on Main Street (€2.60/20 min, Apr–Sept Mon–Fri 10:00–19:00, Sat 10:00–18:00, Sun 13:00–18:00, shorter hours Oct–March, tel. 066/915-2478).

Bike Rental: Bike-rental shops abound. The best is Paddy's Bike Hire (€10/day or 24 hrs, €12 for better bikes, daily 9:00–19:00, helmets €1 extra, on Dykegate next to Grapevine Hostel, tel. 066/915-2311). Foxy John's (Main Street), Mountain Man (no helmets), and the Ballintaggert Hostel also rent bikes. If you're biking the peninsula, get a bike with skinny street tires, not slow and fat mountain-bike tires. Plan on leaving a credit card, driver's license, or passport as a security deposit.

Dingle Activities: The Mountain Man, a hiking shop run by a local guide, Mike Shea, is a clearinghouse for information, local tours, and excursions (July–Sept daily 9:00–21:00, Oct–June 9:00–18:00, just off harbor at Strand Street, tel. 066/915-2400, e-mail: irasc@eircom.net). Stop by for ideas on biking, hiking, horseback riding, climbing, peninsula tours, and trips to the Blaskets. They are the Dingle town contact for the Dunquin–Blasket Islands boats and shuttle-bus rides to the harbor (see "Blasket Islands," below).

Travel Agency: Maurice O'Connor at Galvin's Travel Agency can book train, long-distance bus, and plane tickets, and boat rides to France (Mon–Fri 9:30–18:00, Sat 9:30–17:00, closed Sun, John Street, tel. 066/915-1409).

Farmers Market: Every Saturday (10:00–14:00), local farmers fill the St. James churchyard (on Main Street) with their fresh produce and homemade marmalade.

Dingle Hotels and Services

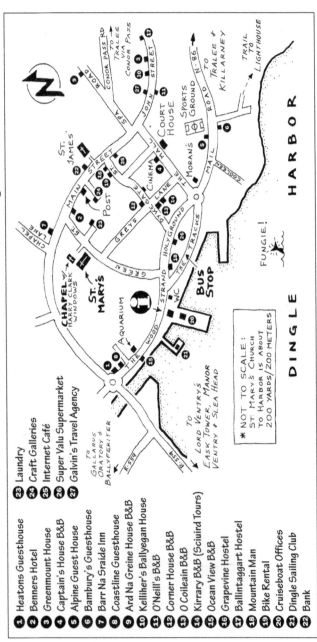

1 Heatons Guesthouse
2 Benners Hotel
3 Greenmount House
4 Captain's House B&B
5 Alpine Guest House
6 Bambury's Guesthouse
7 Barr Na Sraide Inn
8 Coastline Guesthouse
9 Ard Na Greine House B&B
10 Kelliher's Ballyegan House
11 O'Neill's B&B
12 Corner House B&B
13 O Coileain B&B
14 Kirrary B&B (Sciuird Tours)
15 Ocean View B&B
16 Grapevine Hostel
17 Ballintaggart Hostel
18 Mountain Man
19 Bike Rental
20 Cruiseboat Offices
21 Dingle Sailing Club
22 Bank
23 Laundry
24 Craft Galleries
25 Internet Café
26 Super Valu Supermarket
27 Galvin's Travel Agency

Sights—Dingle Town

▲▲**The Harry Clark Windows of Diseart**—Just behind Dingle's St. Mary Church stands St. Joseph's Convent and Diseart (pron. dee-ZHART). The sisters of this order, who came to Dingle in 1829 to educate local girls, worked heroically during the famine. Their neo-Gothic chapel, built in 1884, was graced in 1922 with 12 windows—the work of Ireland's top stained-glass man, Harry Clark. Long enjoyed only by the sisters, these special windows—showing six scenes from the life of Christ—are now open to the public. The convent has become a center for sharing Christian Celtic culture and spirituality (free, Mon–Sat 10:00–17:00, closed Sun, www.diseart.ie).

Enjoy a meditative 15 minutes following the free audioguide that explains the chapel one window at a time. The scenes (clockwise from the back entrance): the visit of the Magi, the Baptism of Jesus, "Let the little children come to me," the Sermon on the Mount, the Agony in the Garden, and Jesus appearing to Mary Magdalene. Each face is lively and animated in the imaginative, devout, medieval, and fun-loving art of Harry Clark, whom locals talk about as if he's the kid next door. While the Mother Superior sat in the covered stall in the rear, the sisters—filling the carved stalls—would chant responsively.

▲**Oceanworld**—The only place charging admission in Dingle is worth considering. This aquarium offers a little peninsula history, 300 different species of local fish in thoughtfully described tanks, and the easiest way to see Fungie the dolphin . . . on video. Walk through the tunnel while fish swim overhead. The only creatures not local—other than you—are the sharks. The aquarium's mission is to teach, and you're welcome to ask questions. The petting pool is fun. Splashing attracts the rays, which are unplugged (€7.50, families-€20, July–Aug daily 10:00–20:30, May, June, and Sept 10:00–18:00, Oct–April 10:00–17:00, cafeteria, just past harbor on west edge of town, tel. 066/915-2111).

▲**Fungie**—In 1983 a dolphin moved into Dingle Harbor and became a local celebrity. Fungie (pron. FOON-gee, with a hard *g*) is now the darling of the town's tourist trade and one reason you'll find so many tour buses parked along the harbor. With a close look at Fungie as bait, tour boats are thriving. The hardy little boats motor 7–40 passengers out to the mouth of the harbor, where they troll around looking for Fungie. You're virtually assured of seeing the dolphin, but you don't pay unless you do (€10, kids-€5, 1-hour trips depart 10:00–19:00 depending upon demand, book a day in advance, behind TI at Dolphin Trips office, tel. 066/915-2626). To actually swim with Fungie, rent wetsuits and catch the early-morning 8:00–10:00 trip (€35 includes wetsuits—unless you've packed your own).

Dingle Area

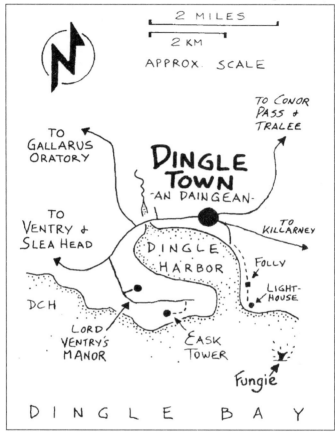

2 MILES

2 KM

APPROX. SCALE

TO CONOR PASS & TRALEE

TO GALLARUS ORATORY

DINGLE TOWN

-AN DAINGEAN-

TO VENTRY & SLEA HEAD

TO KILLARNEY

DINGLE HARBOR

FOLLY

LIGHT-HOUSE

DCH

LORD VENTRY'S MANOR

EASK TOWER

Fungie

D I N G L E   B A Y

▲**Short Harbor Walk from Dingle**—For an easy stroll along the harbor out of town (and a chance to see Fungie, 90 min round-trip), head east from the roundabout past the Esso station. Just after Bambury's B&B, take a right, following signs to Skelligs Hotel. At the beach, climb the steps over the wall and follow the seashore path to the mouth of Dingle Harbor (marked by a tower—some 19th-century fat cat's folly). Ten minutes beyond that is a lighthouse. This is Fungie's neighborhood. If you see tourist boats out, you're likely to see the dolphin. The trail continues to a dramatic cliff.

The Harbor: The harbor was built on land reclaimed (with imported Dutch expertise) in 1992. The string of old stone shops facing the harbor was the loading station for the narrow-gauge railway that hauled the fish from Dingle to Tralee (1891–1953). Make a point to walk out to the end of the breakwater—newly paved and lit at night. The Eask Tower on the distant hill is a marker built in 1847 during the famine as a make-work project. In preradar days, it helped ships locate Dingle's hidden harbor. The fancy mansion across the harbor is Lord Ventry's 17th-century manorhouse (see "Circular Tour," page 133).

Sailing—The Dingle Marina Centre offers diving, sailing, traditional currach rowing, and a salty little restaurant. Sailors can join the club for a day to sail (€22, July–Aug, tel. 066/915-1984). Currachs—stacked behind the building—are Ireland's traditional lightweight fishing boats, easy to haul and easy to make. Cover a wooden frame with canvas (originally cowhide) and paint with tar—presto. The currachs, owned by the Dingle Rowing Club, go out many summer evenings (tel. 087-699-2925).

Dingle Pitch & Putt—For 18 scenic holes and a driving range, hike 10 minutes past Oceanworld (€5 with gear, driving range €5 for 100 balls, daily 10:00–20:00, over bridge take first left and follow signs, Milltown, tel. 066/915-1819).

Horseback Riding—Dingle Horse Riding takes out beginners (€26/hr with instruction) and experienced riders for half-day (€76) and longer excursions. Bob along beaches or mountains on an English-style ride. Book at Greenlane Gallery (Green Street, tel. 066/915-2018, www.dinglehorseriding.com).

Shopping—Dingle is filled with shops showing off local craftsmanship. The **West Kerry Craft Guild**—a co-op selling the work of 15 local artists—is a delight even if you're just browsing. The prices here are very good since you're buying directly from "low-overhead craftspeople" (18 Main Street). The **Niamh Utsch Jewelry** shop next door is much respected for its unique work. **Lisbeth Mulcahy Weaver,** filled with traditional but stylish woven wear, is also the Dingle sales outlet of the well-known potter from out on Slea Head (Green Street, tel. 066/915-1688).

Nightlife in Dingle Town

▲▲▲**Folk Music in Dingle Pubs**—Even if you're not into pubs, take a nap and then give these a whirl. Dingle is renowned among traditional musicians as a place to get work ("€40 a day, tax-free, plus drink"). The town has piles of pubs. There's music every night and rarely a cover charge. The scene is a decent mix of locals, Americans, and Germans. Music normally starts around 21:30, and the last call for drinks is "half eleven" (23:30), sometimes later on weekends. For a seat near the music, arrive early. If the place is chockablock, power in and find breathing room in the back. By midnight the door is usually closed and the chairs are stacked. For more information, see "Traditional Irish Music" on page 29 in the Introduction, or check the fine local-music Web site www.celticwave.com.

While two pubs, the Small Bridge Bar (An Droighead Beag) and O'Flaherty's, are the most famous for their good beer and folk music, make a point to wander the town and follow your ear. Smaller pubs may feel a bit foreboding to a tourist, but people—locals as well as travelers—are out for the *craic*. Irish culture is very accessible in the pubs; they're like highly interactive museums waiting to be explored. But if you sit at a table, you'll be left alone. Stand or sit at the bar and you'll be engulfed in conversation with new friends. Have a glass in an empty, no-name pub and chat up the publican. Pubs are smoky and hot (leave your coat home). The more offbeat pubs are more likely to erupt into leprechaun karaoke.

Pub crawl: The best pub crawl is along Strand Street to O'Flaherty's. Murphy's is lively, offering rock as well as ballads and traditional music. O'Flaherty's has a high ceiling and less smoke, and is dripping in old-time photos and town memorabilia—it's touristy but lots of fun, with nightly music in the summer.

Then head up Green Street. Dick Mack, across from the church, is nicknamed "the last pew." This is a tiny leather shop by day, expanding into a pub at night, with several rooms, a fine snug (private booth, originally designed to allow women to drink discreetly), reliably good beer, and a smoky and strangely fascinating ambience. Notice the Hollywood-type stars on the sidewalk recalling famous visitors. Established in 1899, the grandson of the original Dick Mack now runs the place. A painting in the window shows Dick Mack II with the local gang.

Green Street climbs to Main Street where two more Dick Mack–type places are filled with smoke and locals deep in conversation (but no music): Foxy John's (a hardware shop by day) and O Currain's (across the street, a small clothing shop by day).

A bit higher up Main Street is McCarthy's Pub, a smoke-stained relic. It's less touristy and has some fine traditional music sessions and occasional plays on its little stage. Wander downhill to the Small Bridge Bar at the bottom. With live music nightly, it's popular for good reason. While the tourists gather around the music, poke around the back, which leads to a nook actually closest to the musicians. Finally, head up Spa Road a few doors to An Conair—a.k.a. John Benny's, a clean, modern pub that offers good music and is often less crowded than the others. Farther up Spa Road, the big hotel has late-night dancing (see below).

Off-season: From October through April, the bands play on, though at fewer pubs: Small Bridge Bar (live music nightly), An Conair (Mon, Wed, Thu), McCarthy's (Fri, Sat), and Murphy's (Sat).

Music shops: Danlann Gallery sells musical instruments and woodcrafts (Mon–Fri 10:00–18:00, later in summer, "flexible" on weekends, CC, owner makes violins, Dykegate Street). Siopa an Phiobaire, exclusively a music shop, sells traditional wind instruments (Mon–Fri 10:00–17:00, closed Sat–Sun, CC, Craft Centre, on edge of town a few minutes' walk past Oceanworld, tel. 066/915-1778). Dingle Bodhrans sells homemade traditional goatskin drums and gives lessons (1-hour lesson-€25.50–51, rates are on "sliding scale," Mon–Sat 10:30–18:00, closed Sun, Green Street, enter red iron gate of small alley opposite church, tel. 087-245-7689, Andrea).

Folk concerts—Top local musicians offer a quality evening of live, acoustic, classic Irish music in the fine little St. James Church on Main Street (€10, Mon and Thu at 19:30, June–Aug only, see sign on church gate or drop by Murphy's Ice Cream for details).

Dancing—Some pubs host "set dancing" with live music (An Conair on Mon at 21:30, Small Bridge Bar on Thu). Hillgrove Hotel, up Spa Road a few hundred yards, is a modern hotel with traditional dances every Thursday at 23:00 and pop dancing other nights in summer. Locals say the Hillgrove "is a good time if you're pissed."

Theater—Dingle's great little theater is The Phoenix on Dyke-gate. Its film club (50–60 locals) meets here Tuesdays year-round at 20:30 for coffee and cookies, followed by a film at 21:00 (€6 for film, anyone is welcome). The leader runs it almost like a religion, with a sermon on the film before he rolls it. The regular film schedule for the week is posted on the door.

Sleeping in Dingle Town
**(€1 = about $1, country code: 353,
area code: 066, mail: Dingle, County Kerry)**

Sleep Code: **S** = Single, **D** = Double/Twin, **T** = Triple, **Q** = Quad, **b** = bathroom, **s** = shower only, **CC** = Credit Cards accepted, **no CC** = Credit Cards not accepted. Prices vary with the season, with winter cheap and August tops.

To help you easily sort through these listings, I've divided the rooms into three categories, based on the price for a standard double room with bath:

Higher Priced—Most rooms more than €100.
Moderately Priced—Most rooms under €100.
Lower Priced—Most rooms €60 or less.

HIGHER PRICED

Heatons Guesthouse, big, peaceful, and American in its comforts, is on the water just west of town at the end of Dingle Bay—a five-minute walk past Oceanworld on The Wood. The 16 thoughtfully appointed rooms come with all the amenities (Db-€76–118, suite Db-€125–165, CC, creative breakfasts, parking, The Wood, tel. 066/915-2288, fax 066/915-2324, www.heatonsdingle.com, e-mail: heatons@iol.ie, Cameron and Nuala Heaton).

Benners Hotel was the only place in town a hundred years ago. It stands bewildered by the modern world on Main Street, with sprawling public spaces and 52 abundant, overpriced rooms— only its non-smoking rooms smell fresh (Db-€196 July–Aug, €154 May–June, €140 Sept–May, kids under 7-€19 extra, CC, tel. 066/915-1638, fax 066/915-1412, e-mail: benners@eircom.net).

MODERATELY PRICED

Greenmount House sits among chilly palm trees in the country-side at the top of town. A five-minute hike up from the town center, this guest house commands a fine view of the bay and mountains. John and Mary Curran run one of Ireland's best B&Bs, with five superb rooms (Db-€75–90—top price through the summer) and seven sprawling suites (Db-€100–130) in a modern building with lavish public areas and breakfast in a solarium (CC, reserve in advance, no children under 8, most rooms at ground level, parking, top of John Street, tel. 066/915-1414, fax 066/915-1974, e-mail: mary@greenmounthouse.com).

Captain's House B&B is a shipshape place in the town center, fit for an admiral, with eight classy rooms, peat-fire lounges, a stay-awhile garden, and a magnificent breakfast. Mary, whose mother ran a guest house before Dingle was discovered, loves her work and is very good at it (Sb-€50–55 Db-€80–100, great suite-€135, super breakfast in conservatory, CC, The Mall, tel. 066/915-1531, fax 066/915-1079, e-mail: captigh@eircom.net, Jim and Mary Milhench).

Alpine Guest House looks like a monopoly hotel, but that means comfortable and efficient. Its 13 spacious, bright, and fresh rooms come with wonderful sheep-and-harbor views, a cozy lounge, great breakfast, and friendly owners (Db-€55–84, Tb-€76–120, prices vary with room size and season, 10 percent discount with this book, CC, parking, Mail Road, tel. 066/915-1250, fax 066/915-1966, www.alpineguesthouse.com, e-mail: alpinedingle@eircom.net, Paul). Driving into town from Tralee, you'll see this a block uphill from the Dingle roundabout and Esso station.

Bambury's Guesthouse, big and modern with views of grazing sheep and the harbor, rents 12 airy, comfy rooms (Db-€70–100, prices depend on size and season, family deals, CC; coming in from Tralee it's on your left on Mail Road, 2 blocks before Esso station; tel. 066/915-1244, fax 066/915-1786, http://bamburysguesthouse .com/, e-mail: info@bamburysguesthouse.com).

Barr Na Sraide Inn, central and hotelesque, has 22 comfortable rooms (Db-€70–100, family deals, CC, self-service laundry, bar, parking, past McCarthy's pub, Upper Main Street, tel. 066/915-1331, fax 066/915-1446, e-mail: barrnasraide@eircom.net).

Coastline Guesthouse, on the water next to Heaton's Guesthouse (listed above), is a modern, sterile place with seven bright, spacious rooms (Sb-€60, Db-€82, Tb-€115, deals for 3-night stays, CC, non-smoking, parking, The Wood, tel. 066/915-2494, fax 066/915-2493, www.coastlinedingle.com, e-mail: coastlinedingle@eircom.net, Vivienne O'Shea).

Ard Na Greine House B&B is a charming, windblown, modern house on the edge of town. Mrs. Mary Houlihan rents four well-equipped, comfortable rooms (with fridges) to non-smokers only (Sb-€50, Db-€50–64, Tb-€76, CC, parking, 8-min walk up Spa Road, 3 doors beyond Hillgrove Hotel, tel. 066/915-1113).

Kelliher's Ballyegan House is a big, plain building with six fresh, comfortable rooms on the edge of town and great harbor views (Db-€62, Tb-€90, family deals, 10 percent off through 2003 with this book except in July & Aug, no CC, non-smoking, parking, TVs in rooms, Upper John Street, tel. 066/915-1702, Hannah and James Kelliher).

LOWER PRICED

O'Neill's B&B is a homey, friendly place with six decent rooms on a quiet street at the top of town (Db-€54 with this book through 2003, family deals, no CC, strictly non-smoking, parking, John Street, tel. 066/915-1639, Mary O'Neill).

Corner House B&B is my longtime Dingle home. It's a simple, traditional place with five large, uncluttered rooms run with a twinkle and a grandmotherly smile by Kathleen Farrell (S-€30, D-€60, T-€80, plenty of plumbing but it's down the hall, no CC, reserve with a phone call and reconfirm a day or 2 ahead, central as can be on Dykegate Street, tel. 066/915-1516). Mrs. Farrell, one of the original three B&B hostesses in a town now filled with them, is a great storyteller.

The following two B&Bs, which take up a quiet corner in the town center, are run by the same Collins—Coileain in Gaelic—family that does archaeological tours of the peninsula (below). Both offer pleasant rooms (O Coileain's are a bit bigger), bike rental (€8), identical prices (Db-€58–60), and a homey friendliness. **O Coileain B&B** is run by a young family—Rachel, Michael, and their two cute little girls (tel. 066/915-1937, e-mail: archeo @eircom.net). **Kirrary B&B,** just over the fence, is grandma's place, with a homey charm (tel. 066/915-1606, e-mail: collinskirrary @eircom.net, Eileen Collins).

Ocean View B&B rents three tidy rooms (2 with views) in a humble little waterfront row house overlooking the bay (S-€25, D-€42, CC, welcome treat on arrival, 5-min walk from center, 100 yards past Oceanworld at 133 The Wood, tel. 066/915-1659, e-mail: thewood@gofree.indigo.ie, Mrs. Brosnan).

Hostels: **Grapevine Hostel** is a clean and friendly establishment, quietly yet very centrally located, with a cozy fireplace lounge and a fine members' kitchen. Each three- to eight-bed dorm has its own bathroom. Dorms are coed, but there's a girls' room established (29 beds, €12–14 each, laundry-€5, open all day, Dykegate Lane, tel. 066/915-1434, www.dinglehostel.com, e-mail: grapevine@dingleweb.com, run by Siobhan—pron: sheh-vahn).

Ballintaggart Hostel, a backpacker's complex, is housed in a stylish old manorhouse used by Protestants during the famine as a soup kitchen (for those hungry enough to renounce Catholicism). It comes complete with laundry service (€6.50), a classy study, a family room with a fireplace, and a resident ghost (130 beds, €12.50 in 10-bed dorms, €15 beds in Qb, Db-€45, no breakfast but there's a kitchen, a mile east of town on Tralee Road, tel. 066/915-1454, fax 066/915-2207, www .dingleaccommodation.com, e-mail: info@dingleaccommodation .com). Ask the Tralee bus to drop you here before arriving in Dingle. The hostel's shuttle bus does a nightly pub run in summer.

Eating in Dingle Town

For a rustic little village, Dingle is swimming in good food.

Budget tips: The Super Valu supermarket/department store, at the base of town, has everything and stays open late (Mon–Sat 8:00–21:00, Sun 8:00–19:00, until 22:00 in summer); consider a grand view picnic out on the end of the new pier walk. Smaller groceries are scattered throughout the town, such as Centra on Main Street (Mon–Sat 8:00–21:00, Sun 8:00–18:00).

Fancy restaurants serve early-bird specials from 18:00 to 19:00. Many "cheap and cheery" places close at 18:00, and pubs do good €10 dinners all over town. Most pubs stop serving food around 21:00 (to make room for their beer drinkers).

Lunch? **Adam's Bar and Restaurant** is a tight, smoky place popular with locals for traditional food at great prices. Try their stew, corned beef and cabbage, or lemon-chicken sandwiches (May–Sept Mon–Sat €8 lunches 12:00–17:00, dinners 18:00–21:00, closed Sun, Upper Main Street).

The Old Smokehouse, your best moderate-value eating in town with fresh Dingle Bay fish and good vegetables, serves happy locals in a rustic woody setting (€16 plates, Tue–Sun 18:00–22:00, closed Mon, CC, tel. 066/915-1061).

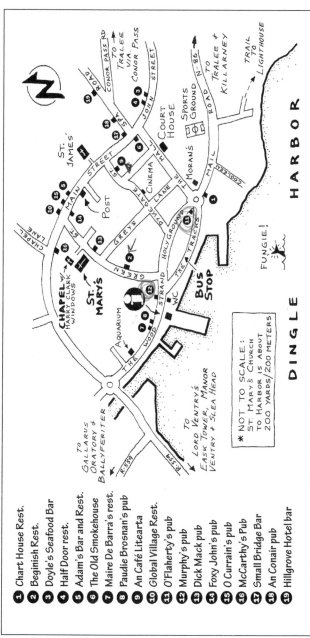

Dingle Restaurants

1. Chart House Rest.
2. Beginish Rest.
3. Doyle's Seafood Bar
4. Half Door rest.
5. Adam's Bar and Rest.
6. The Old Smokehouse
7. Maire De Barra's rest.
8. Paudie Brosnan's pub
9. An Café Liteartta
10. Global Village Rest.
11. O'Flaherty's pub
12. Murphy's pub
13. Dick Mack pub
14. Foxy John's pub
15. O Currain's pub
16. McCarthy's Pub
17. Small Bridge Bar
18. An Conair pub
19. Hillgrove Hotel bar

dinner?

Maire De Barra's is a smoky pub serving the best €10 fresh-fish dinners in town, and traditional Irish fare as well (daily 12:30–21:30, music after 21:30, The Pier). **Paudie Brosnan's** pub, a few doors down, is also popular (and smoky).

Lunch

An Café Litearta, a popular eatery hidden behind an inviting bookstore, serves tasty soup and sandwiches to a good-natured crowd of Gaelic-speaking smokers (daily 10:00–17:00, Dykegate Street).

sounds good also

The **Global Village Restaurant** is where Martin Bealin serves his favorite dishes, gleaned from his travels around the world. It's an eclectic, healthy, meat-eater's place popular with locals for its interesting cuisine (€18 dinners, good salads and great Thai curry, daily 18:00–22:00, CC, top of Main Street, tel. 066/915-2325).

Dingle's Four Fancy Restaurants

Chart House Restaurant serves contemporary cuisine with a menu dictated by what's fresh and seasonal. Settle back into the sharp, clean, lantern-lit harborside ambience (€26 dinners, CC, Wed–Mon 18:30–22:00, closed Tue, at roundabout at base of town, tel. 066/915-2255).

Reserve – Tues?

Beginish Restaurant, serving modern European fare with a fish forte in an elegant Georgian setting, is probably your best dressy splurge meal in town (€25 plates, €30 daily 3-course meal, dinner only, Tue–Sun 18:00–22:00, closed Mon, CC, you'll be glad you reserved ahead, Green Street, tel. 066/915-1321).

Two of Dingle's long-established top-notch restaurants—**Doyle's Seafood Bar** (more famous, with excellent seafood and service, tel. 066/915-1174) and **The Half Door** (heartier portions, tel. 066/915-1600)—are neighbors on John Street. They're in the guidebooks for good reason (and therefore filled with tourists), as they serve good food. Both take credit cards, have the same hours (Mon–Sat 18:00–22:00, closed Sun), offer an early-bird special (3-course meal-€30, 18:00–19:00), and take reservations (wise).

Transportation Connections—Dingle Town

The nearest train station is in Tralee.

By bus from Dingle to: Galway (4/day, 6.5 hrs), **Dublin** (3/day, 8 hrs), **Rosslare** (2/day, 9 hrs), **Tralee** (4/day, 75 min, €8); fewer departures on Sundays. Most bus trips out of Dingle require at least one or two (easy) transfers. Dingle has no bus station and only one bus stop, on the waterfront behind the Super Valu supermarket (bus info tel. 01/830-2222 or Tralee station at 066/712-3566). For more information, see "Transportation Connections—Tralee," below.

Make Res: Lunch – An Café Lit—
Dinner – Beginish Rest

By car: Drivers choose two roads into town, the easy southern route or the much more dramatic, scenic, and treacherous Conor Pass (see "Transportation Connections—Tralee," below). It's 30 miles from Tralee either way.

Dingle Peninsula:
Circular Tour by Bike or Car

A sight worth ▲▲▲, the Dingle Peninsula loop trip is about 30 miles long (go in clockwise direction). It's easy by car, or it's a demanding three hours by bike—if you don't stop.

While you can take the basic guided tour of the peninsula (see "Dingle Peninsula Tours," below), the route described in this section makes it unnecessary. A fancy map is also unnecessary with my instructions. I've keyed in mileage to help locate points of interest. If you're driving, as you leave Dingle, reset your odometer at Oceanworld. Even if you get off track or are biking, derive distances between points from my mileage key. To get the most out of your circle trip, read through this entire section before departing. Then go step by step (staying on R559 and following The Slea Head Drive signs). Roads are very congested in August.

The Dingle Peninsula is 10 miles wide and runs 40 miles from Tralee to Slea Head. The top of its mountainous spine is Mount Brandon—at 3,130 feet, the second-tallest mountain in Ireland. While only tiny villages lie west of Dingle Town, the peninsula is home to 500,000 sheep.

Leave Dingle Town west along the waterfront (0.0 miles at Oceanworld). There's an eight-foot tide here. The seaweed was used to make formerly worthless land arable. (Seaweed is a natural source of potash—organic farming before that was trendy.) Across the water, the fancy Milltown House B&B (with flags) was Robert Mitchum's home for a year during the filming of *Ryan's Daughter*. Look for the narrow mouth of this blind harbor (where Fungie frolics) and the Ring of Kerry beyond that. Dingle Bay is so hidden, ships needed the tower (1847) on the hill to find its mouth.

0.4 miles: At the roundabout, turn left over the bridge. The hardware-store building on the right was a corn-grinding mill in the 18th century.

0.8 miles: The Milestone B&B is named for the stone pillar (*gallaun* in Gaelic) in its front yard. This may have been a prehistoric grave or a boundary marker between two tribes. The stone goes down as far as it sticks up. The peninsula, literally an open-air museum, is dotted with more than 2,000 such monuments dating from the Neolithic Age (4,000 B.C.) through early Christian times. Another stone pillar stands in the field across the street in the direction of the yellow manorhouse of Lord Ventry (in the distance).

Dingle Peninsula Tour

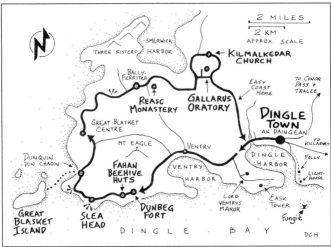

Lord Ventry, whose family came to Dingle as post–Cromwell War landlords in 1666, built this mansion about 1750. Today it houses an all-Gaelic boarding school for 140 high school girls.

As you drive past the Ventry estate, you'll pass palms, magnolias, fuchsias, and exotic flora introduced to Dingle by Lord Ventry. The mild climate—it never snows—is produced by the Gulf Stream and is fine for subtropical plants. Consequently, fuchsias—imported from Chile and spreading like weeds—line the roads all over the peninsula and redden the countryside from June to September. And over 100 inches of rain a year gives this area its "40 shades of green."

Ten yards past the Tobair Michael B&B (on left) a tiny white wall with a blue marker marks the St. Michael's Well. A Christianized Celtic holy well, it's still the site of a Mass on St. Martin's day. St. Martin was the Christian antidote to pagan holy places. Generally, when you see something dedicated to him, it sits upon something that pre-Christian people worshiped.

3 miles: Stay off the "soft margin" as you enjoy views of Ventry Bay, its four-mile-long beach (to your right as you face the water), and distant Skellig Michael, which you'll see all along this part of the route. Skellig Michael—jutting up like France's Mont St. Michel—contains the rocky remains of an eighth-century monastic settlement. Hermit monks lived here in obscure beehive huts—their main contact with the outside world being trading ships stopping between Spain and Scandinavia. Next to it is a smaller island, Little Skellig—a breeding ground for gannets (seagull-like birds with 6-foot wingspans). In 1865 Western Union laid the first transatlantic cable from here to Newfoundland. It was in use until 1965. Mount Eagle (1,660 feet), rising across the bay, marks the end of Ireland. In the village of Ventry, Gaelic is the first language. The large hall at the end of the village is used as a classroom by big-city students who come here on field trips to be immersed in the Gaelic language.

4.7 miles: The rushes on either side of the road are the kind used to make the local thatched roofs. Thatching, which nearly died out because of the fire danger, is more popular now that anti-flame treatments are available. Black-and-white magpies fly.

5.3 miles: The Irish football star Paidi O Se (Paddy O'Shea) is a household name in Ireland. He now trains the Kerry team and runs the pub on the left. (Easy beach access from here.)

5.6 miles: The blue house hiding in the trees 100 yards off the road on the left (view through the white gate) was kept cozy by Tom Cruise and Nicole Kidman during the filming of *Far and Away*.

6.6 miles: *Taisteaal go Mall* means "go slowly"; there's a peach-colored, two-room schoolhouse on the right (20 students, 2 teachers). On the left is the small Celtic and Prehistoric Museum, a strange private collection of prehistoric artifacts with no real connection to Dingle (overpriced at €5, daily 10:00–17:00).

6.9 miles: The circular mound on the right is a late–Stone Age ring fort. In 500 B.C. it was a petty Celtic chieftain's head quarters, a stone-and-earth stockade filled with little stone houses. These survived untouched through the centuries because of super-stitious beliefs that they were "fairy forts." While this is unexca-vated, recent digging has shown that people have lived on this peninsula since 4000 B.C.

7.3 miles: Look ahead up Mount Eagle at the patchwork of stone-fenced fields

7.7 miles: Dunbeg Fort, a series of defensive ramparts and ditches around a central *clochan*, though ready to fall into the sea, is open to tourists. There are no carvings to be seen, but the small *(beg)* fort *(dun)* is dramatic (€2, daily 9:30–20:00, descriptive hand-out). Forts like this are the most important relics left from Ireland's Iron Age (500 B.C. to A.D. 500). Since erosion will someday take this fort, it has been excavated. Alongside the road, the new stone-roofed house was built to blend in with the landscape and the region's ancient rock-slab architecture (A.D. 2000, tea inside, traditional currach in parking lot). Just 50 yards up the hill is a cottage abandoned by a family named Kavanaugh 150 years ago during the famine (€2, tel. 066/915-6241).

8.2 miles: A group of beehive huts, or *clochans*, is a short walk uphill (€2, daily 9:30–19:00, WC). These mysterious stone igloos, which cluster together within a circular wall, are a better sight than the similar group of beehive huts a mile down the road. Look over the water for more Skellig views.

Farther on, you'll ford a stream. There has never been a bridge here; this bit of road—nicknamed the "upside-down bridge"—was designed as a ford.

9.2 miles: Pull off to the left at this second group of beehive huts. Look downhill at the scant remains of the scant home that was burned as the movie equivalent of Lord Ventry tried to evict the tenants in *Far and Away*. Even without Hollywood, this is a bleak and godforsaken land. Look above at the patches of land slowly made into farmland by the inhabitants of this westernmost piece of Europe. Rocks were cleared and piled into fences. Sand and seaweed were laid on the clay, and in time it was good for grass. The created land, generally if at all tillable, was used for growing potatoes; otherwise it was only good for grazing. Much has fallen out of use now. Look behind at the Ring of Kerry in the distance and ahead at the Blasket Islands.

9.9 miles: At Slea Head, marked by a crucifix, a pullout, and great views of the Blasket Islands (described below), you turn the corner on this tour. On stormy days, the waves are "racing in like white horses."

10.4 miles: Pull into the little parking lot (at Dunchaoin sign) to view the Blaskets and Dunmore Head (the westernmost point in Europe) and to review the roadside map (which traces your route) posted in the parking lot. The scattered village of Dunquin has many ruined rock homes abandoned during the famine. Some are fixed up, as this is a popular place these days for summer homes. You can see more good examples of land reclamation, patch by patch, climbing up the hillside. Mount Eagle was the first bit of land Charles Lindberg saw after crossing the Atlantic on his way to Paris in 1927. Villagers here were as excited as he was—they had never seen anything so big in the air. Ahead, down a road on the left, a plaque celebrates the 30th anniversary of the filming of *Ryan's Daughter*.

11.9 miles: The Blasket Islanders had no church or cemetery on the island. This was their cemetery. The famous Blasket story-teller Peig Sayers (1873–1958) is buried in the center. At the next intersection, drive down the little lane that leads left (100 yards) to a small stone marker commemorating the 1588 shipwreck of the *Santa Maria de la Rosa* of the Spanish Armada. Below that is the often-tempestuous Dunquin Harbor, from which the Blasket ferry departs. Island farmers—who on a calm day could row across in

20 minutes—would dock here and hike 12 miles into Dingle to sell their produce. When transporting sheep, farmers would lash the sheep's pointy little hoofs together and place them carefully upside down in the currach—so they wouldn't puncture the frail little craft's canvas skin.

12 miles: Back on the main road, follow signs to the Great Blasket Centre.

13.5 miles: Leave the Slea Head Road left for the Great Blasket Centre (described below).

13.7 miles: Back at the turnoff, head left (sign to Louis Mulcahy Pottery).

14.5 miles: Passing land that was never reclaimed, think of the work it took to pick out the stones, pile them into fences, and bring up sand and seaweed to nourish the clay and make soil for growing potatoes. Look over the water to the island aptly named the "Sleeping Giant"—see his hand resting happily on his beer belly.

15.1 miles: The view is spectacular. Ahead, on the right, study the top fields, untouched since the planting of 1845, when the potatoes didn't grow, but rotted in the ground. The faint vertical ridges of the potato beds can still be seen—a reminder of the famine (easier to see a bit later). Before the famine, 50,000 people lived on this peninsula. After the famine, the population was so small that there was never again a need to farm so high up. Today only 10,000 live on the peninsula. Coast downhill. The distant hills are crowned by lookout forts built back when Britain expected Napoleon to invade.

18.3 miles: Ballyferriter (Baile an Fheirtearaigh), established by a Norman family in the 12th century, is the largest town on this side of Dingle. The pubs serve grub, and the old schoolhouse is a museum (€2, Easter–Sept daily 10:00–16:30, closed off-season). The early-Christian cross next to the schoolhouse looks real. Tap it... it's fiberglass—a prop from *Ryan's Daughter*.

19.1 miles: At the T-junction, signs direct you to Dingle ("An Daingean, 11 km") either way. Go left, via Gallarus (and still following Slea Head Way). Take a right over the bridge, still following signs to Gallarus.

19.5 miles: Just beyond the bridge and a few yards before the sign to Mainistir Riaise (Reasc Monastic enclosure), detour right up the lane. After 0.2 miles (the unsigned turnout on your right), you'll find the scant remains of the walled Reasc Monastery (dating from the 6th–12th centuries). The inner wall divided the community into sections for prayer and business (cottage industries helped support the monastery). In 1975 only the stone pillar was visible, as the entire site was buried. The layer of black felt marks where the original rocks stop and the excavators' reconstruction begins. The stone pillar is Celtic (c. 500 B.C.). When the Christians arrived in the fifth century, they didn't throw out the Celtic society. Instead, they carved a Maltese-type cross over the Celtic scrollwork. The square building was an oratory (church—you'll see an intact oratory at the next stop). The round buildings would have been *clochans*—those stone igloo-type dwellings. The monastery ran cottage industries with a double-duty kiln. Just outside the wall (opposite the oratory, past the duplex *clochan*, at the bottom end), find a stone hole with a passage facing the southwest wind. This was the kiln—fanned by the wind, it was used for cooking and drying grain. Locals would bring their grain to be dried and ground, and the monks would keep a tithe. With the arrival of the Normans in the 12th century, these small religious communities were replaced by relatively big-time state and church governments.

20 miles: Return to the main road, continue to the right.

21.1 miles: At the big hotel (Smerwick Harbor), turn left following the sign to Gallarus Oratory.

21.8 miles: At the big building (with camping sign), go right up a lane marked with a sign for the oratory. Another sign directs you to a small tourist center—with a shop, WC, and video theater. For €2 you get a 17-minute video overview of Dingle Peninsula's historic sights. (Bikers and hikers can avoid the entry fee by ignoring the visitors center sign and continuing up the lane 200 yards to a free entrance.)

The Gallarus Oratory, built about 1,300 years ago, is one of Ireland's best-preserved early-Christian churches. Shaped like an upturned boat, its finely fitted drystone walls are still waterproof. Notice the holes once used to secure covering at the door and the fine alternating stonework on the corners.

From the oratory the little lane leads directly up and over the hill, home to Dingle. To complete this tour, however, you should return to the main road and continue (following sign to An Mhuirioch).

22.9 miles: Turn right at the fork and immediately take a right (at the blue Shop sign) at the next fork. Pass a 19th-century church.

24.2 miles: The ruined Kilmalkedar church was the Norman center of worship for this end of the peninsula. It was built when England replaced the old monastic settlements in an attempt to centralize their rule. The 12th-century Irish Romanesque church is surrounded by a densely populated graveyard (which has risen noticeably above the surrounding fields over the centuries). In front of the church, you'll find the oldest medieval tombs, a stately early-Christian cross (substantially buried by the rising graveyard and therefore oddly proportioned), and a much older Ogham stone. This stone, which had already stood here 900 years when the church was built, is notched with the mysterious Morris code–type script the Celts used from the 3rd to 7th centuries. It marked a grave, indicating this was a pre-Christian holy spot. The hole was drilled through here centuries ago as a place where people would come to seal a deal—standing on the graves of their ancestors and in front of the house of God, they'd "swear to God" by touching fingers through this stone. You can still use this to renew your marriage vows (free, B.Y.O. spouse). The church fell into ruin during the Reformation. As Catholic worship went underground until the early 19th century, Kilmalkedar was never rebuilt.

24.6 miles: Continue uphill, overlooking the water. You'll pass another "fairy fort" (Ciher Dorgan) dating back to 1000 B.C. (free, go through the rusty "kissing gate").

25.5 miles: At the crest of the hill, enjoy a three-mile coast back into Dingle town (in the direction of the Eask Tower).

28.3 miles: *Tog Bog E* means "take it easy." At the T-junction, turn left. Then turn right at the roundabout.

29 miles: You're back into Dingle town. Well done.

Dingle Peninsula Tours

▲▲**Sciuird Archaeology Tours**—Sciuird (pron. SCREW-id) tours are offered by a father-son team with Dingle history—and a knack for sharing it—in their blood. Tim Collins (a retired Dingle police officer) and his son Michael give serious 2.5-hour minibus tours (€15, departing at 10:30 and 14:00, depending upon demand). Drop by the Kirrary B&B (Dykegate and Grey's Lane) or call 066/915-1606 to put your name on the list. Call early. Tours fill quickly in summer. Off-season (Oct–April) you may have to call back to see if the necessary five people signed up to make a bus go. While skipping the folk legends and the famous sights (such as Slea Head), your guide will drive down tiny farm roads (the Gaelic word for road literally means "cow path"), over hedges, and up ridges to hidden Celtic forts, mysterious stone tombs, and forgotten castles with sweeping seaside views. The running commentary gives an intimate peek into the history of Dingle. Sit as close to the driver as possible to get all the information. They do two completely different tours: west (Gallarus Oratory) and east (Minard Castle and a wedge tomb). I enjoyed both. Dress for the weather. In a literal gale with horizontal winds, Tim kept saying, "You'll survive it."

More Minibus Tours—Moran's Tour, which does a quickie minibus tour around the peninsula, offers meager narration and a short stop at the Gallarus Oratory (€15 to Slea Head, normally May–Sept at 10:00 and 14:00 from Dingle TI, 2.5 hrs; Moran's is at Esso station at roundabout, tel. 066/915-1155 or cellular 087-275-3333). There are always enough seats. But if no one shows up, consider a private Moran taxi trip around the peninsula (€45 for 3 people, cabby narrates 2.5-hour ride). The **Mountain Man** also runs three-hour minibus tours of the peninsula (€14/3 hrs, 3 tours daily June–Aug with demand, tel. 066/915-2400).

Eco-Cruises—Dingle Marine Eco Tours offers a two-hour birds-and-rocks boat tour of the peninsula. The guided tour sails either east toward Minard Castle or west toward the Blasket Islands (€25, April–Sept, departs 16:00, office around corner from TI, tel. 066/915-0768).

Blasket Islands

This rugged group of six islands off the tip of Dingle Peninsula seems particularly close to the soul of Ireland. The population of Great Blasket Island, home to as many as 160 people, dwindled until the government moved the last handful of residents to the mainland in 1953. Life here was hard. Each family had a cow, a few sheep, and a plot of potatoes. They cut their peat from the high ridge and harvested fish from the sea. There was no priest, pub, or doctor. These people formed the most traditional Irish community of the 20th century—the symbol of antique Gaelic culture.

Their special closeness to their island—combined with their knack for vivid storytelling—is inspirational. From this primitive but proud fishing/farming community came three writers of inter-national repute whose Gaelic work—basically tales of life on Great Blasket—is translated into many languages. You'll find *Peig* (by Peig Sayers), *Twenty Years a-Growing* (Maurice O'Sullivan), and *The Islander* (Thomas O'Crohan) in shops everywhere.

In the summer there's a café and hostel (cellular 086-852-2321) on the island, but it's little more than a ghost town overrun with rabbits on a peaceful, grassy, three-mile-long poem. The Blasket ferry runs hourly, and in summer every half hour, depend-ing on weather and demand (€20 round-trip, May–Oct). There may be a bus from Dingle town to Dunquin—leaving in the morning and picking up in the late afternoon—coordinated with the ferry schedule (€15 taxi service by Moran, tel. 066/915-1155; Dunquin ferry tel. 066/915-6422). Dunquin has a fine hostel (tel. 066/915-6121).

In summer, a fast boat called the *Peig Sayers* runs between Dingle town and the Blaskets. The ride (which may include a quick look at Fungie) traces the spectacular coastline all the way to Slea Head in a boat designed to slice expertly through the ocean chop. Because of the tricky landing at Great Blasket's primitive, tiny boat ramp, any substantial swell can make actually going ashore impossible (€35 round-trip, departing at 9:00, 11:00, 13:00, and 15:00, includes 40-min ride with free time to explore island, or €70 overnight trip includes dinner, a bed in the island's hostel, and breakfast; for info, call Mary at 066/915-1344).

▲▲**Great Blasket Centre**—This state-of-the-art Blasket and Gaelic heritage center gives visitors the best look possible at the language, literature, and way of life of the Blasket Islanders. See the fine 20-minute video (shows on the half hour), hear the sounds, read the poems, browse through old photos, and then gaze out the big windows at those rugged islands and imagine. Even if you never got past limericks, the poetry of these people—so pure and close to each other and nature—will have you dipping your pen into the cry of the birds (€3.20, Easter–Oct daily 10:00–18:00, until 19:00 July–Aug, cafeteria, on the mainland facing the islands, well-signposted, tel. 066/915-6444). Visit this center before visiting the islands.

Sights—East of Dingle Town

▲**Minard Castle**—Three miles southwest of Annascaul (off Lispole Road) is Minard Castle, the largest fortress on the peninsula. Built by the Norman Knights of Kerry in 1551, it was destroyed by Cromwell in about 1650.

Wander around the castle. With its corners undermined by Cromwellian explosives, it looks ready to split. Look up the garbage/toilet chute. As you enter the ruins, find the faint scallop in the doorway—the symbol of St. James. The castle had a connection to Santiago de Compostela in Spain. Medieval pilgrims would leave from here on a seafaring pilgrimage to northern Spain. Inside, after admiring the wall flowers, re-create the floor plan: ground floor for animals and storage; main floor with fireplace; thin living-quarters floor; and, on top, the defensive level.

The setting is dramatic, with the Ring of Kerry across the way and Storm Beach below. Storm Beach is notable for its sandstone boulders that fell from the nearby cliffs. Grinding against each other in the wave and tidal action, the boulders eroded into cigar-shaped rocks.

Next to the fortress, look for the "fairy fort," a Stone-Age fort from about 500 B.C.

▲**Puicin Wedge Tomb**—While pretty obscure, this is worth the trouble for its evocative setting. Above the hamlet of Lispole in Doonties, park your car and hike 10 minutes up a ridge. At the summit is a pile of rocks made into a little room with one of the finest views on the peninsula. Beyond the Ring of Kerry you may just make out the jagged Skellig Rock, noted for its eighth-century monastery.

Inch Strand—This four-mile sandy beach, shaped like a half moon, was made famous by *Ryan's Daughter.*

TRALEE

While Killarney is the tour-bus capital of county Kerry, Tralee is its true leading city. Except for the tourist complex around the TI and during a few festivals, Tralee feels like a bustling Irish town. A little outdoor market combusts on The Square (Thu–Sat).

Tralee's famous Rose of Tralee International Festival (usually mid-August), while a celebration of arts and music, climaxes with the election of the Rose of Tralee—the most beautiful woman at the festival. While the rose garden in the Castle Gardens sur-rounding the TI is in bloom from summer through October, Tralee's finest roses are going about their lives in the busy streets of this workaday town.

Orientation (area code: 066)

For the tourist, the heart of Tralee is Ashe Memorial Hall, housing the TI and Kerry the Kingdom, located near the rose garden and surrounded by the city park. Beyond the park is the Aqua Dome and steam railway that, if you were here 50 years ago, would chug-chug you to Dingle. Today it goes only to the touristy windmill.

Tourist Information: The TI is in Ashe Memorial Hall (July–Aug daily 9:00–19:00, Sept–June daily 9:00–17:00, tel. 066/712-1288).

Arrival in Tralee: From the train and bus station (both are located in the same building, with bike rental available), the Ashe Memorial Hall is a 10-minute walk through the center of town. Exit the station right, take a near-immediate left on Edward Street, then turn right on Castle Street and left on Denny. The Hall is at the end of Denny. Drivers should knock around the town center until they find a sign to the TI. Parking on the street requires a disk (€0.75/hr, sold at TI and newsstands—have them date it for you—or from machines on the street).

Sights—Tralee

▲▲**Kerry the Kingdom**—This is the place to learn about life in Kerry. The museum has three parts: Kerry slide show, museum, and medieval-town train ride. Get in the mood by relaxing for 15 minutes through the Enya-style, continuous slideshow of Kerry's spectacular scenery, then wander through 7,000 years of Kerry history in the museum (well described, no need for free headphones). The Irish say that when a particularly stupid guy moved from Cork to Kerry, he raised the average IQ in both counties—but this museum is pretty well done. It starts with good background on the archaeological sites of Dingle and goes right up to a video showing highlights of the Kerry football team (a fun look at Irish football). The lame finale is a 12-minute, four-person train ride back in time to 1450 down a re-creation of Tralee's Main Street (€8, daily 9:30–17:30, closed Jan & Feb, €0.75 disk at TI for 1-hour parking, tel. 066/712-7777). Before leaving, horticulture enthusiasts will want to ramble through the rose garden in the adjacent park.

Blennerville Windmill—On the edge of Tralee, just off the Dingle road, spins a restored mill originally built in 1800. Its eight-minute video tells the story of the windmill, which ground grain to feed Britain as the country steamed into the Industrial Age (€4.50 gets you a 1-room emigration exhibit, the video, and a peek at the spartan interior of the working windmill, April–Oct daily 9:30-17:30, closed Nov–March, tel. 066/712-1064); heritage researchers can scan the famine-ship records database upstairs above the emigration exhibit.

A restored narrow-gauge steam railway runs hourly between Tralee's Ballyard Station and the windmill (€4.50 round-trip, save 10 percent if you buy windmill and steam railway tickets together, tel. 066/712-1064). In the 19th century, Blennerville was a major port for America-bound emigrants.

Siamsa Tire Theatre—The National Folk Theater of Ireland, Siamsa Tire (pron. shee-EM-sah TEE-rah), stages two-hour dance and theater performances based on Gaelic folk traditions. The songs are in Irish, but there's no dialogue (€16, April–Oct Mon–Sat at 20:30, next to Kingdom of Kerry building in park, tel. 066/712-3055, e-mail: siamsatire@eircom.net).

Swimming—The Aqua Dome is a modern-yet-fortified swim center—the largest indoor water world in Ireland—at the Dingle end of town, near the Ashe Memorial Hall. Families enjoy the huge slide, wave pool, and other wet amusements (€9, kids-€8, locker-€1, June–Aug daily 10:00–22:00, less off-season, tel. 066/712-8899 or 066/712-9150).

Music and Other Distractions—Tralee has several fine pubs within a few blocks of each other (on Castle Street and Rock Street) offering live traditional music most evenings. There's greyhound racing (Tue and Fri year-round plus Sat in summer, 20:00–22:15, 10 30-second races every 15 min, 10-min walk from station or town center, tel. 066/718-0008). Entry to the track costs €5—plus what you lose gambling (kids free). At just about any time of day, you can drop into a betting office to check out the local gambling scene.

Sleeping in Tralee
(€1 = about $1, country code: 353, area code: 066, mail: Tralee, County Kerry)

The first two places—a pleasant B&B and a fancy guest house—are located a 10-minute walk from the station up Oakpark Road (which turns into Oakpark Drive). A cab runs €4.

HIGHER PRICED

Meadowlands is a classy 58-room guest house with a bar serving great pub meals. If you want to splurge in Tralee, do it here (Db-€160–200, suites-€210, CC, Oakpark Road, leaving the station, walk up Oakpark Road, tel. 066/718-0444, fax 066/718-0964, e-mail: medlands@iol.ie).

LOWER PRICED

O'Shea's B&B, a simple, tidy, modern house, rents four comfy rooms (Sb-€35–40, Db-€56–60, Tb-€80, CC, non-smoking, 2 Oakpark Drive, nearly across street from Meadowlands—listed above, tel. 066/718-0123, fax 066/718-0188, e-mail: osheasofkerry@eircom.net, Mairead O'Shea).

Hostels: Cheap hostels abound in Tralee, some offering doubles as well as dorm beds. These two are central. The **Courthouse Lodge** is on 5 Church Street (€14 dorm beds, Db-€32, no CC, 5-min walk from station toward town center, take Ashe Street, tel. & fax 066/712-7199). **Finnegan's Hostel,** in a stately Georgian house from 1826, is a block from TI at 17 Denny Street (€16 beds in 3-bed dorm rooms, rustic cellar restaurant serving fine meals, CC, tel. 066/712-7610, e-mail: imptralee@indigo.ie).

A mile out of town—in different directions—you'll find the homey **Lisnagree Hostel** (€14 beds in shared quads, D-€32, no CC, a mile east of center just off N21, follow Boherboy to Ballinorig Road, tel. 066/712-7133) and the **Collis-Sandes House,** a run-down, neo-Gothic mansion in a peaceful forest with 100 cheap beds (€12 beds in 4- to 8-bed rooms, D-€39, Db-€44, includes sheets, breakfast-€2.50, CC, a mile north of station and town center; from the station head up Oakpark Drive, after about 8 blocks you'll see sign on left, tel. & fax 066/712-8658, www.colsands.com, e-mail: colsands@indigo.ie). They have a free shuttle service from the station—ring them upon arrival—and a Tralee pub run on summer evenings.

Eating in Tralee

The Cookery is good (€9 lunches Tue–Sat 12:30–17:30, €15–23 dinners Tue–Sat from 18:00, closed Sun–Mon, CC, a block off

The Square, 16 Abbey Street, tel. 066/712-8833), but it's cheaper to shop for a picnic at **Tesco,** the big grocery off The Square (Mon–Sat 8:30–20:00, Sun 10:00–18:00).

Transportation Connections—Tralee

Day trippers, beware: The station has lockers, but not enough.

By train to: Dublin (4/day, 3/day on Sun, 4 hrs, €47), **Rosslare** (1/day except Sun, 5 hrs, €21.50). Train info: tel. 066/712-3522.

By bus to: Dingle (6/day, less off-season and on Sun, 75 min, €8 one-way, €12 round-trip), **Galway** (8/day, 4 hrs), **Limerick** (8/day, 2 hrs), **Doolin/Cliffs of Moher** (2/day, 4 hrs), **Ennis** (9/day, 3 hrs, change in Limerick), **Rosslare** (3/day, 7 hrs, €21.50), **Shannon** (9/day, 2.5 hrs). Tralee's bus station is at the train station. Bus info: tel. 066/712-3566.

Car rental: Duggan's Garage Practical Car Hire rents Fiat Puntos (€100/48 hrs, includes everything but gas, must be 25 years old, CC, 2 blocks from train station on Ashe Street, tel. 066/ 712-1124, fax 066/712-7527).

Airports

Kerry Airport, a 45-minute drive from Dingle town, offers direct flights to **Dublin** and **London** (daily, €109 to London, €72 to Dublin; airport tel. 066/976-4644 or 066/976-4350, Ryanair tel. 01/609-7878, Aer Arann Express tel. 1-890-462-726, www.kerryairport.ie).

Shannon Airport, the major airport in Western Ireland, has direct flights to **Dublin** (2–3/day, 30 min) and **London** (6/day, 1 hr). Ryanair (www.ryanair.com) and Aer Lingus (www.aerlingus.ie) fly out of Shannon. Airport info: tel. 061/ 471-444. Shannon Airport TI: tel. 061/471-664 (daily 6:30–17:30, June–Sept until 19:00). Shannon Airport also has easy bus connections to **Limerick** (nearly hrly, 1 hr, can continue to Tralee— 2 hrs, and Dingle—1.25 hrs more), **Ennis** (nearly hrly, 1 hr) and **Galway** (every 2 hrs, 2 hrs). Bus info: tel. 061/313-333.

Route Tips for Drivers

From Tralee to Dingle: Drivers choose between the narrow, but very exciting, Conor Pass road or the faster, easier, but still narrow N86 through Lougher and Anascaul. On a clear day Conor Pass comes with incredible views over Tralee Bay and Brandon Bay, the Blasket Islands, and the open Atlantic. Pull over at the summit viewpoint to look down on Dingle town and harbor. While in Kerry, listen to Radio Kerry FM 97. To practice your Gaelic, tune in to FM 94.4.

Between Tralee and Galway/Burren/Doolin: The Killimer–Tarbert ferry connection allows those heading north for the Cliffs of Moher (or south for Dingle) to avoid the 80-mile detour around the Shannon River. If you're going to Galway, the Limerick route is faster, but the ferry route is more scenic (1 trip/hr, 20 min, €13/carload, leaves on the half-hour going north and on the hour going south, until 21:00 April–Sept, until 19:00 Oct–March, no need to reserve, tel. 065/905-3124, www.shannonferries.com).

GALWAY

Galway feels like a boomtown—rare in Western Ireland. With 65,000 people, it's the area's main city—a lively university town and the county's industrial and administrative center. Amid the traditional regions of Connemara and the Aran Islands, it's also a Gaelic cultural center.

Galway offers tourists plenty of traditional music, easy bus connections to Dublin (1/hr, 3.5 hrs, €12), and a convenient jumping-off point for a visit to the Aran Islands.

While Galway has a long and interesting history, its British overlords (who ruled until 1922) had little use for anything important to the Irish heritage. Consequently, precious little from old Galway survives. What does survive has the interesting disadvantage of being built in the local limestone, which, even if medieval, looks like modern stone construction. The city's quincentennial celebration in 1984 prompted a spirit of preservation.

What Galway lacks in sights it makes up for in ambience. Spend an afternoon just wandering its medieval streets, with their delightful mix of colorful facades, labyrinthine pubs, weather-resistant street musicians, and steamy eateries.

Blustery Galway heats up after dark, with fine theaters and a pub scene Dubliners travel for. Visitors mix with old-timers and students as the traditional music goes round and round.

If you hear a strange language on the streets and wonder where those people are from ... it's Irish, and so are they.

Planning Your Time
Galway's sights are little more than pins on which to hang the old town. The joy of Galway is its street scene. You can see its sights in three hours, but without an evening in town, you've

Galway History

The medieval fishing village of Galway went big time when the Normans captured the territory from the O'Flaherty family in 1234. Making the town a base, the Normans invited in their Angle friends, built a wall (1270), and kicked out the Irish. Galway's Celtic name (Gaillimh) comes from an old Irish word, *gall*, which means "foreigner." Except for a small section in the Eyre Square Shopping Centre and a chunk at the Spanish Arch, that Norman wall is gone.

In the 14th century, 14 merchant families, or tribes, controlled Galway's commercial traffic, including the lucrative wine trade with Spain and France. These English families constantly clashed with the local Irish. Although the wall was built to "keep out the O's and the Macs," it didn't always work. A common prayer at the time was, "From the fury of the O'Flaherty's, good Lord deliver us."

Galway's support of the English king helped it prosper. But with the rise of Oliver Cromwell, Galway paid for that prosperity. After sieges in 1651 by Cromwell and in 1691 by the Protestant King William of Orange, Galway declined. It wasn't until the last half of the 20th century that it regained some of its importance and wealth.

missed the best. Many spend three nights here and two days: one for the town and another for a side-trip to the Burren, the Aran Islands, or Connemara (see next chapter). Tour companies make day trips to all three regions cheap and easy.

Orientation (area code: 091)

The center of Galway is Eyre Square. Within two blocks of the square you'll find the TI, Aran boat offices, a bike-rental shop, a tour pick-up point, the best cheap beds, and the train station. The train and bus station butt up against the Great Southern Hotel, a huge gray railroad hotel that overlooks and dominates Eyre Square. The lively old town lies between Eyre Square and the river. From Eyre Square, Williamsgate Street leads right through the old town (changing names several times) to Wolfe Tone Bridge. Nearly everything you'll see and do is within a few minutes' walk of this spine.

Tourist Information: The TI, located a block from the bus/train station in the ground floor of the Forster Court Hotel, has a bookshop and many booking services (May–June Mon–Sat

9:00–17:45, Sun 9:00–12:45; July–Aug daily 9:00–19:45; Sept–April Mon–Fri 9:00–17:45, Sat 9:00–12:45, closed Sun, tel. 091/537-700, www.irelandwest.ie). Pick up the TI's *Galway Magazine* (€2, persistent readers will find several maps and walking tours amid the ads).

Arrival in Galway: Trains and most buses share the same station, virtually on Eyre Square (which has the nearest ATMs). To get to the TI, turn right on Forster Street as you exit the station. Some buses from Dublin and Dublin's airport use the Forster Street Bus Park, next to the TI.

Parking: The most central and handiest pay garage is under Jurys Inn in the town center. To park nearby for free, look across the bridge along the Claddagh Quay or by the Siamsa Theatre.

Helpful Hints

Crowd Control: Expect huge crowds—and higher prices—during the Galway Arts Festival (last half of July), Galway Oyster Festival (4 days near end of Sept), and the three sets of Galway Races (a week in late July/early Aug, 3 days in mid-Sept, and 3 days in late Oct).

Bike Rental: Celtic Rent-a-Bike has good bikes and long hours (€20/day, daily 8:00–20:00, on Queen Street, a block past Kinlay House, 2 blocks off Eyre Square, if no one's there, buzz Celtic Tourist Hostel upstairs, tel. 091/566-606).

Markets: A fun market clusters around St. Nicholas' Church all day on Saturday (best 9:00–12:00). An antique market clinks and clanks at the base of the medieval wall in the Eyre Square Shopping Centre (daily, best Thu–Sat).

Internet Access: Try Internet Arcade in FunWorld at the top of Eyre Square (€5/hr, daily 10:00–23:00, tel. 091/561-415). There are also several good places along High Street near Jurys Inn.

Laundry: These two laundrettes are both centrally located. Launderland is conveniently close to the recommended B&Bs on College Road (Mon–Fri 8:30–18:30, Sat 9:00–18:00, closed Sun, €10 drop-off, Forster Court, 2 min up hill from TI, tel. 091/568-393). Prospect Hill Launderette is 100 yards off Eyre Square (Mon–Fri 8:30–18:00, Sat 8:30–17:00, closed Sun, €6.50 self-serve, €10 drop-off, 44 Prospect Hill, tel. 091/568-343).

Tours of Galway

▲**Walking Tour**—Kay Davis enjoys taking small groups on grandmotherly two-hour walks through old Galway. Starting at the TI, she covers Eyre Square, the cathedral, and the old town, and then finishes up at the Spanish Arch (€5, tickets at TI, June–Sept Mon, Wed, Fri at 11:30; Kay also does private walks, tel. 091/792-431).

Galway

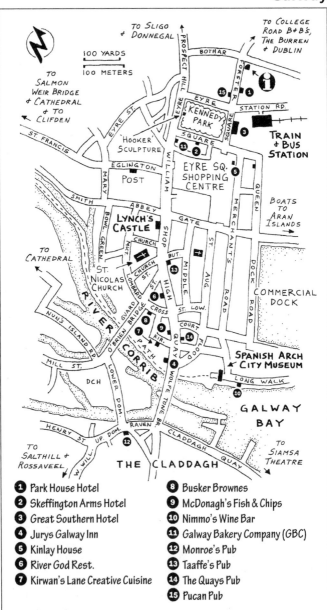

1. Park House Hotel
2. Skeffington Arms Hotel
3. Great Southern Hotel
4. Jurys Galway Inn
5. Kinlay House
6. River God Rest.
7. Kirwan's Lane Creative Cuisine
8. Busker Brownes
9. McDonagh's Fish & Chips
10. Nimmo's Wine Bar
11. Galway Bakery Company (GBC)
12. Monroe's Pub
13. Taaffe's Pub
14. The Quays Pub
15. Pucan Pub

▲**Hop-on, Hop-off City Bus Tours**—Several companies run guided, 60-minute, hop-on, hop-off double-decker buses from Eyre Square, making nine stops—including the cathedral, Salthill, and the Spanish Arch. You're allowed to get off and explore and hop back on later (€9, daily 10:30–16:30, longer hours in summer, 4/day, buses usually depart every 90 min from TI on Forster Street or top of Eyre Square—near Hooker's Monument, different companies honor other companies' tickets).

Sights—Medieval Galway's "Latin Quarter"

From the top of Eyre Square, Williamsgate Street (named for the old main gate of the Norman town wall that once stood here) is the spine of medieval Galway, leading downhill straight to the Corrib River. While the road changes names several times (William, Shop, High, and Quay Streets), it leads generally downhill and straight past these sights:

Lynch's Castle—Now the Allied Irish Bank, Galway's best 16th-century fortified townhouse was the home of the Lynch family—the most powerful of the town's 14 tribes. More than 60 Lynch mayors ruled Galway in the 16th and 17th centuries.

Collegiate Church of St. Nicholas—This church, located a half-block off the main street on the right, is the finest surviving medieval building in town (1320) and is dedicated to St. Nicholas of Myra, the patron saint of sailors. Columbus is said to have worshiped here in 1477, undoubtedly while contemplating a scary voyage. Its interior is littered with obscure town history (€2 donation for admission). On Saturday, a wonderful market surrounds the church.

The Quay Pub—This pub, once owned by "Humanity Dick," an 18th-century member of Parliament who was the original animal-rights activist, is worth a peek inside for its lively interior. The lane just before it leads to the . . .

Druid Theatre—This 100-seat theater offers top-notch contemporary Irish theater. Drop by to see if anything's playing tonight (€15 tickets, CC, Chapel Lane, tel. 091/568-660, www.druidtheatre.com).

Spanish Arch and City Museum—Overlooking the Corrib River, these make up the best surviving chunk of the old city wall. The Spanish Arch (1584), the place where Spanish ships would unload their cargo, is a reminder of Galway's former importance in trade. The tiny museum is humble—but if you're looking for fragments of old Galway, this is where they're kept (€3, April–Oct daily 10:00–13:00 & 14:00–17:00, closed off-season, tel. 091/567-641).

Corrib River Sights—At the Corrib River, you'll find a riverside park perfect for a picnic (or get take-out from the town's best chippie, McDonagh's, across the street). Over the river (southeast of the bridge) is the modern housing project that, in the 1930s,

Galway Legends

Because of the dearth of physical old stuff, the town milks its legends. Here are a few you'll encounter repeatedly:

In the 15th century, the mayor, one of the Lynch tribe, condemned his son to death for the murder of a Spaniard. When no one in town could be found to hang the popular boy, the dad—who loved justice more than his son—did it himself.

Columbus is said to have stopped in Galway in 1477. He may have been inspired by tales of the voyage of St. Brendan, the Irish monk who is thought by some (mostly Irish) to have beaten Columbus to the New World by nearly a thousand years.

On the main drag you'll find a pub called the King's Head. It was originally given to the man who chopped off the head of King Charles I in 1649. For his safety he settled in Galway, about as far from London as an Englishman could go back then.

Every sight in town finds a way to tell you the story about the Claddagh ring—so I won't.

replaced the original Claddagh. Claddagh (pron. CLA-dah) was a picturesque, Gaelic-speaking fishing village with a strong tradition of independence—and open sewers. This gaggle of thatched cottages actually functioned as an independent community with its own "king" until early in the 1900s. Nothing survives today except for the tradition of the popular claddagh ring—two hands holding a heart.

Notice the monument (just before the bridge) given to Galway by the people of Genoa, celebrating Columbus' visit here in 1477. (That acknowledgment, from a town known in Italy for its stinginess, helps to substantiate the murky visit.) From the bridge, look up the river. The green copper dome marks the city's Cathedral of St. Nicholas (listed below). Down the river is a tiny harbor with a few of Galway's famous square-rigged "hooker" fishing ships tied up and on display. Beyond that a huge park of reclaimed land is popular with the local kids for Irish football and hurling. From there the promenade leads to the resort town of Salthill.

Sights—Galway

▲**Eyre Square**—In the Middle Ages, this was a green just outside the town wall. The square is named for the mayor who gave the land to the city in 1710. While still called Eyre Square, it now contains John F. Kennedy Park—established in memory of the Irish-American president's visit in 1963, a few months before he was assassinated. (Though Kennedy is celebrated as America's first Irish-Catholic president, there have been several presidents who are descendants of Protestant Ulster stock.) On a sunny day Eyre Square is a popular grassy hangout. Walk to the rust-colored Quincentennial Fountain (built in 1984 to celebrate the 500th anniversary of the incorporation of the city). The sails represent Galway's square-rigged fishing ships and the vessels that made Galway a trading center so long ago. The Browne Doorway, from a 1627 fortified townhouse, is a reminder of the 14 family tribes that once ruled the town. Each had a town castle—much like the towers that characterize the towns of Tuscany with their feuding noble families. So little survives of medieval Galway that the town makes a huge deal of any surviving window or crest. The cannons are from the Crimean War (1854). The statue is of Patrick O'Connor, Galway's favorite Gaelic poet, who'd sit on a limestone wall, as sculpted, recording the local life.

The Eyre Square Shopping Centre—a busy, modern shopping mall (see the arcaded entry from the square)—leads to a surviving piece of the old town wall that includes two reconstructed towers (and an antiques market).

▲▲**Cathedral of St. Nicholas**—Opened by American Cardinal Cushing in 1965, this is one of the last great stone churches built in Europe. The interior is a treat—mahogany pews set on green Connemara marble floors under a Canadian cedar ceiling. The acoustically correct cedar enhances the church's fine pipe organ. Two thousand worshipers sit in the round facing the central altar. A Dublin woman carved 14 larger-than-life stations of the cross. The carving above the chapel (left of entry) is from the old St. Nicholas church. Explore the modern stained glass. Find the Irish holy family—with Mary knitting and Jesus offering Joseph a cup of tea. The window depicting the Last Supper is particularly creative—find the 12 apostles. Church bulletins at the doorway tell of upcoming Masses and concerts (located across Salmon Weir Bridge on outskirts of town, tel. 091/563-577).

Salmon Weir Bridge—This bridge was the local "bridge of sighs." It led from the courthouse (opposite the church) to the prison (torn down to build the church—unlikely in the United States). Today the bridge provides a fun view of the fishing action. Salmon run up this river most of the summer (look for them). Fishermen, who wear waders and carry walking sticks to withstand the strong current, book long in advance to get half-day appointments for a casting spot.

Canals multiplied in this city (sometimes called the Venice of Ireland) to power more water mills.

Sights—Outer Galway

▲**Galway Irish Crystal Heritage Center**—This is a grand-sounding name for a sight in a grand new building made-to-order for big bus groups. Still, this cheap tour (handy for drivers) is the place to see the making of Irish crystal. Tours go every half-hour. After a guided tour through the museum and a quick look at craftsmen cutting crystal (Mon–Fri only), you sit for 10 minutes while a video subliminally sells you crystal and wows you with Galway sights. The museum, more interesting than Galway's City Museum, gives you a good rundown on Claddagh village and a chance to see a large hooker named *Fiona* (€4, May–Sept Mon–Sat 9:00–18:00, Sun 11:00–17:00, Oct-April Mon–Sat 10:00–17:30, Sun 11:00–17:00, good cafeteria, 5 min out of Galway on Dublin road N6, or take Merlin Park bus—every 20 min—from Eyre Square, tel. 091/757-311, www.galwaycrystal.ie).

▲**Salthill**—This small resort packs pubs, discos, a splashy water park, amusement centers, and a fairground up against a fine mile-long beach promenade. At the new Atlantaquaria aquarium, which features solely Irish water life, kids can help feed the fish at 15:00 (€7, daily 10:00–17:00, touch tanks, Toft Park, tel. 091/585-100). For sunny time on the beach, a relaxing sunset stroll, late-night traditional music, or later-night disco action, Salthill hops. To get to Salthill, catch bus #1 from Eyre Square in front of the IAB bank next to the Great Southern Hotel (€1, runs 7:00–23:00).

Dog Racing—Join the locals and cheer on the greyhounds on Tuesday and Friday evenings from 20:15 to 22:00 (€4, barking distance from my recommended B&Bs, a 10-min walk from Eyre Square, tel. 091/562-273).

Nightlife in Galway

Folk Theater—Galway's folk theatre, **Siamsa**, features Irish music, folk drama, singing, and dancing, including the step-dancing popularized by Riverdance (€18, late-June–Aug Mon–Fri at 20:45, Claddagh Hall, Nimmos Pier, tel. 091/755-479).

▲**Traditional Irish Music in Pubs**—Galway (like Dingle and Doolin) is a mecca for good Irish music (nightly 21:30–23:30). Unlike Dingle and Doolin, this is a university town (enrollment: 12,000), and many pubs are often overrun with noisy students. Still, the chances of landing a seat close to a churning band surrounded by new Irish friends are good any evening of the year. Touristy and student pubs are found and filled along the main drag down from Eyre Square to the Spanish Arch and across Wolfe Tone Bridge along William Street West and Dominick Street. Across the bridge, start at **Monroe's**, with its vast, music-filled interior (live music nightly, set-dancing Tue, Dominick

Street, tel. 091/583-397). Several other pubs within earshot also feature almost-nightly traditional music.

Pubs known for Irish music along the main drag include **Taaffe's** (nightly music, plus Thu–Sat at 17:30, Shop Street, across from St. Nicholas Church, tel. 091/564-066) and **The Quays** (traditional music at 21:30 Mon–Wed, 17:00 Fri–Sun, young scene, Quay Street, tel. 091/568-347).

Pucan Pub, a smoky cauldron of music and beer-drinking with an older crowd—including lots of tourists—is worth a look (music nightly at 22:00, sometimes traditional, just off Eyre Square on Forster Street, tel. 091/561-528).

Sleeping in Galway
(€1 = about $1, country code: 353, area code: 091)

Sleep Code: **S** = Single, **D** = Double/Twin, **T** = Triple, **Q** = Quad, **b** = bathroom, **s** = shower only, **CC** = Credit Cards accepted, **no CC** = Credit Cards not accepted.

To help you easily sort through these listings, I've divided the rooms into three categories, based on the price for a standard double room with bath:

Higher Priced—Most rooms more than €100
Moderately Priced—Most rooms €60–100.
Lower Priced—Most rooms €60 or less.

There are three price tiers for most beds in Galway: high season (Easter–October), off-season, and charge-what-you-like festival times (e.g., race weekends and the last half of July). I've listed high-season rates. B&Bs simply play the market. If you're on a tight budget, call around and see where the prices are. All B&Bs include a full fried breakfast.

Hotels

For a fancy hotel, Park House Hotel offers the best value. For a budget hotel, go to Jurys.

HIGHER PRICED

Park House Hotel, a plush, business-class hotel, is ideally located a block from the train station and Eyre Square. Its 68 spacious rooms come with all the comforts you'd expect (Db-€160 is the "corporate rate" you should get most of the year, ask if there's a discount, Sun night is slow and rooms can rent for Db-€95–125, includes breakfast, CC, good restaurant, elevator, free garage, helpful staff, Forster Street, tel. 091/564-924, fax 091/569-219, www.parkhousehotel.ie, e-mail: parkhouse@eircom.net).

The **Skeffington Arms Hotel,** which feels more Irish (and a bit smokier) than the Park House or Jurys, escapes most of the tour-group scene because it has only 23 rooms. Centrally located on Eyre Square, it's furnished in a dark-wood Victorian style (Db-€102–140, CC, pub downstairs, Eyre Square, tel. 091/ 563-173, fax 091/ 561-679, e-mail: info@skeffington.ie).

Great Southern Hotel, filled with palatial Old World elegance and 90 rooms, marks the end of the Dublin–Galway train line and the beginning of Galway. Since 1845 it has been Galway's landmark hotel (Db-€240, some discounts during slow times, breakfast-€12.75, CC, sauna, indoor rooftop pool, stuffy staff, at the head of Eyre Square, tel. 091/564-041, fax 091/ 566-704, e-mail: res@galway-gsh.ie).

MODERATELY PRICED

Jurys Galway Inn offers 128 American-style rooms in a modern hotel centrally located where the old town hits the river. The big, bright rooms have two double beds and huge modern bathrooms (€98 per room, depending on season, whether filled by a single, a couple, 3 adults, or a family of 4, continental breakfast-€6, full Irish breakfast-€9, CC, elevator, lots of tour groups, non-smoking floor, parking-€8.50, Quay Street, tel. 091/566-444, fax 091/568-415, U.S. tel. 800/843-3311, www.jurys.com, e-mail: galway_inn@jurysdoyle.com).

B&Bs

Drivers, following city-center signs into Galway, pass right by a string of B&Bs just after the greyhound-racing stadium. These are a five-minute walk from Eyre Square (from the station, walk up Forster Street, which turns into College Road). All of the listings are on College Road except for the two lower-priced listings (Flanagan's and Kinlay House).

HIGHER PRICED

Ardawn House is a classy B&B with nine comfortable rooms (Db-€76–120, CC, College Road, near stadium on right, tel. 091/568-833, fax 091/563-454, e-mail: ardawn@iol.ie).

MODERATELY PRICED

The first two B&Bs listed are the best values.

College Crest Guest House is a proud establishment with 12 big, fresh rooms and a cushy lounge (Sb-€60-70, Db-€80-90, Tb-€120, CC, non-smoking, parking, closest to town at 5 College Road, tel. & fax 091/564-744, www.collegecrest.com, e-mail: inquiries@collegecrest.com). Marion Fitzgerald enjoys her work and runs this place with flair.

Petra House, a peaceful-feeling brick building, rents six great

Galway B&Bs

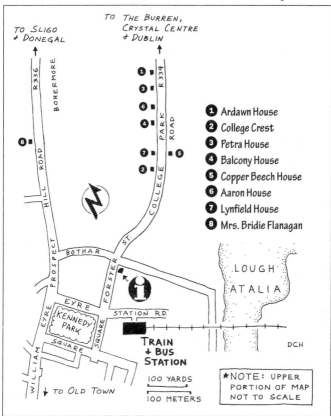

TO THE BURREN,
CRYSTAL CENTRE
& DUBLIN

TO SLIGO
& DONEGAL

R 336

BOHERMORE

R 339

COLLEGE PARK ROAD

1 Ardawn House
2 College Crest
3 Petra House
4 Balcony House
5 Copper Beech House
6 Aaron House
7 Lynfield House
8 Mrs. Bridie Flanagan

HILL ROAD

PROSPECT

BOTHAR

FORSTER ST.

EYRE

EYRE SQUARE

KENNEDY PARK

WILLIAM

STATION RD.

LOUGH
ATALIA

TRAIN
& BUS
STATION

DCH

↓ TO OLD TOWN

100 YARDS
100 METERS

★NOTE: UPPER
PORTION OF MAP
NOT TO SCALE

rooms, including a family room. The owners, Joan and Frank Maher, keep everything lovingly maintained (Sb-€50–55, Db-€76–89, CC, elegant sitting room, next door to Ardawn House—listed above, 29 College Road, tel. & fax 091/566-580, www.galway.net/pages /petra-house, e-mail: petrahouse@eircom.net).

Balcony House B&B rents nine pleasant rooms (Db-€70–80, family deals in quads, 27 College Road, tel. & fax 091/563-438, Michael and Teresa Coyne).

Copper Beech House B&B rents five rooms a bit cheaper than its neighbors but with no lounge, tight quarters, and an absentee owner (Db-€64–90, CC, 26 College Road, tel. 091/ 569-544, e-mail: oceanbb@iol.ie).

Aaron House B&B rents 14 decent rooms (Sb-€32–50,

Db-€63–100, CC, 25 College Road, tel. 091/563-315, e-mail: aaron@indigo.ie).

Lynfield House B&B rents five plain, practical rooms (Db-€70, CC, 9 College Road, tel. & fax 091/567-845, e-mail: info@adriaguesthouse.com).

LOWER PRICED

On Prospect Hill Road: This road (leaving Eyre Square from Richardson's Bar on Prospect Hill Road) is lined with small row houses, many of which do B&B. **Mrs. Bridie Flanagan's B&B** is a humble, friendly, old home with a welcoming living room and four bedrooms—two big and two cramped (tiny D-€50, fine Db-€60, T-€65, 85 Prospect Hill, tel. 091/561-515).

Hostel: **Kinlay House** is a no-nonsense place just 100 yards from the train station, with 180 beds (1–8 beds per room) in bare, clean, and simple rooms, including 15 doubles. The lounge/reception area is enveloped in a haze of smoke, but the rooms are smoke-free. Easygoing people of any age feel comfortable here, but if you want a double, book well in advance—several months in advance for weekends (dorm bed-€14.50, Sb-€40, Db-€48, includes continental breakfast, CC, elevator, self-service kitchen, Internet access, launderette, luggage storage, on Merchants Road, just off Eyre Square, tel. 091/565-244, fax 091/565-245, e-mail: kinlay.galway@usitworld.com).

Sleeping in Salthill

MODERATELY PRICED

Carraig Beag B&B, the classiest, friendliest, and most peaceful of all, is a big brick home on a residential street a block off the beach just beyond the resort town of Salthill. Catherine Lydon, with the help of her husband Paddy, rents six big, bright, fresh, and comfy rooms with a welcoming living room and a social breakfast table (Sb-€40–65, Db-€60–70, family room-€70–95; 8-min drive from Galway, follow the beach past Salthill, take second right after golf course on Knock-nacarra Road and go 2 blocks to 1 Burren View Heights, tel. 091/521-696). The #2 bus (€1, 3/hr) goes from Eyre Square (picks up in front of Skeffington pub) to the Knocknacarra stop at the B&B's doorstep. Catherine can arrange for day-tour pick-ups at her place.

Eating in Galway

Being a tourist and college town, the city is filled with colorful, inexpensive eateries. People everywhere seem to be enjoying their food. Each of these places is at the bottom of the old town within a block or two of Jurys Inn.

River God is a bistro/restaurant passionately run by Patric Juillet, who cooks fine "world French" cuisine. He slices, dices, and prices as if his bottom line were filling people with very good food (€8 2-course lunch deals, €15 3-course dinners, daily 17:00–23:00 plus Sat lunch 12:30–17:00, CC, reservations recommended; above Bunch of Grapes pub at 2 High Street, tel. 091/565-811).

Kirwan's Lane Creative Cuisine, considered Galway's best restaurant, is a dressy place where reservations are required (€19 lunches, €32 dinners, Mon–Sat 12:30–14:30 and dinner from 18:00, closed Sun, Kirwan's Lane a block from Jurys, tel. 091/568-266).

Busker Brownes has three eateries in a smoky, sprawling place popular for its good, cheap food. Enter on Cross Street for the restaurant (and walk to the back for better seating) or enter on Kirwan's Lane for the ground-floor pub; upstairs from the pub is the third and smokiest section (€9 meals, daily 11:00–21:00, "Sunday-morning jazz session" at 13:00, Cross Street and Kirwan's Lane, tel. 091/563-377).

McDonagh's Fish & Chips is a favorite chippie. It has a fast, cheap section and a classier restaurant. If you're determined to try Galway oysters, remember that they're in season September through April only. Other times you'll eat Pacific oysters—which doesn't make much sense to me (€7 cheap lunch, €13–19 in restaurant, Mon–Sat 12:00–24:00, Sun 17:00–23:00, non-smoking section, 22 Quay Street, tel. 091/565-001).

Nimmo's Wine Bar Bistro lurks peacefully in an old stone warehouse behind the Spanish Arch with great €5 fish soup and a diverse wine list. The candlelit ambience is great even for a cup of coffee (€13–23 meals, Tue–Sat 12:30–15:00 & 18:30–23:00, Sun only 18:30–23:00, Long Walk Street, tel. 091/561-114).

The **Galway Bakery Company (GBC)** is a popular and basic place for a quick Irish meal (€4–8 meals in the ground-floor cafeteria, pricier restaurant upstairs, daily 8:00–21:00, CC, 7 Williamsgate Street, near Eyre Square, tel. 091/563-087).

Supermarkets: A Super Valu is in Eyre Square Shopping Centre (Mon–Sat 9:00–18:30, Thu–Fri until 21:00, closed Sun) and Dunne's is just moments away, accessed through the Eyre Square Shopping Centre or around the corner at tiny Castle Street, off the pedestrian street, Williamsgate (Mon–Sat 9:00–18:30, Thu until 21:00, Sun 12:00–18:00, supermarket in basement). Lots of smaller grocery shops are scattered throughout town.

Medieval Banquet: If you have a car, consider a **Dunguaire Castle medieval banquet** in Kinvarra, a 30-minute drive south of Galway (for more information, see next chapter). The 17:30 banquet can be done very efficiently as you're driving into or out of Galway (B&Bs are accustomed to late arrivals if you call).

Transportation Connections—Galway

By train to: Dublin (4/day, 3 hrs). For **Belfast, Tralee,** and **Rosslare,** you'll change in or near Dublin. Train info: tel. 091/561-444.

By bus to: Ennis (14/day, 1.25 hr), **Doolin/Cliffs of Moher** (4/day, 1.5 hrs), **Limerick** (12/day, 2 hrs), **Rosslare** (2/day, 6.5 hrs), **Belfast** (3/day, 7 hrs, €28), **Dublin** (15/day, 3.5 hrs, €12). Bus info: tel. 091/562-000. Nestor Travel and Citylink, among other companies, run cheap and fast bus services from Galway (Forster Street Bus Park) to Dublin (Tara Street DART Station at George's Quay) and the Dublin airport (7/day; €10 and 3 hrs for Dublin; €15 and 3.5 hrs for airport, Nestor tel. 091/797-144, Citylink tel. 091/564-163).

By car: For ideas on driving from Galway to Derry or Portrush in Northern Ireland, see the end of the Derry chapter.

SIGHTS NEAR GALWAY

In three different directions, Galway has interesting sights: County Clare and the Burren to the south, the Aran Islands to the west, and the Connemara region to the north. To see the Burren by car, visit it en route between Galway and Dingle; otherwise you can take a tour from Galway. The Aran Islands (use public transportation) and Connemara (easy by car or tour) each take a day.

Bus Tours of the Burren and Connemara

Two companies—Lally and O'Neachtain—in Galway run all-day, €25 tours of nearby regions. Tours of the Burren do a loop south of Galway, covering Kinvarra, Aillwee Cave, Portal (Poulnabrone) Dolmen, and the Cliffs of Moher. Tours of Connemara include the *Quiet Man* Cottage, Kylemore Abbey, Clifden, and the "Famine Village." Tours go most days from about 10:00 to 17:30 (depart near Galway's TI, call to confirm exact itinerary, Lally tel. 091/562-905, O'Neachtain tel. 091/553-188). Drivers take cash only; to pay with a credit card, book at the TI.

COUNTY CLARE AND THE BURREN

Those connecting Dingle in the South with Galway, the urban center of the West, can entertain themselves along the way by joyriding through the fascinating landscape and tidy villages of County Clare. Ennis, the major city of the county, with a medieval history and a market bustle, is a workaday Irish town ideal for anyone tired of the tourist crowds. The dramatic Cliffs of Moher overlooking the Atlantic offer tenderfeet a thrilling hike. The Burren is a unique, windblown, limestone wasteland that hides an abundance of flora, fauna, caves, and history. For your evening entertainment, you can join a tour-bus group in a castle for a medieval banquet at Kinvarra

County Clare and the Burren

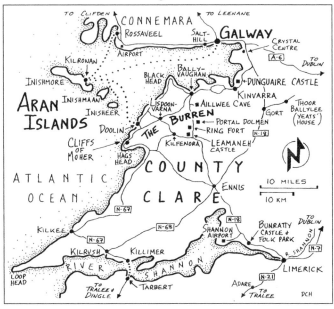

or join traditional-Irish-music enthusiasts from around Europe for tin-whistling in Doolin.

Planning Your Time

By train and bus, your gateways to this region are Ennis from the south and Galway from the north (consider a tour from Galway; see "Bus Tours," above).

By car, the region can be an enjoyable daylong drive-through or a destination in itself. None of the sights has to take much time. But do get out and walk a bit.

If driving between Dingle/Tralee in the south and Galway/Aran Islands in the north, I'd recommend this day plan rather than the fast road via Limerick: Drive north from Tralee to catch the Tarbert–Killimer car ferry (avoiding the 80-mile drive around the Shannon estuary; see "Route Tips" at the end of Dingle chapter), then drive the scenic coastal route to the Cliffs of Moher for an hour break. The scenic drive through the Burren, with a couple of stops and a tour of the caves, takes about two hours. There's a 17:30 medieval banquet at **Dunguaire Castle** near Kinvarra (just 30 min south of Galway).

Skip the **Bunratty Castle and Folk Museum.** I'd leave this most commercial and least lively of all European open-air folk museums to the jet-lagged, big-bus American tour groups (located just a potty stop from the Shannon Airport, past Limerick on the road to Ennis).

Cliffs of Moher

A visit to the Cliffs of Moher, a ▲▲▲ sight, is one of Ireland's great natural thrills. For five miles, the dramatic cliffs soar as high as 650 feet above the Atlantic.

Drivers park at the lot for €2.50 (or catch a bus from Galway: 3/day in summer, 1.5 hrs, €15 round-trip). You'll find a TI office (daily 9:30–17:30, July–Aug until 19:00, tel. 065/708-1171), shop, and cafeteria. Walk 200 meters past harpists and accordion players along a low wall of the local Liscannor slate (notice squiggles made by worms, eels, and snails long ago when the slate was still mud on the sea floor) to the cliff's edge. O'Brien's Tower (1853) marks the highest point (€1.50).

For the best thrill, read the warning, consider the risk, then step over the slate barrier and down onto the stone platform. Here there are no crowds. If you're a risk-taking fool, belly out and take a peek over the ledge. You'll find yourself in a dramatic world where the only sounds are the waves, the wind, the gulls, and your stomach signaling frantically for help. There's a particularly peaceful corner of the platform over on the far right. On the far left, watch the birds play in the updrafts. In the distance, on windy days, the Aran Islands can be seen wearing their white necklace.

Before leaving the area, take 10 minutes to check out the holy well of St. Brigid, located beside the tall column about two miles south of the cliffs on the main road to Liscannor. In the short hall leading into the hillside spring, you'll find a treasure of personal and religious memorabilia left behind by devoted visitors seeking cures and blessings. The gray column outside was a folly erected 150 years ago by a local landlord with money and ego to burn.

Doolin

This town is a strange phenomenon. Tourists go directly from Paris or Munich to Doolin. It's on the tourist map for its three pubs that feature Irish folk music. A few years ago, this was a mecca for Irish musicians. They came together here to jam before a few lucky aficionados. But now the crowds and the foreigners are overwhelming the musicians, and the quality of music is not as reliable. Still, as Irish and European music-lovers alike crowd the pubs, the *bodhrán* beat goes on. The Michael Russell Heritage Centre may eventually become a museum of traditional music. For now, some *ceilidh* dances are held here. Ask at a pub if anything's scheduled.

Doolin has plenty of accommodations, several good restaurants, and a Greek-island-without-the-sun ambience. Each pub serves decent dinners before the music starts. The "town" is just a few homes and shops strung out along a valley road from the tiny harbor. Nearest the harbor, the Lower Village (Fisherstreet) has **O'Connor's Pub** (tel. 065/707-4168) and is the closest thing to a commercial center. A mile farther up the road, the Upper Village (Roadford) straddles a bridge with the other two destination pubs, **McGann's** (tel. 065/707-4133) and **McDermott's** (tel. 065/707-4328). Music starts around 21:30 and finishes around midnight. On my last trip, I hit Doolin on a mediocre music night. The *craic* is fine regardless.

From Doolin you can hike or bike (rentals in town) up Burren Way for three miles to the Cliffs of Moher. (Get advice locally on the trail condition and safety.)

Ferries: The boats from Doolin to the Aran Islands (described below) can be handy but are often canceled. Even a balmy day can be too windy (or the tide can be too low) to allow for a sailing from Doolin's crude little port. If you're traveling by car and have time limits, don't risk sailing from Doolin. Without a car, you can travel on from the Aran Islands to Galway by the bigger boats, so Doolin might work for you. But it's a longer trip to Inishmore (some sailings make a stop at Inisheer en route), so consider an overnight stay on the islands (to Inishmore: €20 one-way, €35 round-trip, 2/day, 2.5 hrs, leaving at 10:00 and 13:00, depending on season, returning at 11:30 and 16:00; to Inisheer: €15 one-way, €25 round-trip, 5/day, 30 min, leaving roughly hrly 10:00–14:00; CC, tel. 065/707-4455 to see what's sailing).

Sleeping in Doolin (area code: 065): Harbour View B&B is a fine modern house with four rooms a mile from the Doolin fiddles, overlooking the valley. Mrs. Cullinan keeps the guests' living room stocked with books and games (Sb-€35, Db-€52, Tb-€72, larger family room deals, includes classy breakfast, CC, on main road halfway between Lisdoonvarna and the Cliffs of Moher, next to Statoil gas station, tel. 065/707-4154, fax 065/707-4935, www .harbourviewdoolin.com, e-mail: kathlen@eircom.net). **Doolin Hostel,** right in Doolin's Lower Village, caters creatively to the needs of backpackers in town for the music (dorm bed-€12, Db-€33, Qb-€52, Lower Village, tel. 065/707-4006, fax 065/707-4421, www.kingsway.ie/doolinhostel, e-mail: doolinhostel@eircom.net).

Lisdoonvarna

This town of 1,000 was known for centuries for its spa and its matchmakers. Today, except for a couple of September weeks during its Matchmaking Festival, it's pretty sleepy. (The bank is only open one day a week.) Still, it's more of a town than Doolin and, apart from festival time, less touristy. Lisdoonvarna has good traditional music in its pubs. I'd stay here rather than in Doolin and commute.

Sleeping in Lisdoonvarna (area code: 065): Each of these three places is on the main Galway road near the main square and church. **Marchmont B&B** rents two large twin/family rooms and two small doubles in a fine old house (Db-€54, just past post office, tel. 065/707-4050, Eileen Barrett). **Banner County Lodge** (S-€25, D/Db-€50–60, Tb-€75, tel. & fax 065/707-4340) and **St. Genevieve's B&B** (D-€33–39, Db-€39–43, T-€46, CC, open May–Sept only, tel. 065/707-4074) are closer to the square but bigger, scruffier, and less personal.

The Burren

Literally the "rocky place," the Burren is just that. The 50-square-mile limestone plateau, a two-star sight, is so barren a disappointed Cromwellian surveyor of the 1650s described it as "a savage land, yielding neither water enough to drown a man, nor a tree to hang him, nor soil enough to bury him." But he wasn't much of a botanist, because the Burren is a unique ecosystem, with flora that has changed little since the last ice age 10,000 years ago. It's also rich in prehistoric and early Christian sites. The first human inhabitants of the Burren came about 6,000 years ago. Today this limestone land is littered with more than 2,000 historic sites, including about 500 Iron Age stone forts.

Sightseeing the Burren: The drive from Kilfenora to Ballyvaughan offers the best quick swing through the historic Burren.

Kilfenora (5 miles southeast of Lisdoonvarna) is a good starting point. Its hardworking, community-run **Burren Centre** shows an intense 18-minute video explaining the geology and botany of the region and then ushers you into its enlightening new museum exhibits (€5, March–May and Oct daily 10:00–17:00, June–Sept daily 9:30–18:00, closed Nov–Feb, tel. 065/708-8030, www.theburrencentre.ie). You'll see copies of a fine eighth-century golden collar and ninth-century silver brooch (now in Dublin's National Museum). The ruined church next door has a couple of 12th-century crosses but isn't much to see. Mass is still held in the church, which claims the pope as its bishop. Kilfenora, as the smallest and poorest diocese in Ireland, was almost unable to function after the famine, so in 1866 Pope Pius the IX supported the town as best he could—by personally declaring himself its bishop. For lunch in Kilfenora, consider the cheap and cheery Burren Centre lunchroom or the more atmospheric Vaughan's Pub (tel. 065/708-8004).

The Burren

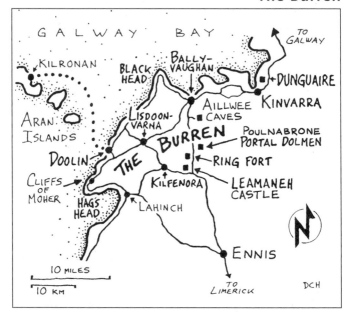

At **Leamaneh Castle,** a ruined shell of a fortified 17th-century house not open to anyone these days, turn north on R480 (direction: Ballyvaughan). After about five miles you'll hit the start of the real barren Burren and see a stone table a few hundred yards off the road (to the east, toward an ugly gray metal barn).

This is the **Portal Dolmen** (also called the Poulnabrone Dolmen—a stone table). Two hundred years ago, locals called this a "druid's altar." Four thousand years ago, it was a grave chamber within a cairn of stacked stones that have since been eroded or carried away. Wander over for a look. (It's crowded in midday with tour buses, but it's all yours early or late.)

Be a geologist. Wander for some quiet time with the wild-flowers. You're walking across a former seabed. Look for fossils: White smudges were coral. Scratches on rocks were ground by other rocks embedded in the belly of a retreating glacier. The boulders were carried on a giant conveyor belt of ice, then left behind by the melting glaciers. V-shaped valleys were carved by the swift glacial runoff.

The **Cahercommaun ring fort** (one of 500 or so in the area) can be seen on the crest of a hill just off the road about a half mile south of the Portal Dolmen. (You can park at the

Botany of the Burren in Brief

The Burren is a story of water, rock, geological force, and time. It supports the greatest diversity of plants in Ireland. Like nowhere else, Mediterranean and Arctic wildflowers bloom side by side in the Burren. It's an orgy of cross-pollination that attracts more insects than Doolin does music-lovers—even beetles help out. Limestone, created from layers of coral, sea shells, and mud, is the basis of the Burren. (This same basic slab resurfaces 10 miles or so out to sea to form the Aran Islands.) The earth's crust heaved it up and the glaciers swept it bare—dropping boulders as they receded. Rain, reacting naturally with the limestone to create a mild but determined acid, slowly drilled potholes into the surface. Rainwater cut through weak parts in the limestone, leaving crevices on the surface and Europe's most extensive system of caves below. These puddles grew algae, which dried into a powder. That, combined with bug parts and rabbit turds (bunnies abound in the Burren), created a very special soil. Plants and flowers fill the cracks in the limestone. Grasses and shrubs don't do well here, and wild goats eat any trees that try to grow, giving tender little flowers a chance to enjoy the sun. Different flowers appear in different months, sharing space rather than competing. The flowers are best in June and July.

intersection and walk up the gray farm's driveway and through the gate marked "stone fort" for a look, but there's little to see.) The stretch from Portal Dolmen north to Ballyvaughan offers the starkest scenery.

The **Aillwee Caves** are touted as "Ireland's premier showcaves." I couldn't resist a look. While fairly touristy and not worth the time or money if you've seen a lot of caves, they offer your easiest look at the massive system of caves that underlie the Burren. Your guide walks you 300 meters into the plain but impressive cave, giving a serious 40-minute geology lesson. During the ice age, underground rivers carved countless caves such as these. Brown bears, which became extinct in Ireland a thousand years ago, found this cave great for hibernating. But the caves are a constant 50 degrees, and I needed my sweater (€7, €18 family deal, open daily at 10:00, last tour at 18:30 July–Aug, otherwise 17:30, Dec–Feb call ahead for limited tours, clearly signposted just south of Ballyvaughan, tel. 065/707-7036).

Ballyvaughan

Really just a crossroads, Ballyvaughan is the closest town to
the Burren and an ideal rural oasis for those intending to really
explore the Burren.

In Ballyvaughan, the **Burren Exposure** is your best first stop
if you're entering the Burren from Galway. Located in a modern
little building overlooking Galway Bay, at the edge of the bleakness,
its excellent three-part audiovisual presentation tells the geological,
human, and floral story of this unique chunk of Ireland (€4.50,
April–Oct 10:00–17:30, shows every 12 min, closed in winter,
plush sea-view cafeteria, tel. 065/707-7277, fax 065/707-7278).

Shane Connolly leads in-depth, three-hour guided walks
through the Burren explaining the diverse flora and geology.
Wear comfortable shoes for wet, rocky fields, and prepare to
meet a proud farmer who really knows his stuff (€15.25, daily
at 10:00 from Corkscrew Hill, 4 miles west of Ballyvaughan, tel.
065/707-7168, http://homepage.eircom.net/~burrenhillwalks).

Sleeping and Eating in Ballyvaughan (area code: 065):
Rusheen Lodge, near the fringe of the Burren, offers nine prim
rooms and a great breakfast (Sb-€63, Db-€89, CC, tel. 065/
707-7092, fax 065/707-7152, www.rusheenlodge.com, e-mail:
rusheen@iol.ie). Your best bet for meals is **Tri na cheile** in
the middle of town, serving good food in a colorful, laidback
atmosphere (€16–24 dinners, daily 18:00–22:00, CC, Main
Street, tel. 065/707-7029).

Kinvarra

This tiny town, between Ballyvaughan and Galway (half an hour
from each), is waiting for something to happen in its minuscule
harbor. It faces Dunguaire Castle, a four-story tower house from
1520 standing a few yards out in the bay.

The **Dunguaire Castle medieval banquet** is Kinvarra's
most tourist-worthy sight. The 500-year-old Dunguaire Castle
hosts a touristy but fun medieval banquet (€42, April–Oct almost
nightly at 17:30 and 20:30, CC, reservations tel. 061/360-788,
castle tel. 091/637-108, www.shannonheritage.com). The evening
is as intimate as 55 tourists gathered under one time-stained,
barrel-vaulted ceiling can be. You get a decent four-course meal
with wine (or mead if you ask sweetly), served amid an entertaining evening of Irish tales and folk songs. Remember that in medieval times it was considered polite to flirt with wenches. It's a
small and multitalented cast: One harpist and three singer/actors
who serve the "lords and ladies" between tunes. The highlight is
the 40-minute stage show, featuring songs and poems by local
writers, that comes with dessert.

Sleeping in Kinvarra (area code: 091): Cois Cuain B&B
is a small but stately house with a garden, overlooking the square
and harbor of the most charming village setting you'll find. Mary
Walsh rents three super-homey rooms for non-smokers (Db-€56,
The Harbour, tel. & fax 091/637-119).

Ennis

This bustling market town, the main town of County Clare (population 25,000), provides those relying on public transit with a handy
transportation hub (good connections to Limerick, Dublin, and Galway; see "Transportation Connections," below) and a chance to wander around a workaday Irish town that is not reliant upon the tourist
dollar (though not shunning it either). The **TI** is just off O'Connell
Street Square (June–Sept daily 9:30–17:30, Sat–Sun closed for lunch
13:00–14:00, Oct–May closed Sun, tel. 065/682-8366). The large
building also houses the worthwhile **Riches of Clare** museum, which
has displays of ancient ax heads, submarine development, and local
boys who made good—from 10th-century High King Brian Boru
to 20th-century statesman Eammon DeValera (€3.80, Mon–Sat
9:30–13:00 & 14:00–17:30, Sun 14:00–17:00, tel. 065/682-3382).

The Franciscan monks arrived here in the 13th century and
the town grew up around their friary. The **Ennis Friary,** with
some fine limestone carvings in its ruined walls, is worth a look
(€1.20, sometimes includes tour, April–Sept daily 10:00–18:00,
closed off-season, tel. 065/682-9100). Ask the guide to fully explain
the crucifixion symbolism in the 15th-century *Ecce Homo* carving.

The town's new **Glór** (Irish for "sound") **Irish Music Centre**
connects you with Irish culture without the pub smoke haze. It's
worth considering for traditional music, dance, or storytelling
performances (€12–20, June–Aug usually at 20:00, 5 minutes
behind TI, Friar's Walk, tel. 065/684-3103, www.glor.ie).

You'll also find live, traditional music in the pubs. The best
is **Cruise's** on Abbey Street, with music nightly year-round and
good food (bar is cheaper than restaurant, tel. 065/684-1800).
Other pubs offering traditional music are **Quinn's** on Lower
Market Street (Sat year-round, tel. 065/682-8148), the rough-
and-tumble **Kelly's** on Carmody Street (Sat–Sun in summer,
Sat in winter, at intersection with Dumbiggle Road, tel. 065/628-
8155), and **May Kearney's**, across the bridge from the friary
(Fri–Sat, 100 yards up Newbridge Road, tel. 065/682-4888).
The **Old Ground Hotel** hosts live music year-round at its pub
(Thu–Sun, open to anyone); though tour groups stay at the
hotel, the pub is low-key and feels real, not staged.

For an easy pub-free place for dinner, try the simple
Numero Uno Pizzeria (Tue–Fri 12:00–23:30, Sun–Mon 17:00–

Daniel O'Connell (1775–1847)

Elected in Ennis as the first Catholic member of the British Parliament, O'Connell was the hero of Catholic emancipation in Ireland. Educated in France at a time when the anti-Catholic Penal Laws limited schooling for Irish Catholics in Ireland, he witnessed the carnage of the French Revolution. Upon his return to Ireland, he saw more bloodshed during the futile 1798 Uprising. He chose law as his profession and reluctantly killed a man who challenged him to a duel. Abhorring all this violence, he dedicated himself to peacefully gaining equal rights for Catholics in an Ireland dominated by a wealthy Protestant minority. He formed the Catholic Association with a 1 penny per month membership fee and quickly gained a massive following (especially among the poor) with his persuasive speaking skills. Although Catholics weren't allowed to hold office, he ran for election to Parliament anyway and won the County Clare seat in 1828. His unwillingness to take the anti-Catholic Oath of Supremacy kept him out of Westminster, but the moral force of his victory caused the government to give in and concede Catholic emancipation the following year. Known as "the Liberator," he was making progress toward his next goal of repealing the Act of Union with Britain when the Potato Famine hit in 1845. He died two years later in Genoa on his way to Rome. Today his statue towers above O'Connell Square in Ennis.

23:30, tel. 065/684-1740, on Old Barrack Street off Market Place). Also on Old Barrack Street is the **White Knights** self-service launderette.

Sleeping in Ennis
(€1 = about $1, country code: 353, area code: 065)
Sleep Code: **S** = Single, **D** = Double/Twin, **T** = Triple, **Q** = Quad, **b** = bathroom, **s** = shower only, **CC** = Credit Cards accepted, **no CC** = Credit Cards not accepted. Breakfast is included unless otherwise noted.

To help you easily sort through these listings, I've divided the rooms into categories, based on the price for a standard double room with bath:

Higher Priced—Most rooms €70 or more.
Moderately Priced—Most rooms €50–70.
Lower Priced—Most rooms €50 or less.

HIGHER PRICED

These are both fancy places that you'll share with tour groups. The stately, ivy-covered, 18th-century **Old Ground Hotel** has 82 rooms with a family feel (Sb-€95–121, Db-€118–152, suite-€152–180, rates vary with season, 2-night weekend stays include a dinner, CC, at intersection of Station Road and O'Connell Street, a few blocks from station, tel. 065/682-8127, fax 065/682-8112, e-mail: oghotel.iol.ie). The **Temple Gate Hotel** is more modern and less personal (Db-from €140, rates lower off-season, CC, non-smoking floor, O'Connell Street Square, in courtyard with TI, tel. 065/682-3300, fax 065/682-3322, e-mail: templegh@iol.ie).

LOWER PRICED

These two places are on Station Road, a block or two in toward the town center from the train/bus station. **Grey Gables B&B** is a bit more upscale and has nine rooms (1 small D-€50, 7 large Db-€56, parking, Station Road, tel. 065/682-4487, e-mail: marykeane.ennis@eircom.net, Mary Keane). **Rockfield B&B**, nearer to town on Station Road, has four decent, simple rooms (S-€20, Db-€50, parking, tel. 065/682-4749, Pauline O'Driscoll).

Transportation Connections—Ennis

By train to: Limerick (2/day, 40 min), **Dublin** (2/day, 3 hrs). Train info: tel. 065/684-0444.

By bus to: Galway (14/day, 1 hr), **Dublin** (11/day, 4 hrs), **Rosslare** (3/day, 5 hrs), **Limerick** (15/day, 60 min), **Doolin/Lisdoonvarna** (3/day, 60–90 min), **Tralee** (6/day, 3 hrs). Bus info: tel. 065/682-4177.

ARAN ISLANDS

The Aran Islands consist of three limestone islands: Inishmore, Inishmaan, and Inisheer. The largest, Inishmore (9 miles by 2 miles), is by far the most populated, interesting, and visited. The landscape of all three islands is harsh: steep, rugged cliffs, and windswept, rocky fields divided by stone walls. During the winter, severe gales sweep the islands; because of this, most of the settlements on Inishmore are found on its more peaceful eastern side.

There's a stark beauty about these islands and the simple lives its inhabitants eke out of six inches of topsoil and a mean sea. Precious little of the land is productive. In the past, people made a precarious living from fishing and farming. The layers of limestone rock meant that there was little natural soil. Farming soil has been built up by the islanders—the result of centuries of layering seaweed with sand. The fields are small, divided by several thousand miles of drystone wall. Most of these are built in the Aran "gap" style, in which angled upright stones are filled with smaller stones. This allows a farmer who wants to move stock to dismantle and rebuild the walls easily. Nowadays tourism boosts the local economy.

The islands are a Gaeltacht area. While the islanders speak Irish among themselves, they happily speak English for their visitors. Many of them have direct, personal connections with America and will ask you if you know their cousin Paddy in Boston.

Today the 800 people of Inishmore (literally, "the big island") greet as many as 2,000 visitors a day. The vast majority of these are day-trippers. They'll hop on a minibus at the dock for a 2.5-hour tour to Dún Aenghus, then spend an hour or two browsing through the few shops or sitting at a picnic table outside a pub with a pint of Guinness.

The other islands, Inishmaan and Inisheer, are smaller, much less populated, and less touristy. While extremely quiet, they do have B&Bs, daily flights, and ferry service. For most, the big island is quiet enough. For more information, look up an old issue of *National Geographic* on the Aran Islands (April 1981).

Kilronan, on Inishmore

By far the Aran Islands' largest town, Kilronan is still just a village. Groups of backpackers wash ashore with the landing of each ferry. Minibuses, bike shops, and a few men in pony carts sop up the tourists. There are about 10 shops and about as many pubs, restaurants, and B&Bs. Most of Kilronan huddles around the pier. A few blocks inland you'll find the Heritage Centre (Internet access upstairs, €2.50/15 min, €4/30 min, 10:00–17:00), the best folk-music pubs, a post office, and a bank (open only on Wed 10:00–12:30 & 13:30–15:00, plus Thu June–Aug). The huge SPAR supermarket, two blocks inland from the harbor, seems too big for the tiny community. Several huts near the pier rent bikes (€10/day). Bring cash: Some B&Bs and other businesses don't accept credit cards. There are no ATMs on the island, and the bank is rarely open.

Tourist Information: The TI is helpful, but don't rely on it for accommodations. The B&B owners who work with the TI are out-of-town and desperate. Ask the TI for a good map of the island showing rough trails, as there are some remote sites worth seeking out (daily 10:00–17:00, June–Aug until 19:00, shorter winter hours, faces the harbor, public WCs next door, tel. 099/61263).

Getting around Inishmore

Just about anything rolling functions as a taxi. A trip from Kilronan to Dún Aenghus to the Seven Churches and back to Kilronan costs €10 in a shared minibus. Flag them down and don't hesitate to bargain. Pony carts cost about €35 for two people (€50 for 4) for a trip to the west end of the island. Biking is great though hilly, with occasional headwinds (30 min to start of trailhead up to Dún Aenghus). Bikers take the high road over and the low road back— fewer hills, scenic shoreline, and, at low tide, 50 seals sunbathing. Keep a sharp lookout along the roads for handy modern stone signposts (with distances in kilometers) that point the way to important sites. They're in Irish, but you'll be clued in by the small metal depictions of the site embedded within them.

Sights—Inishmore

▲**Aran's Heritage Centre**—This little museum, while nothing impressive, offers a worthwhile introduction that covers the island's traditional lifestyle, its geology, and its archaeological wonders (€3.50 includes *Man of Aran* movie, daily 10:00–17:00, June–Aug until 19:00, tel. 099/61355).

Man of Aran: This 1934 movie, giving a good look at traditional island life with an all-local cast, is shown at the Heritage Centre (1 hr, 6 shows/day in summer). The movie features currachs (canoe-like boats) in a storm, shark-fishing with hand-held harpoons, cultivation of the fields from bare rock, and life in the early 1900s when you couldn't rent bikes.

▲**Island Minibus Tours**—There can't be more than 100 vehicles on the island, and the majority of them seem to be minibuses. A line of buses awaits the arrival of each ferry, offering 2.5-hour, €10 island tours. Chat with several to find a driver who likes to talk. I learned that 800 islanders live in 14 villages, with three elementary schools and three churches. Most own a small detached field where they keep a couple of cows (sheep are too much trouble). When pressed for more information, my guide explained that there are 400 different flowers and 19 different types of bees on the island. The tour, a convenient time-saver, zips you to the end of the island for a quick stroll in the desolate fields, gives you 10 minutes to wander through the historic but visually unimpressive "seven churches," and then drops you for 90 minutes at Dún Aenghus (20 min to hike up, 30 min at the fort, 20 min back, 20 min in café or shops at drop-off point) before running you back to Kilronan. Ask your driver to take you back along the smaller coastal road (scenic beaches and sunbathing seals at low tide).

▲▲▲**Dún Aenghus**—This is the island's blockbuster sight. The stone fortress hangs spectacularly and precariously on the edge of a cliff 90 meters (300 feet) above the Atlantic. The crashing waves seem to say, "You've come to the end of the world." Little is known about this 2,000-year-old Celtic fort. Its concentric walls are 13 feet thick and 10 feet high. As an added defense, the fort is

Inishmore Island

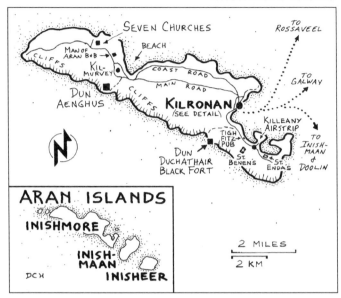

ringed with a commotion of spiky stones, sticking up like lances, called a *chevaux-de-frise* (literally, "Frisian horses," named for the Frisian soldiers who used pikes like these to stop charging cavalry). Slowly, as the cliff erodes, hunks of the fort fall into the sea. Dún Aenghus doesn't get crowded until after 11:00. I enjoyed a half-hour completely alone at 10:00 in the tourist season. Be there early (you can slip through the fence anytime) or late, if you can (€1.30, April–Oct daily 10:00–18:00, Nov–March 10:00–16:00, guides at fort June–Aug answer questions and sometimes give free tours, 5.5 miles from Kilronan, tel. 099/61008). A small museum displays findings from recent digs and tells the story of the fort. Advice from rangers: Wear walking shoes and watch your kids closely; there's no fence.

Seven Churches (Na Seacht Teampaill)—Close to the western tip of the island, this gathering of ruined chapels, monastic houses, and fragments of a high cross dates from the 8th–11th centuries. The island is dotted with reminders that Christianity was brought to the islands in the fifth century by St. Enda, who established a monastery here. Many great monks studied under Enda. Among these "Irish apostles," who started Ireland's "Age of Saints and Scholars" (A.D. 500–900), was Columba, the founder of a monastery on the island of Iona in Scotland.

Kilmurvey—The island's second village sits below Dún Aenghus. With a gaggle of homes, a B&B, a great sheltered beach, and a pub, this is the place for peaceful solitude (except for the folk music in the pub).

Ancient Sites near Killeany—The quiet eastern end of Inishmore offers three ancient sights in evocative settings for overnight visitors with more time, or for those seeking rocky hikes devoid of crowds. First, get a good hiking map from the Kilronan TI. Then consider a soup-and-sandwich lunch at Tigh Fitz pub to fuel up either before or after a half-day spent exploring these sights on foot. Ask the folks at the pub for directions (almost always a memorable experience in Ireland).

Closest to the road, amid the dunes 200 meters past Tigh Fitz pub and just south of the airport, is **St. Enda's Church** (Teaghlach Einne). Protected from wave erosion by a stubborn breakwater, it sits half-submerged in a sandy graveyard surrounded by a sea of sawgrass peppered with tombstones. St. Enda is said to be buried here along with 125 other saints who flocked to Inishmore in the fifth century to learn from him.

St. Benen's Church (Teampall Bheanáin) perches high on a desolate ridge opposite Tigh Fitz pub. Walk up the stone-walled lane, passing a holy well and the stubby remains of a round-tower base. Then take another visual fix on the church's silhouette on the horizon and zigzag up the stone terraces to the top. The 20-minute hike from Tigh Fitz pub pays off with a great view. Dedicated to St. Benen, a young disciple of St. Patrick himself, this tiny sixth-century oratory is aligned north-south (instead of the usual east-west) to protect the doorway from prevailing winds.

Hidden on a remote, ragged headland an hour's walk from Kilronan to the south side of the island, you'll find the **Black Fort** (Dún Duchathair). Next to Dún Aenghus, this is Inishmore's most dramatic fortification. Built on a promontory with cliffs on three sides, its defenders would have held out behind drystone ramparts, facing the island's interior attackers. Watch your step on the uneven ground, be ready to course-correct as you go, and chances are you'll have this windswept ruin all to yourself.

Ragus—Irish for "desire," this is a riveting hour of quality Irish song-and-dance performed in the small Halla Ronain community center in Kilronan. Ten energetic young Irish adults give you an opportunity to see Irish step-dancing up close, accompanied by a small group of musicians earnestly playing traditional Irish instruments. The center is a five-minute walk from the boat dock and offers day-trippers a mid-afternoon performance you can plan as your last stop before catching the late-afternoon boat back to the mainland. Buy tickets at the Aran Fisherman Restaurant in

Kilronan or at the door of the Halla Ronain community center
(€12.50, daily at 14:45, 17:00, and 21:00, mid-June–Aug, tel.
099/61104 or 091/572-525).

Pub Music—Several pubs in Kilronan offer live music nearly
nightly in summer. Off-season you're likely to find music on
Wednesday, Friday, and Saturday evenings. Joe Watty's Pub,
just past the post office, has good Irish folk music. Tigh Fitz,
on the airport road, has folk music and dancing on Fridays,
Saturdays, and Sundays.

Other pubs offer Irish tunes but with musical detours beyond
the tin whistle. The Halla Ronain community center becomes
a dance hall on some Saturday and Sunday nights, when from
midnight to 2:00 locals have a *ceilidh* (pron. KAY-lee), the Irish
equivalent of a hoedown.

Sleeping in Kilronan, Inishmore
(€1 = about $1, country code: 353,
area code: 099, mail: Kilronan, Aran Islands)

Remember, this is a poor island. Most rooms are plain with
sparse plumbing. Few places take credit cards.

HIGHER PRICED

The Pier House stands solidly a hundred yards beyond the pier,
offering 12 decent rooms, a good restaurant downstairs, a dramatic
setting, and sea views from most of its rooms (Sb-€45–55, Db-€70–
80, CC, tel. 099/61417, fax 099/61122, e-mail: pierh@iol.ie).

Clai Ban, about the only really cheery place in town, is
worth the 10-minute walk from the pier (Sb-€50, Db-€50–60,
Tb-€75–90, walk past the bank out of town and down a lane on
the left, tel. 099/61111, fax 099/61423, Marion Hernon).

While Kilronan is getting pretty touristy, you can get out
into the Aran countryside and find peace. The **Man of Aran B&B**
is as classy as a thatched cottage can be. Rooms are quiet and rustic,
with fireplaces. The restaurant uses all-organic, homegrown vegetables and herbs (€25–30 meals). The setting is pristine—this is
where the movie was filmed (S-€41, D-€64, Db-€70, reserve
well in advance, bear right just 100 yards after passing Kilmurvey
beach before Dún Aenghus turnoff, 4 miles from Kilronan, tel.
099/61301, fax 099/61324, e-mail: manofaran@eircom.net).

MODERATELY PRICED

Costello's B&B has four plain rooms in a plain home in a fine
garden setting (D-€50, Db-€60, with your back to the SPAR
supermarket's entrance, take little alley at 1:00—ahead slightly
to right—to last house, tel. 099/61241, Sally Costello).

Kilronan

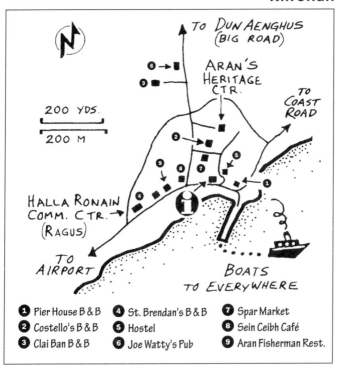

1. Pier House B & B
2. Costello's B & B
3. Clai Ban B & B
4. St. Brendan's B & B
5. Hostel
6. Joe Watty's Pub
7. Spar Market
8. Sein Ceibh Café
9. Aran Fisherman Rest.

LOWER PRICED

St. Brendan's B&B, hiding a cozy living room behind ivy-covered walls and a windblown garden, rents eight rooms (Sb-€25.50, D-€46, Db-€50, about €2.50 less per person off-season, save €2.50 if you have the continental breakfast, from TI walk uphill and go left when road forks, tel. 099/61149).

Kilronan Hostel, run by friendly Jeanette and overlooking the harbor near the TI, is cheap but noisy above Joe Mac's Pub (€13 beds, 4- to 6-bed rooms, includes breakfast, self-service kitchen, tel. 099/61255, e-mail: kilronanhostel@ireland.com).

Eating in Kilronan

Kilronan's cafés dish up soup, soda bread, sandwiches, and tea. **Lios Aengus,** next door to the SPAR market, does simple lunches (daily 9:30–17:00, tel. 099/61030).

Sein Ceibh, which seems to slam out more meals than the

rest of the town combined, is popular for its fish and chips and great clam chowder (eat in or take out).

Aran Fisherman serves a good dinner (daily 10:00–16:00 & 17:00–22:00, arrive before 19:00 to avoid a wait, CC, tel. 099/61104).

The **Pier House** operates a quality restaurant below its guest house (€16–20 dinners, Tue–Sat 18:00–22:00, closed Sun–Mon, CC, tel. 099/61417).

The **SPAR supermarket** has all the groceries you'll need (Mon–Sat 9:00–20:00, Sun 10:00–17:00).

Transportation Connections—Aran Islands

By ferry from Rossaveel: Three companies sail to the Islands, and the first two below sell tickets side by side from small counters in the Galway TI and run shuttle buses from Galway to the docks (see below for details).

Island Ferries sails to Inishmore from Rossaveel, a port 20 miles west of Galway (3/day April–Oct, 2/day Nov–March, 40-min crossing; if you're coming from Galway, allow 2 hours one-way including 45-minute bus ride, €19 round-trip boat crossing plus €6 round-trip for Galway–Rossaveel shuttle bus, CC, ask about getting discount if you prebook in the high season). Shuttle buses depart Galway (from Merchants Road in front of Kinlay House) 60 minutes before the sailing and return to Galway immediately after each boat arrives. Ferry schedule for April–Oct: from Rossaveel at 10:30, 13:30, and 18:30; from Inishmore at 9:00, 12:00, and 17:00 (plus 19:30 July–Aug, WCs on board). Island Ferries has two offices, one at the Galway TI and the other in a little alley across from Kinlay House on Merchants Road (tel. 091/568-903, www.aranislandferries.com).

InisMor Ferries takes pride in being owned by islanders and operates the *Queen of Aran II*, which offers service, schedule, and prices similar to Island Ferries' (shuttle bus departs across street from Galway TI, tel. 091/566-535, www.queenofaran2.com).

Drivers should go straight to the ferry landing in Rossaveel, passing several ticket agencies and pay parking lots. At the boat dock, you'll find a convenient €4-per-day lot and two small competing offices selling tickets for Island Ferries and InisMor Ferries. Check both and see what's going when and for how much.

O'Brien Shipping operates smaller boats to all three Aran Islands on slower rides from Galway, not Rossaveel (€15, Tue, Thu, Fri, Sat, New Docks Road, tel. 091/567-676). Boats carry cargo as well, so they go in anything less than a gale—only a couple departures a year are canceled, but call to confirm schedule. For drivers, there's a €3 parking lot at the dock.

By ferry from Doolin: This ferry is handy if you're in

Doolin, but it's notorious for being canceled because of wind or tides (for specifics, see "Doolin," above).

By plane: Aer Arann, a friendly and flexible little airline, flies three planes a day (every hour during peak season) and stops at all three islands (€44 round-trip, groups of 4 or more €37 each, CC, 10-min flight). These flights get booked up—reserve a day or two in advance with a credit card. Their nine-seat planes take off from the Connemara Regional Airport, 20 miles (32 km) west of Galway (not the Galway airport). A minibus shuttle—€6 round-trip—runs from Kinlay House on Merchants Road an hour before each flight. The Kilronan airport is small (baggage is transported from the plane to the "gate" in a shopping cart). A minibus shuttle to and from Kilronan costs €3 round-trip (2 miles from the airport). For reservations and seat availability, contact the airline (tel. 091/ 593-034, fax 091/593-238, www.aerarann.ie). Ask for a 10 percent discount—they distribute lots of coupons.

CONNEMARA

If you have a car, consider spending a day exploring the wild western Irish fringe known as Connemara. Gaze up at the peak of Croagh Patrick, the mountain from which St. Patrick supposedly banished the snakes from Ireland. Pass through the desolate Doo Lough valley on a road stained with tragic famine history. Bounce on a springy peat bog, and drop in at a Westport pub owned by a member of the Chieftains traditional-Irish-music group. This beautiful area also claims a couple of towns—Cong and Leenane— where classic Irish movies were filmed, as well as photogenic Kylemore Abbey.

Connemara makes an easy day trip by car from Galway. Without a car, you can take a tour from Galway (see above). Public transportation in this region is patchy and some areas are not served at all. Trains connect Galway and Westport to Dublin but not to each other.

This is a full day of driving (about 150 miles using Galway as your base). With an early start, your day will be less rushed. Those wanting to slow down and linger can sleep in Westport. These country roads, punctuated by blind curves and surprise bumps, are shared by trucks, tractors, and sheep. Drive sanely and bring rain gear and your sense of humor. This is the real Ireland.

Take along a good map (Michelin's are widely sold in Ireland) and study a loop connecting these points before you start: Galway, Cong, Westport, Louisburgh, Leenane, Kylemore Abbey, and back to Galway (for specifics, see "Route Summary" on page 187).

Driving from Galway to Cong: From Galway's Eyre Square, head north out of town on Prospect Hill Road. Follow the signs at each roundabout in the direction of Castlebar onto N84. You'll soon be out of Galway's suburbs and crossing miles of flat bog-land laced with simple rock walls. You may notice the flags on the phone poles changing colors: from burgundy and white to green and red. These are the colors of the local hurling and football teams. You've just crossed the border from County Galway into County Mayo. At Cross, take R346 into Cong. You'll pass the grand, gray gateway of Ashford Castle as you approach the town.

Sights—Connemara

Cong—Plan to spend an hour in Cong. Cross the small bridge and park in front of the abbey. Drop into the **TI** across from the abbey entrance for a map (March–Nov daily 10:00–18:00, July–Aug until 20:00, closed Dec–Feb, tel. 092/46542). Public WCs are 50 yards down the street across from the *Quiet Man* cottage. That's right, pilgrim, this town is where John Wayne and Maureen O'Hara made the famous John Ford film *The Quiet Man* 50 years ago. The cottage's modest historical exhibits (upstairs) and film props (downstairs) are really only worth it for diehard fans of the Duke (€3.80, daily 10:00–17:00, tel. 092/46089).

We're here for the ruins of **Cong Abbey** (free and always open). The abbey was built in the late 1100s, when Romanesque was going out of style and Gothic was coming in; you'll see the mixture of rounded Romanesque and pointy Gothic arch styles in the doorway. The famous Cross of Cong (an Irish art treasure now on display in Dublin's National Museum), which held a holy relic of what was supposedly a splinter of the True Cross, was held aloft at the front of processions of Augustinian monks during High Masses in this church. Rory O'Connor, the last Irish high king, died in this abbey in 1198. After O'Connor realized he could never outfight the superior Norman armies, he retreated to Cong and spent his last years here in monastic isolation.

Take a walk through the cloister and down the path behind the abbey. The forested grounds are lush, and the stream water is incredibly clear. Cong's salmon hatchery contributes to western Ireland's reputation for great fishing. The monks fished for more than sinners. They built the modest **Monk's Fishing Hut** (just over the footbridge) right on the bank so that the river flowed underneath. They lowered a net though the floor and attached a bell to the rope; whenever a fish was netted, the bell would ring.

Next stop is **Ashford Castle.** To reach the castle from the abbey, face the abbey entrance, then go left, walking 10 minutes down the lane onto the grounds of the castle, which is hidden behind the trees. Garden-lovers happily pay the stiff €5 entry fee to stroll the lakeside paradise once owned by the Guinness beer family. The

Connemara

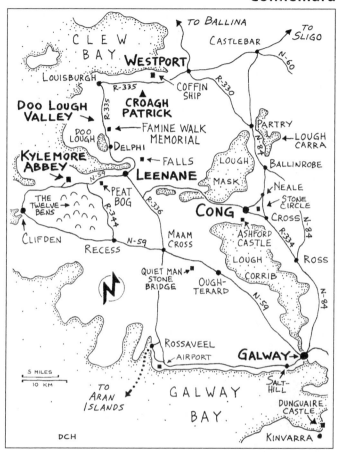

TO BALLINA
TO SLIGO
CASTLEBAR
N-60
CLEW BAY
WESTPORT
LOUISBURGH   R-335   COFFIN SHIP
R-335   CROAGH PATRICK   R-330
DOO LOUGH VALLEY   DOO LOUGH   FAMINE WALK MEMORIAL   PARTRY
DELPHI   LOUGH CARRA
N-84
KYLEMORE ABBEY   ←FALLS   LOUGH   BALLINROBE
N-59   LEENANE   MASK   NEALE
THE TWELVE BENS   PEAT BOG   STONE CIRCLE
R-344   R-336   CONG   CROSS
N-84
CLIFDEN   N-59   MAAM CROSS   ASHFORD CASTLE   R-334
RECESS   LOUGH   ROSS
QUIET MAN STONE BRIDGE   OUGH-TERARD   CORRIB   N-84
N   N-59
ROSSAVEEL
AIRPORT   GALWAY→
5 MILES
10 KM   TO ARAN ISLANDS   G A L W A Y   SALT-HILL
B A Y   DUNGUAIRE CASTLE
DCH   KINVARRA

renovated Victorian castle rents some of the finest rooms in all of Ireland. President Reagan stayed here in 1984 and actor Pierce Brosnan chose these grounds for his wedding reception in 2001.

From Cong to Neale: Cong (from *conga*, the Irish word for "isthmus") lies between two large lakes. Departing Cong over the same bridge by which you entered, look through the thick vegetation to see a dry canal. Built between 1848 and 1854, this canal was a famine work project that stoked only appetites. The canal, complete with locks, would have linked Lough Mask to the north with Lough Corrib to the south. But the limestone bedrock was too porous and the canal wouldn't hold water.

Take R345 out of Cong. Heading north, you'll pass through the tiny hamlet of...

Neale—About 120 years ago, a retired army captain named Boycott was hired to manage the nearby estate of Lord Erne. But the strict captain harshly treated the tenants who worked his lands. So they unified to ostracize him by deserting their jobs and isolating his estate. Over time the agitation worked, and eventually "boycotting" became a popular tactic in labor conflicts.

From Neale to Westport: At Neale, go north on R334, then take N84 from Ballinrobe to Partry. At Partry, turn left off N84 onto R330 in the direction of Westport (the easy-to-miss turnoff is immediately after you pass the thatch-roofed Village Inn). Just over 200 years ago, in the countryside a few miles to your right, a French invasion force supported by locals dealt the British an embarrassing loss in the **Battle of Castlebar.** The surprised British forces were routed and their rapid retreat is slyly remembered in Irish rebel lore as the "Castlebar races." Unfortunately for the rebels, this proved to be the last glimmer of hope for Irish victory in the Uprising of 1798. The British reorganized, defeating the small force of 1,300 Frenchmen and the ill-equipped Irish rebels within weeks. The captured French soldiers were treated as prisoners of war while the Irish rebels were executed.

Westport—On arrival in Westport, park along the Mall under the trees that line the canal-like river. This is a planned town, built in Georgian style in the late 1700s to support the adjacent estate of Westport House (skip it for better manors at Powerscourt and Muckross). The town once thrived on the linen industry created by local Irish handlooms. But after the Act of Union with Britain in 1801, the town was unable to compete with the industrialized British linenmakers and fell into decline. The town is still pretty and a good place for a relaxed lunch and some exploration on foot. The **TI** is on James Street (Mon–Sat 9:00–17:00, July–Aug daily until 19:00, tel. 098/25711). Laundry can be dropped off early at **Gills** and picked up late the same day (€7, Mon–Sat 8:30–18:30, closed Sun, tel. 098/25819).

Eating in Westport: Most of your best bets are clustered on Bridge Street. For lunch try the Cove (€7–10 lunches, €12–16 dinners, Mon–Sat 10:00–15:00 & 18:00–21:30, Sun 10:00–16:00, Bridge Street, tel. 098/27096), or O'Cee's Coffeeshop (cafeteria-style lunches €8, Mon–Sat 8:30–19:00, Sun 10:00–16:00, Shop Street, tel. 098/27000). A couple of good dinner choices are J. J. O'Malleys (€12–22 meals, daily 17:00–22:00, Bridge Street, tel. 098/27307) or the Urchin (€12–22 dinners, daily 18:00–22:00, Bridge Street, tel. 098/27532). Fans of the Chieftains' traditional Irish music will seek out Matt Molloy's pub (Bridge Street) since

Irelands' Misunderstood Nomads

When you see a small cluster of trailers at the side of an Irish road, you're looking at a dying way of life. These are Travellers, a nomadic throwback to the days when wandering craftsmen, musicians, and evicted unfortunates crowded rural Ireland. Often mislabeled as Gypsies, they have no ethnic ties to those Eastern European nomads but instead have Irish heritage going back centuries.

There were once many more Travellers, living in tents and using horse-drawn carts as they wandered the countryside in search of work. Before the famine, when Irish hospitality was a given, Travellers filled a niche in Irish society. They would do odd jobs repairing furniture, sweeping chimneys, and selling horses. Skilled tinsmiths, they mended pots, pans, and *poitín*—Irish moonshine—stills. (Travellers used to be called "tinkers," but they now consider this label derogatory.) But post-famine rural depopulation and the gradual urbanization of the countryside forced this nomadic group to adapt to an almost sedentary existence on the fringes of towns.

Today the 30,000 remaining Travellers are outsiders, usually treated with suspicion by the traditionally conservative Irish. Locals often complain that petty thefts go up when Travellers set up camp in a nearby "halting site" and that they leave their refuse behind when they depart. Travellers tend to keep to themselves, marry young, have large families, and speak their own Gaelic-based language (called Shelta, Gammon, or Cant). Attempts to settle Travellers in government housing and integrate their children into schools have met with mixed success.

he's not just the owner of the pub—he's also flutist for the Chieftans, the group credited with the resurgence of interest in Irish music worldwide over the past 25 years.

Sleeping in Westport: For those wanting extra time to explore, Westport is the best place along this route to spend a night. All of the following listings are centrally located. Prices vary quite a bit depending on the season. **Westport Inn** has a fresh feel with 33 comfortable rooms and convenient, free underground parking (Sb-€40–80, Db-€65–150, CC, Mill Street, tel. 098/29200, fax 098/29250, www.westportinn.ie). The classy **Clew Bay Hotel** is a couple doors down from the TI with large modern

rooms (Sb-€60–90, Db-€80–140, CC, James Street, tel. 098/
28088, fax 098/25783, www.clewbayhotel.com). Right on the leafy
Mall is the **Olde Railway Hotel** with a "retire to the study to
drink port and smoke your pipe" kind of feel (Db-€140 July–
Sept, less off-season, CC, The Mall, tel. 098/25166, fax 098/25090,
www.anu.ie/railwayhotel). The homey **Teallach an Ghabha
B&B** has comfy, modest rooms (S-€30, Db-€65, Altamount
Street, tel. 098/25704).

From Westport to Murrisk: Leave Westport heading
west on R335. After about eight km (5 miles), as you're driving
along scenic Clew Bay, you'll reach a wide spot in the road
called Murrisk. Stop here. In the field on your right (opposite
Campbell's Pub) is the . . .

Coffin Ship—This bronze ship sculpture is one of the most powerful famine memorials you'll see in Ireland. It's a "coffin ship,"
like those of the 1840s that carried the sick and starving famine
survivors across the ocean in hope of a new life. Unfortunately,
many of the ships contracted to take the desperate immigrants
were barely seaworthy, no longer fit for dependable commerce.
The poor were weak from starvation and vulnerable to "famine
fever," which they then spread to others in the putrid, cramped
holds of these awful ships. Many who lived through the six- to
eight-week journey died shortly after reaching their new country.
Pause a moment to look at the silent skeletons swirling around the
ship's masts. Now contemplate the fact that famine exists today.
And before judging the lack of effective relief intervention by the
British government of that time, consider the rich world's ability
to ignore similar suffering today.

Across the road from the coffin ship is . . .

Croagh Patrick—This small mountain rises 2,500 feet above the
bay. In the fifth century, St. Patrick is said to have fasted on its summit for 40 days. It's from here that he supposedly rang his bell,
driving all the snakes out of Ireland. The snakes never existed, of
course, but they represent the pagan beliefs that Patrick's newly
arrived Christianity replaced. Every year on the last Sunday of July,
"Reek Sunday" (a "reek" is a mountain peak), more than 50,000 pilgrims hike two hours up the rocky trail to the summit in honor of
St. Patrick. The most penitent hike barefoot. On that Sunday, Mass
is celebrated throughout the day in a modest chapel on the top.

A few years ago, valuable gold deposits were discovered within
Croagh Patrick. Luckily, public sentiment has kept the sacred
mountain free of any commercial mining activity.

From Croagh Patrick to Doo Lough Valley: Continue
on R335. Passing through Louisburgh, you'll turn south to enter
some of the most rugged and desolate country in Ireland.

Doo Lough Valley—Signs of human habitation vanish from the bogland and ghosts begin to appear beside the road. About eight miles beyond Louisburgh, stop at the simple gray stone cross on the left. The lake ahead is Doo Lough (Irish for Black Lake) and this is the site of one of the saddest famine tales.

In the early 1800s, County Mayo's rural folk were almost exclusively dependent on the potato for food. They were hardest hit when the Great Famine came in 1845. During "Black '47," the worst winter of the century, about 600 starving Irish walked 12 miles in the snow from Louisburgh to Delphi Lodge. They hoped to get food from their landlord, but were turned away. On the walk back, almost 400 of them died along the side of this road. Today, the road still seems to echo with the despair of those hungry souls and inspires an annual walk that commemorates the tragedy. Archbishop Desmond Tutu made the walk in 1991, shortly before South Africa ended its apartheid system.

From Doo Lough Valley to Leenane: Continue south on R335. You'll get a fine view of **Aasleagh Falls** on the left. In late May, the banks below the falls explode with lush, wild rhododendron blossoms. Cross the bridge after the falls and turn right onto N59 toward Leenane. You'll drive along Killary Harbor, Ireland's version of a fjord. This long, narrow body of water was carved by a receding glacier.

Leenane—This town is a good place for a break. The 1990 movie *The Field*, starring Limerick-born Richard Harris, was filmed here. Take a glance at the newspaper clippings of the making of the movie on the wall of Hamilton's Pub. While you're there, find the old photo of the British battleships that filled Killary Harbor when the king of England visited 100 years ago. Drop into the **Leenane Cultural Centre** (on the left as you enter town) to see an interesting wool-spinning and weaving demonstration (€2.50, April–Sept).

From Leenane to a Peat Bog: As you continue west on N59, notice the rows of blue floats in Killary Harbor. They're there to mark mussel farms growing in the cold seawater. Climbing out of the fjord valley about eight km (5 miles) past Leenane, you'll pass some good areas to get a close look at a turf cut in a peat bog.

A Slog on the Bog—Walk a few yards onto the spongy green carpet. Watch your step on wet days to avoid squishing into a couple inches of water. Find a dry spot and jump up and down to get a feel for it. Have your companion jump; you'll feel the vibrations a few feet away.

These bogs once covered almost 20 percent of Ireland. As the climate got warmer at the end of the last ice age, plants began growing along the sides of the many shallow lakes and ponds.

When the plants died in these waterlogged areas, there wasn't enough oxygen for them to fully decompose. The moss built up, layer after dead layer, over the centuries. It's this wet, oxygen-starved ecosystem that preserved ancient artifacts so well, many of which can be seen in Dublin's National Museum. Even forgotten containers of butter, churned centuries ago and buried to keep cool, have been discovered. Since these acidic bogs contain few nutrients, unique species of carnivorous plants have adapted themselves to life here by trapping and digesting insects. Take a moment to find a mossy area and look closely at the variety of tiny plants. In summer you'll see white tufts of bog cotton growing in marshy areas.

People have been cutting, drying, and burning peat as a fuel source for over a thousand years. The cutting usually begins in April or May when drier weather approaches. You'll probably see stacks of "turf" piled up to dry along recent cuts. Pick a brick up and fondle it. Dried peat is surprisingly light and stiff. In central Ireland, there are even industrial peat cuts that were begun after World War II to fuel power stations. But in the past decade, recognition of the rare habitat that the bogs provide has encouraged conservation efforts and the smell of burning peat is becoming increasingly rare.

From Peat Bog to Kylemore Abbey: Continue west on N59 and pass the junction with R344 (direction: Recess) on the left; you'll come back to this junction after the next stop. We've got one last picture-postcard view to locate. The road soon crosses a shallow lake, with a wonderful view of Kylemore Abbey to the right. You'll get a better photo from the parking lot a couple hundred yards ahead, so don't stop here. Pull into the parking lot and take a few minutes to enjoy the view.

Kylemore Abbey—This neo-Gothic country house was built by a wealthy English businessman in the 1860s, after he and his wife had honeymooned in the area. After her death in 1874, he sold it. During World War I, refugee Benedictine nuns from Belgium took it over, and today it's an exclusive girls' boarding school. The best thing about the abbey is the view of it from the lakeshore. Tours inside are a letdown, so just enjoy its setting. WCs are in the gift shop next to the parking lot (€8.50 combo-ticket for abbey and gardens, €4.50 audioguide, daily 9:00–17:30, tel. 095/41146, www.kylemoreabbey.com).

Returning to Galway: Drive back the way you came. Turn right on the R344 (direction: Recess). Off to the right is Connemara's Twelve Bens mountains, but it's late and we're headed for home. At the junction with the N59, turn left and follow the signs back to Galway.

Route Summary of Connemara Loop Trip

Take N84 north out of Galway. At Cross, take R346 into Cong and R345 back out again. At Neale, go north on R334 and pick up N84 again from Ballinrobe to Partry. Take R330 from Partry to Westport. After lunch in Westport, go west on R335 through Louisburgh and south through Doo Lough Valley all the way to Leenane. Pick up N59 in Leenane and take it as far as Kylemore Abbey. Double back from Kylemore and take R344 south to the junction with N59. The N59 will take you back via Maam Cross and Oughterard to Galway.

NORTHERN IRELAND

- Northern Ireland is 5,222 square miles (13,576 square kilometers), a little bigger than Connecticut.
- Population is 1.7 million (about 325 per square mile, 55 percent Protestant, 45 percent Catholic).
- £1 (pound sterling) = about $1.50.

All of Ireland was once part of Great Britain—a colony made more distant from London than its Celtic cousins Scotland and Wales, not so much by the Irish Sea as by its Catholicism. Protestant settlers from England and Scotland were "planted" in Catholic Ireland to help assimilate the island into the British economy. These settlers established their own cultural toehold on the island, but the Catholic Irish held strong to their Gaelic culture.

Over the centuries, British rule has not been easy. By the beginning of the 20th century, the sparse Protestant population could no longer control the entire island. When Ireland won its independence in 1921 (after a bloody guerilla war against British rule), 26 of the island's 32 counties became the Irish Free State, ruled from Dublin with dominion status in the British Commonwealth—like Canada. In 1949, they left the Commonwealth and became the Republic of Ireland, removing all political ties with Britain.

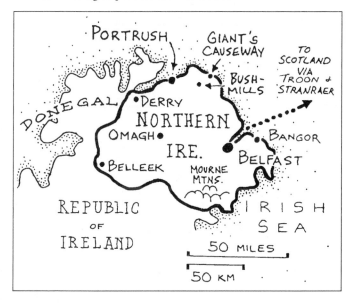

Meanwhile, the six remaining northeastern counties (the only ones with a Protestant majority), who had voted not to join the Irish Free State in 1922, remained part of the United Kingdom. In this new political entity called Northern Ireland, the long-established Orange Order and the military muscle of the newly mobilized Ulster Volunteer Force (UVF) worked to defend the union with Britain—so their political philosophy was "Unionist." This was countered on the Catholic side by the Irish Republican Army (IRA). They wanted all 32 of Ireland's counties to be united in one Irish nation—so their political goals were "Nationalist."

In World War II, the Republic stayed neutral while the North enthusiastically supported the Allied cause, and the North won a spot close to London's heart. After the war, the split between North and South seemed permanent, and Britain invested heavily in Northern Ireland to bring it solidly into the United Kingdom fold.

As 94 percent of the Republic of Ireland (the South) was Catholic and only 6 percent Protestant, there was no question as to who was dominant. But in the North, the Catholics, although a minority, were a sizable 35 percent and demanded attention. Discrimination was considered necessary to maintain the Protestant status quo in the North, and this led to the Troubles that have filled headlines since the late 1960s.

It is not a fight over Protestant and Catholic religious differences. It's about whether Northern Ireland will stay part of the United Kingdom or become part of the Republic of Ireland. The indigenous Irish of Northern Ireland, who generally want to unite with Ireland, happen to be Catholic. The descendants of Scottish and English settlers, who generally want to remain part of Britain, happen to be Protestant.

Partly inspired by the Civil Rights movement in America in the 1960s, the Catholic minority in Northern Ireland claimed they were discriminated against in gaining better jobs and housing. Extremists polarized issues, and demonstrations became violent. Unionists were afraid that if the island became one nation, the relatively poor Republic of Ireland would drag down the North, and the high percentage of Catholics could mean repression of the Protestants. As Protestants and Catholics clashed in 1969, the British Army entered the fray. They've been there ever since. In 1972, a watershed year, combatants moved from petrol bombs to guns, and a new, more violent IRA emerged. In this most recent 30-year chapter in the struggle for an independent and united Ireland, more than 3,000 people have been killed.

A 1985 agreement granted Dublin a consulting role in the Northern Ireland government. Unionists bucked this, and violence escalated. That same year, Belfast City Hall draped a huge, defiant banner under its dome, proclaiming, "Belfast Says No."

In 1994, the banner came down. In the 1990s, with Ireland's membership in the European Union, the growth of its economy, and the weakening of the Catholic Church's influence, the consequences of a united Ireland were less threatening to the Unionists. Also in 1994, the IRA declared a cease-fire and the Protestant UVF followed suit. Talks are still underway, interrupted by sporadic hostilities.

The Nationalists want British troops out of Ireland, while the Unionists want the IRA to turn in its arms. Optimists hail the signing of the Good Friday Accord in 1998, which led to the emotional release of prisoners on both sides in 2000. Major hurdles to a solid peace persist, but the downtown checkpoints are history, and "bomb damage clearance sales" are over. Statistically, you're safer in Northern Ireland than in most major American cities. And today, more tourists than ever are venturing to Belfast and Derry.

Terminology

Ulster (one of Ireland's 4 ancient provinces) consists of nine counties in the northern part of the island of Ireland. Six of these make up Northern Ireland (pronounced "Norn Iron" by locals), while three counties remain part of the Republic.

Unionists—and the more hard-line **Loyalists**—want the North to remain in the United Kingdom. The **Ulster Unionist Party (UUP),** led by Nobel Peace Prize co-winner David Trimble, is the principal political party representing Unionist views. The **Democratic Unionist Party (DUP),** led by Reverend Ian Paisley, chooses to take a harder stance in defense of Unionism. The **Ulster Volunteer Force (UVF),** the **Ulster Freedom Fighters (UFF),** and the **Ulster Defense Association (UDA)** are the Loyalist paramilitary organizations mentioned most frequently in newspapers and on spray-painted walls.

Nationalists—and the more hard-line **Republicans**—want a united and independent Ireland ruled by Dublin. The **Social Democratic Labor Party (SDLP),** led by Nobel Peace Prize co-winner John Hume, is the principal political party representing Nationalist views. **Sinn Fein** (pron. shin fayn), led by Gerry Adams, takes a harder stance in defense of Nationalism. The **Irish Republican Army (IRA)** is the Nationalist paramilitary organization (linked with Sinn Fein) mentioned most often in the press and in graffiti.

Orange and the red, white, and blue of the Union Jack, are the favored colors of the Unionists. Green is the color of the

Republicans. To gain more insight into the complexity of the Troubles, see the University of Ulster's Conflict Archive at http://cain.ulst.ac.uk/index.html.

Safety

Tourists in Northern Ireland are no longer considered courageous (or reckless). Traveling there is as safe as traveling in England. You really have to look for trouble to find it here. Just don't seek out spit-and-sawdust pubs in working-class Protestant neighborhoods and sing Catholic songs. Tourists notice the tension mainly during the marches. July 12 is Orange Day (for the background, see page 76), when Protestants parade and flex in favor of remaining separate from the Republic of Ireland. Lie low if you stumble onto any big green or orange parades.

Northern Ireland Is a Different Country

When you leave the Republic of Ireland and enter Northern Ireland, you are crossing an international border. You change stamps, phone cards, money—and your Eurailpass is no longer valid. Instead of using euros as in the Republic of Ireland, you need to switch to the British pound sterling. Northern Ireland issues its own Ulster pound and also uses English pounds. Like the Scottish pound, Ulster pounds are interchangeable with English pounds. But if you're heading to England next, it's best to change your Ulster pounds into English ones (free at any bank in Northern Ireland, England, and Scotland).

BELFAST

Seventeenth-century Belfast was only a village. With the influx, or "plantation," of Scottish and English settlers, Belfast boomed, spurred by the success of the local linen, rope-making, and shipbuilding industries. The Industrial Revolution took root with a vengeance. While the rest of Ireland remained rural and agricultural, Belfast earned its nickname, "Old Smoke," when many of the brick buildings you'll see today were built. The year 1888 marked the birth of modern Belfast. After Queen Victoria granted city status to this boomtown of 300,000, its citizens built the city's centerpiece, City Hall.

Belfast is the birthplace of the *Titanic* (and many ships that didn't sink). The two huge, mustard-colored cranes (the biggest in the world, nicknamed Samson and Goliath) rise like skyscrapers above the harbor as a reminder of this town's shipbuilding might.

It feels like a new morning in Belfast. It's hard to believe that the bright and bustling pedestrian zone was once a subdued, traffic-free security zone. Now there's no hint of security checks, once a tiresome daily routine. On my last visit, the children dancing in the street were both Catholics and Protestants. They were part of a community summer-camp program giving kids from both communities reasons to live together rather than apart.

Still, it's a fragile peace and a tenuous hope. Mean-spirited murals, hateful bonfires built a month before they're actually burned, and pubs with security gates are reminders that the island is split—and about a million Protestants prefer it that way.

Planning Your Time
Big Belfast is thin on sights. For most, a day of sightseeing is plenty.

Day trip from Dublin: On the handy two-hour Dublin–Belfast train (and its cheap £21 day-return tickets, £30 on Fri or Sun), you could make Belfast a day trip: 7:40–Catch the early-morning train from Dublin; 10:30–City Hall tour, browse the pedestrian zone, lunch, ride a shared cab up the Falls Road; 15:00–Visit Ulster Museum or side-trip to the Ulster Folk and Transport Museum; Evening–Return to Dublin (last train Mon–Sat at 20:10, Sun at 18:15). Confirm train times at local stations. Note that on Saturday, there's a morning market (at St. George's), a town walk offered by the TI (at 14:00), and only one City Hall tour (at 14:30).

Staying overnight: Belfast makes a pleasant overnight stop, with plenty of cheap hostels, reasonable B&Bs, hotel deals (on Fri–Sun), and a resort neighborhood full of B&Bs 30 minutes away in Bangor.

Two days in small-town Northern Ireland: From Dublin (via Belfast), take the train to Portrush; allow two nights and a day to tour the Causeway Coast (castle, whiskey distilleries, Giant's Causeway, resort fun), then follow the Belfast-in-a-day plan above. With an extra day, add Derry.

Two days in Belfast: Splice in the Living History bus tour, Ulster Museum, and Botanic Gardens, or take a day trip to the Antrim Coast.

Coming from Scotland: With good ferry connections (from Stranraer or Troon in Scotland, details in "Transportation Connections," below), it's easy to begin your exploration of the Emerald Isle in Belfast, then head south to Dublin and the Republic.

Orientation (area code: 028)

For the first-time visitor in town for a quick look, Belfast is pretty simple. There are three zones of interest: central (Donegall Square/City Hall/pedestrian shopping/TI), southern (Ulster Museum/Botanic Gardens/university), and western (working-class sectarian neighborhoods west of the freeway). Belfast's "Golden Mile"—stretching from Hotel Europa to the university district—connects the central and southern zones with many of the best dinner and entertainment spots.

Tourist Information: The modern TI has fine, free city maps and an enjoyable bookshop with Internet access (June–Aug Mon–Sat 9:00–19:00, Sun 12:00–17:00; Sept–May Mon–Sat 9:00–17:30, closed Sun; 47 Donegall Place, 1 block north of City Hall, tel. 028/9024-6609, www.gotobelfast.com). For the latest on evening fun, get *The List* free at the TI or *That's Entertainment* at newsstands (50p).

Arrival in Belfast: Arriving by fast train, you'll go directly to Central Station (with ATMs and free city maps at ticket counter). From the station, a free Centerlink bus loops to Donegall Square, with stops near Shaftesbury Square (recommended hostels), the

Belfast

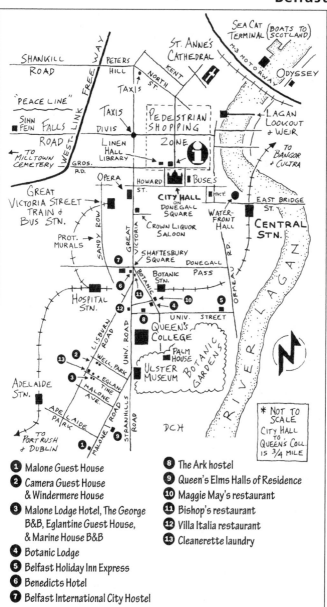

1 Malone Guest House
2 Camera Guest House & Windermere House
3 Malone Lodge Hotel, The George B&B, Eglantine Guest House, & Marine House B&B
4 Botanic Lodge
5 Belfast Holiday Inn Express
6 Benedicts Hotel
7 Belfast International City Hostel
8 The Ark hostel
9 Queen's Elms Halls of Residence
10 Maggie May's restaurant
11 Bishop's restaurant
12 Villa Italia restaurant
13 Cleanerette laundry

bus station (recommended hotels), and the TI (free with any train or bus ticket, 4/hr, never on Sun, during morning rush hour bus runs only between station and Donegall Square). Allow about £3 for a taxi from Central Station to Donegall Square.

Slower trains arc through Belfast, stopping at several downtown stations, including Central Station, Great Victoria Station (most central, near Donegall Square and most hotels), Botanic (close to the university, Botanic Gardens, and some recommended hostels), and Adelaide (near several recommended B&Bs). It's easy and cheap to connect stations by train (75p).

Helpful Hints

U.S. Embassy: It's at 14 Queen Street, north of the intersection with College Street (Mon–Fri 8:30–17:00, closed Sat–Sun, tel. 028/9032-8239, www.usembassy.org.uk).

Phone Tips: To call the Republic of Ireland from Northern Ireland, dial 00-353 then the area code without its initial 0, then the local number. To call Northern Ireland from the Republic of Ireland, dial 048, then the local eight-digit number.

Irish Tourist Board: Traveling on to the Republic of Ireland, are ye? If it's information you'll be wanting, pop on in (Mon–Fri 9:00–17:00, plus June–Sept Sat 9:00–12:30, Oct–May closed weekends, 53 Castle Street, off Donegall Place, tel. 028/9032-7888).

Post Office: The main P.O., with lots of fun postcards, is at the intersection of Castle Place and Donegall Place (Mon–Sat 9:00–17:30, closed Sun, 2 long blocks north of Donegall Square).

Internet Access: Revelations Internet Café is at 27 Shaftesbury Square, near the City Hostel (£4/hr, Mon–Fri 10:00–22:00, Sat 10:00–18:00, Sun 11:00–19:00, tel. 028/9032-0337).

Laundry: Globe Launderers is at 37 Botanic Avenue (£4.50-self-serve, £6.50-drop-off, Mon–Fri 8:00–21:00, Sat 8:00–18:00, Sun 12:00–18:00). For the B&B neighborhood south of town, the closest is Cleanerette (£6-drop-off, Mon–Fri 9:00–18:00, Sat 9:00–17:00, closed Sun, 160 Lisburne Road, at intersection with Eglantine Avenue, tel. 028/9038-1297).

Bike Rental: McConvey Cycles is at 183 Ormeau Road (£10/24 hrs, Mon–Sat 9:00–18:00, closed Sun, CC, tel. 028/9033-0322).

Market: On Saturday morning, St. George's Market is a commotion of clothes, produce, and seafood (at corner of Oxford and East Bridge Streets, 5 blocks east of Donegall Square).

Getting around Belfast

If you line up your sightseeing logically, you can do most of the town on foot.

If you're here in July and August, you can take advantage of

"Day Tracker" tickets that give individuals one day of unlimited train travel anywhere in Northern Ireland for £5 (making it easy to side-trip to Bangor, the Ulster Folk and Transport Museum in Cultra, or Carrickfergus Castle). Families (up to 2 adults and 2 kids under 16) visiting in July and August get an even better deal: the £12.50 one-day Family Passes, valid for train and bus travel. Buy your pass at any train station in the city.

For information on trains and buses in Belfast, contact Trans Link (tel. 028/9066-6630, www.translink.co.uk).

By Bus: Buses go from Donegall Square East to Malone Road and my recommended B&Bs (#70 and #71, 3/hr, 95p, all-day pass-£3).

By Taxi: Taxis are reasonable and should be considered. Rather than use their meters, many cabs charge a flat £3 rate for any ride up to two miles. It's £1 per mile after that. Ride a shared cab if you're going up the Falls Road (explained below).

Tours of Belfast

▲**Walking Tour**—Offered Saturdays at 14:00, a Town Walk takes you through the historic core of town (£4, 90 min, departs from TI, sometimes more tours added—check with TI, tel. 028/9024-6609).

▲**Big Bus Tours**—Citybus (marked with a rainbow on the side of the bus) offers two different bus tours: The **Living History Tour** offers the best introduction to the city's recent and complicated political and social history. You'll cruise the Catholic and Protestant working-class neighborhoods, with a commentary explaining the political murals and places of interest—mostly dealing with the Troubles of the last 25 years. You see things from the bus and get out only for a tea break (daily at 14:30, 1.5 hrs). The **City Tour,** free of politics and religion, takes you on a 20-mile loop of Belfast's sights, with stops at the Parliament and zoo—and a guide to point out the difference (Mon–Sat at 11:00, 1.5 hrs). Both tours depart from Castle Place (2 blocks north of Donegall Square) and cost £9 apiece (pay at kiosk on Donegall Square West, pay driver cash, or book by phone with CC, tel. 028/9045-8484, www.citybus.co.uk/belfasttours.asp).

Minibus Tours—Rodney's Tours leave from Belfast International City Hostel daily at 10:30 and 14:00 to cover the troubled areas in more depth, with time for photo stops (£8, 2 hrs, book in advance, tel. 028/9032-4733). Rodney also offers a variety of minibus tours, including the Antrim Coast (£16, rope bridge, Giant's Causeway, Bushmills Distillery—£3.50 admission not included—and Dunluce Castle, daily 9:30–17:45 depending on demand, book through and depart from hostel, tel. 028/9096-3534). Rodney also works as a private guide (tel. 028/9086-3976, cellular 0783-667-6258, www.minicoachni.co.uk). Or consider **Alternative Tours** (£8, 2 hrs with small group "walkabouts" of 7 people or less, will pick up on request, cellular 0787-926-8153, e-mail: alternative_tours @hotmail.com).

Bailey's Historical Belfast Pub Walk—Mixing drinks and history, you'll start at Flannigan's pub and end six pubs later (£6, drinks not included, May–Sept Thu at 19:00, Sat at 16:00, 2 hrs, book in advance, pub above Crown Liquor Saloon on 46 Great Victoria Street, across from Hotel Europa, tel. 028/ 9268-3665, Judy Crawford).

Catholic and Protestant Neighborhoods

It will be a happy day when the sectarian neighborhoods of Belfast have nothing to be sectarian about. For a look at a couple of the original home bases of the Troubles, explore the working-class neighborhoods of the Catholic Falls Road and the Protestant Shankill Road and Sandy Row.

You can get tours of Falls Road or Shankill Road (see listings below), but rarely are both combined in one tour. Ken Harper is part of a new breed of Belfast taxi drivers who will give you an insightful private tour of both (£20 minimum or £7.50 per person for a 90-min tour, days-cellular 0771-175-7178, evenings-tel. 028/9074-2711).

▲▲**Falls Road**—At the intersection of Castle Street and King Street, you'll find a building whose ground floor is filled with old black cabs—and the only Irish-language signs in downtown Belfast. These shared black cabs efficiently shuttle residents from outlying neighborhoods up and down the Falls Road and to the city center. This service originated more than 30 years ago at the beginning of the Troubles, when locals would hijack city buses and use them as barricades in the street fighting. When bus service was discontinued, local paramilitary groups established the shared taxi service. Any cab (except those in the "Whiterock" line) goes up the Falls Road, past Sinn Fein headquarters and lots of murals, to the Milltown Cemetery (80p, sit in front and talk to the cabbie). Hop in and out. Easy-to-flag-down cabs run every minute or so in each direction on the Falls Road. Twenty trained cabbies do one-hour tours for £20, cheap for a small group of up to six riders (tel. 028/9059-0800, www.wbta.net).

The Sinn Fein office and bookstore are near the bottom of Falls Road. The bookstore is worth a look. Page through books featuring color photos of the political murals that decorate the buildings. Money raised here supports families of imprisoned IRA members.

A sad, corrugated wall called the Peace Line runs a block or so north of Falls Road, separating the Catholics from the Protestants in the Shankill Road area.

At the Milltown Cemetery, walk past all the Gaelic crosses down to the far right-hand corner (closest to the highway), where the IRA Roll of Honor is set apart from the thousands of other graves by little green railings. They are treated like fallen soldiers. Notice the memorial to Bobby Sands and nine other hunger strikers. They starved themselves to death in the nearby Maze prison in 1981, protesting for political prisoner status as opposed to terrorist criminal treatment. The prison closed in the fall of 2000.

Shankill Road and Sandy Row—You can ride a shared black cab through the Protestant Shankill Road area (departing from the end of North Street, 30-min loop-£1.20, or take a 1-hr tour-£12 for 1–2 people, £15 for 3–6 people, tel. 028/9032-8775).

An easier (and cheaper) way to get a dose of the Unionist side is to walk Sandy Row. From Hotel Europa, walk a block down Glengall Street, then turn left for a 10-minute walk along a working-class Protestant street. A stop in the Unionist memorabilia shop, a pub, or one of the many cheap eateries here may give you an opportunity to talk to a local. You'll see murals filled with Unionist symbolism. The mural of William of Orange's victory over the Catholic King James II (Battle of the Boyne, 1690) thrills Unionist hearts. (From the south end of Sandy Row, it's a 10-min walk to the Ulster Museum, below.)

More Sights—Belfast

▲▲**City Hall**—This grand structure, with its 173-foot-tall copper dome, dominates the town center. Built between 1898 and 1906, with its statue of Queen Victoria scowling down Belfast's main drag and the Union Jack flapping behind her, it's a stirring sight. In the garden, you'll find memorials to the *Titanic* and the landing of the U.S. Expeditionary Force in 1942—the first stop en route to Berlin. Take the free 45-minute tour (June–Sept usually Mon–Fri at 10:30, 11:30, and 14:30, Sat only at 14:30; Oct–May Mon–Sat 14:30 only; for Sat tours, enter back of building—south side, otherwise enter front; call to check schedule and to reserve, tel. 028/9027-0456). The tour gives you a rundown on city government and an explanation of the decor that makes this an Ulster political hall of fame. Queen Victoria and King Edward VII look down on city council meetings. The 1613 original charter of Belfast granted by James I is on display. Its Great Hall—bombed by the Germans in 1941—looks as great as it did the day it was made.

If you can't manage a tour, at least step inside, admire the marble swirl staircase, and drop into the "What's on in Belfast" room just inside the front door.

Linen Hall Library—Across the street from City Hall, the 200-year-old Linen Hall Library welcomes guests. It has a fine,

Belfast Center

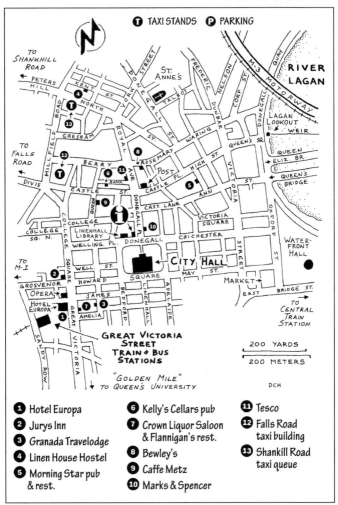

T TAXI STANDS **P** PARKING

TO SHANKHILL ROAD

← PETERS HILL

RIVER LAGAN

ST. ANNE'S

LAGAN LOOKOUT
WEIR

QUEEN'S SQ.

TO FALLS ROAD

GRESHAM

BERRY

POST

QUEEN ELIZ. BR.

QUEEN'S BRIDGE

DIVIS

CASTLE ST.

BANK

CAST. LANE

VICTORIA SQUARE

COLLEGE SQ. N.

LINENHALL LIBRARY

WELLING. PL.

DONEGALL

CHICHESTER

WATERFRONT HALL

TO M-1 ←

WELL. ST.

CITY HALL

SQUARE

MAY ST.

MARKET

BRIDGE ST.

GROSVENOR

HOWARD

EAST

TO CENTRAL TRAIN STATION

OPERA

HOTEL EUROPA

JAMES

AMELIA

BEDFORD

GREAT VICTORIA STREET TRAIN & BUS STATIONS

200 YARDS

200 METERS

"GOLDEN MILE"
↓ TO QUEEN'S UNIVERSITY

DCH

❶ Hotel Europa

❷ Jurys Inn

❸ Granada Travelodge

❹ Linen House Hostel

❺ Morning Star pub & rest.

❻ Kelly's Cellars pub

❼ Crown Liquor Saloon & Flannigan's rest.

❽ Bewley's

❾ Caffe Metz

❿ Marks & Spencer

⓫ Tesco

⓬ Falls Road taxi building

⓭ Shankill Road taxi queue

hardbound ambience, a coffee shop, and a royal newspaper reading room. Described as "Ulster's attic," the library takes pride in being a neutral space where anyone trying to make sense of the sectarian conflict can view the *Troubled Images* historical collection of engrossing political posters (Mon–Fri 9:30–17:30, Sat 9:30–16:00, get free visitor's pass at entrance on Fountain Street, 17 Donegall Square North, tel. 028/9032-1707).

Golden Mile—This is the overstated nickname of Belfast's liveliest dining and entertainment district, which stretches from the Opera House (Great Victoria Street) to the university (University Road).

The **Grand Opera House,** originally built in 1895, bombed and rebuilt in 1991, and bombed and rebuilt again in 1993, is extravagantly Victorian and the place to take in a concert, play, or opera (closed to sightseers, ticket office across street, CC, tel. 028/9024-1919, www.goh.co.uk). **Hotel Europa,** next door, while considered the most bombed hotel in the world, feels pretty casual (listed under "Sleeping," below).

Across the street is the museum-like **Crown Liquor Saloon.** Built in 1849, it's now a part of the National Trust. A wander through its mahogany, glass, and marble interior is a trip back into the day of Queen Victoria (although the privacy provided by the snugs—private booths—allows for un-Victorian behavior; Mon–Sat 11:30–24:00, Sun 12:30–22:00; consider a lunch stop, see "Eating," below). Upstairs, **Flannigan's** serves pub grub, is decorated with historic photos, and is the starting point for a pub walk (see "Tours of Belfast," above).

Lagan Lookout Visitors Centre—This center shows off the fruits of the city's £750 million investment in its harbor. The tides of the River Lagan left the town with unsightly mud flats daily. The weir, built in 1994, controls the tides, stabilizing the depth of the harbor. It also doubles as a free pedestrian bridge over the river, affording walkers a fine view of the harbor area, including the big cranes and the new convention center. The visitors' center, while mildly entertaining and enthusiastically "interactive," is not worth the £1.50 entry fee (Mon–Fri 11:00–17:00, Sat 12:00–17:00, Sun 14:00–17:00, in winter shorter hours and closed Mon, 5-min walk from TI, just past the tipsy, 4-feet-off-center Albert Clock Tower, tel. 028/9031-5444).

▲**Ulster Museum**—While mediocre by European standards, this is Belfast's one major museum. It's free and pretty painless: Ride the elevator to the top floor and follow the spiraling exhibits downhill; there's a cheery café halfway down. You'll find an interesting *Made in Belfast* exhibit just before an arch that proclaims, "Trade is the golden girdle of the globe." The delicately worded history section is given an interesting British slant (such as the implication that the Great Famine of 1845 was caused by the Irish population doubling in 40 years—without a mention of various English contributions to the suffering). After a wander through the *Early Medieval Ireland* exhibit and a peek at a pretty good mummy, top things off with the *Girona* treasure. Soggy bits of gold, silver, leather, and wood were salvaged from the Spanish Armada's shipwrecked *Girona*—lost off the Antrim Coast north of Belfast in 1588 (free, Mon–Fri 10:00–17:00, Sat 13:00–17:00, Sun 14:00–17:00, tel. 028/9038-3000, www.ulstermuseum.org.uk).

▲**Botanic Gardens**—This is the backyard of Queen's University. On a sunny day, you couldn't imagine a more relaxing park setting. On a cold day, step into the Tropical Ravine for a jungle of heat and humidity. Take a quick walk through the Palm House, reminiscent of the one in London's Kew Gardens, but smaller (free, Mon–Fri 10:00–12:00 & 13:00–17:00, Sat–Sun 13:00–17:00, less in winter, tel. 028/9032-4902).

The Odyssey—This huge new complex offers a food pavilion (with Ireland's only Hard Rock Café), a 12-screen cinema (with IMAX), a 10,000-seat arena (where the Belfast Giants professional hockey team plays), and the W5 Science center with stimulating, interactive exhibits for youngsters (2 Queen's Quay, 10-min walk from Central Station, tel. 028/9045-1055, www.theodyssey.co.uk).

Sights—Near Belfast

▲▲**Ulster Folk and Transport Museum**—This 180-acre, two-museum complex straddles the road and rail at Cultra, midway between Bangor and Belfast (8 miles east of town).

The Folk Museum, an open-air collection of 34 reconstructed buildings from all over the nine counties of Ulster, showcases the region's traditional lifestyles. After wandering through the old-town site (church, print shop, schoolhouse, humble Belfast row house, and so on), you'll head off into the country to nip into cottages, farmhouses, and mills. Most houses are warmed by a wonderful peat fire and a friendly attendant. It can be dull or vibrant, depending upon when you visit and your ability to chat with the attendants. Drop a peat brick on the fire.

The Transport Museum (downhill, over the road from the folk section) consists of three buildings. Start at the bottom and trace the evolution of transportation from 7,500 years ago—when people first decided to load an ox—to modern times. The lowest building holds an intriguing section on the sinking of the Belfast-made *Titanic*. In the next two buildings, you roll through the history of bikes, cars, and trains. The car section rumbles from the first car in Ireland (an 1898 Benz) through the "Cortina Culture" of the 1960s to the local adventures of John DeLorean and a 1981 model of his car (£5, £13 for families, CC, July–Sept Mon–Sat 10:00–18:00, Sun 11:00–18:00; March–June Mon–Fri 10:00–17:00, Sat 10:00–18:00, Sun 11:00–18:00; Oct–Feb closes daily at 16:00; check schedule for special events that day, allow 3 hrs, tel. 028/9042-8428, www.nidex.com/uftm.) Expect lots of walking. Drivers can drive from one section to the next.

From Belfast, reach **Cultra** by taxi (£10), bus #1 or #2 (2/hr, 30 min from Laganside Bus Centre), or train (£3.50 round-trip, 2/hr, 15 min, from any Belfast train station or Bangor). Trains and buses stop right in the park. Public transport schedules get skimpy on Saturday and Sunday.

Carrickfergus Castle—This historic castle, built during the Norman invasion of the late 1100s, stands sentry on the shore of Belfast Lough. William of Orange landed here in 1690, when he began his Irish campaign against deposed King James II. These days the castle feels a bit sanitized and geared for kids, but it's an easy excursion if you're seeking a castle experience near the city (£3, April–Sept Mon–Sat 10:00–18:00, Sun 14:00–18:00, Oct–March Mon–Sat 10:00–16:00, Sun 14:00–16:00, 20-min train ride from Belfast on line to Larne, tel. 028/9335-1273).

Sleeping in Belfast

(£1 = about $1.50; country code: 44, area code: 028, to call Belfast from the Republic of Ireland, dial 048 before the local 8-digit number)

Sleep Code: **S** = Single, **D** = Double/Twin, **T** = Triple, **Q** = Quad, **b** = bathroom, **s** = shower only, **CC** = Credit Cards accepted, **no CC** = Credit Cards not accepted).

To help you easily sort through these listings, I've divided the rooms into three categories, based on the price for a double room with bath:

Higher Priced—Most rooms more than £80.

Moderately Priced—Most rooms £50–80.

Lower Priced—Most rooms £50 or less.

Many of Belfast's best budget beds cluster in a comfortable area just south of the Ulster Museum and the university. Two train stations (Botanic and Adelaide) are nearby, and buses zip down Malone Road every 20 minutes. Any bus on Malone Road goes to Donegall Square East. Taxis, cheap in Belfast, zip you downtown for £3 (your host can call one). Belfast is more of a business town than a tourist town, so business-class room rates are lower or soft on weekends.

Sleeping in South Belfast

HIGHER PRICED

Malone Lodge Hotel, by far the classiest listing in this neighborhood, provides slick, business-class comfort and spacious rooms in a charming environment on a quiet, leafy street (Sb-£60–95, Db-£80–115, superior Db-£100–140, weekend deals, includes breakfast, CC, elevator, 60 Eglantine Avenue,

Belfast BT9 6DY, tel. 028/9038-8000, fax 028/9038-8088, www.malonelodgehotel.com).

MODERATELY PRICED

Camera Guest House rents large, smoke-free rooms and comes with an airy, hardwood feeling throughout (S-£25, Sb-£38, Db-£55, CC, 44 Wellington Park, Belfast BT9 6DP, tel. 028/9066-0026, fax 028/9066-7856, e-mail: pauldrumm @hotmail.com, Paul Drumm).

LOWER PRICED

Malone Guest House is a classy, stand-alone Victorian house fronting the busy Malone Road. It's homey and well run by Mrs. Millar, who rents 13 recently refurbished rooms (Sb-£25–35, Db-£40–50, Tb-£55–60 with this book, 79 Malone Road, at inter-section with Adelaide Park and bus stop, Belfast BT9 6SH, tel. 028/9066-9565, fax 028/9022-3020, e-mail: maloneguesthouse @maloneroad.fsnet.co.uk).

Windermere House has 11 rooms, including several small but pleasant singles, in a large Victorian house (S-£24, Sb-£35, very small D-£34, D-£46, Db-£50, T-£54, 60 Wellington Park, tel. 028/9066-2693, fax 028/9068-2218).

On the same quiet street, you'll find these three budget choices: **The George B&B** (6 fine, smallish rooms, S-£24, Sb-£35, Db-£45, no CC, 9 Eglantine Avenue, tel. & fax 028/9068-3212, Hugh McGuinness), **Eglantine Guest House** (7 pleasant rooms, S-£24, D-£44, T-£60, no CC, 21 Eglantine Avenue, tel. 028/9066-7585, fax 028/9066-8203, Lou Cargill will take care of you), and the grand old **Marine House B&B** (10 high-ceilinged rooms, Sb-£35–38, Db-£50, CC, 30 Eglantine Avenue, tel. & fax 028/9066-2828).

Botanic Lodge rents 18 decent rooms on a lively but stylish street, with lots of fun eateries nearby (D-£40, Db-£45, CC, 87 Botanic Avenue, 10-min walk to City Hall, Belfast BT7 1JN, tel. & fax 028/9032-7682).

Sleeping in Hotels

HIGHER PRICED

Hotel Europa is Belfast's landmark hotel—fancy, comfortable, and central—with four stars and good weekend rates. Modern yet elegant, this was Clinton's choice when he visited (Db-£160 plus £12 breakfast Mon–Thu, Db-£110 Fri–Sun including break-fast; President Clinton's suite-£375, CC, 4 non-smoking floors, Great Victoria Street, tel. 028/9032-7000, fax 028/9032-7800, www.hastingshotels.com).

MODERATELY PRICED

Jurys Inn, an American-style place that rents its 190 identical modern rooms for one simple price, is perfectly located two blocks from the City Hall (up to 3 adults or 2 adults and 2 kids for £71, breakfast-£7, CC, 3 non-smoking floors, Fisherwick Place, tel. 028/9053-3500, fax 028/9053-3511, www.jurys.com, e-mail: info@jurys.com).

Granada Travelodge is a basic Jurys-style business hotel with 90 cookie-cutter rooms high on value, low on character (Db-£65, often huge weekend discounts—such as Db-£48 for Fri, Sat, or Sun nights, no breakfast, CC, quiet but extremely central, a block from Hotel Europa and City Hall at 15 Brunswick Street, Belfast BT2 7GE, tel. 08700-850-950 or 028/9033-3555, fax 028/9023-2999, www.travelodge.co.uk).

Belfast Holiday Inn Express is cheaper but not as central as Jurys Inn, with the same basic formula (Db-£60 Mon–Thu, Db-£55 Fri–Sun, kids free, includes continental breakfast, CC, non-smoking floors, elevator, 106 University Street, tel. 028/9031-1909, fax 028/9031-1910, e-mail: express@holidayinn-ireland.com).

Benedicts Hotel has a local feel in a good location at the northern fringe of the Queen's University district, with a popular bar that's a maze of polished wood (Sb-£65, Db-£75–80, Tb-£100, CC, elevator, 7-21 Bradbury Place, tel. 028/9059-1999, fax 028/9059-1990, e-mail: info@benedictshotel.co.uk).

Sleeping in Hostels and Dorms

LOWER PRICED

Belfast International City Hostel, providing the best value among Belfast's hostels, is big and creatively run, with 40 twins and quads. It's located near the Botanic train station, in the heart of the lively university district and close to the center. Features include free lockers, left luggage, Internet access, videos, kitchen, self-serve laundry (£3), cheap breakfast-only cafeteria, elevator, 24-hour reception, and no curfew (beds in 6-bed dorm-£8.50, beds in quad-£10, S-£17, D-£26, CC, 22 Donegall Road, tel. 028/9032-4733, fax 028/9043-9699, www.hini.org.uk, e-mail: info@hini.org.uk). Paul, the manager of the hostel, is a veritable TI with a passion for his work. The hostel is the starting point for Rodney's Tours (see "Tours of Belfast," page 197).

The Ark, a smaller, hipper, more youthful and easygoing hostel, is in the university district near the Botanic train station (beds in 4-bed dorms-£8.50, D-£32, kitchen, 18 University Street, tel. 028/9032-9626, fax 028/9032-9647, www.arkhostel.com, e-mail: info@arkhostel.com).

Linen House Youth Hostel fills an old linen factory with a 130-bed industrial-strength hostel. It's on a dark, scary-at-night street in a very central location (dorm bed-£9, S-£15, D-£24, no breakfast, plenty of facilities, kitchen, Internet access, 18 Kent Street, tel. 028/9058-6400, fax 028/9058-6444, e-mail: info@belfasthostel.com).

Queen's Elms Halls of Residence is a big brick Queen's University dorm renting 300 basic, institutional rooms (mainly singles) to travelers during summer break. Singles should book in advance and ask for a "self-catering room" to snare a spot in the newer building (mid-June–early-Sept only, S-£12.50, Sb-£17.50, D-£22, cheaper for students, CC, coin-op laundry, self-serve kitchen, building is set back about 250 yards from street, 78 Malone Road, tel. 028/9038-1608, fax 028/9066-6680, e-mail: qehor@qub.ac.uk).

Eating in Belfast

Eating Downtown

If it's £5 pub grub you want, consider these places. The **Morning Star** is woody and elegant (daily 12:00–22:00, restaurant upstairs, CC, 17 Pottinger's Entry, tel. 028/9023-5986). The very Irish **Kelly's Cellars** is 300 years old and hard to find, but worth it (Mon–Wed 11:30–20:00, Thu–Sat 11:30–24:00, closed Sun, live traditional music Fri–Sat nights and Sat at 15:30, restaurant upstairs Mon–Sat 12:00–18:00, 32 Bank Street, behind Tesco supermarket, tel. 028/9024-2628). The small, antique **Crown Liquor Saloon,** mentioned in "More Sights" on page 199, has a mesmerizing mishmash of mosaics and shareable snugs (booths), topped with a smoky tin ceiling (Mon–Sat lunch only 12:00–17:00, 46 Great Victoria Street, across from Hotel Europa, tel. 028/9027-9901). **Flannigan's** upstairs offers dependable £10 meals (Mon–Sat 12:00–21:00, Sun 12:30–19:00, tel. 028/9027-9901, use entry on Amelia Street when the Crown is closed).

For cafés, try any of the many popular eateries in the streets north of Donegall Square. **Bewley's,** popular in Ireland, offers a good-value cafeteria with seating under a conservatory-style roof (Mon–Sat 8:00–17:30, Thu until 20:00, closed Sun, north end of Donegall's Arcade); to save money, skip the Coffee House with table service and choose the cafeteria section instead. **Caffe Metz** has a sleek, light-wood design and £4 meals, including salads (Mon–Sat 9:00–17:00, closed Sun, 12 Queen Street, at intersection with College Street, next door to U.S. Embassy, tel. 028/9024-9484).

Marks & Spencer has a coffee shop serving skinny lattes and a supermarket in its basement (Mon–Sat 9:00–18:00, Thu until 21:00, closed Sun, WCs on 2nd floor, Donegall Place, a block north of Donegall Square). **Tesco,** another supermarket, is a block north of M&S and two blocks north of Donegall Square (Mon–Sat 8:00–19:00, Thu until 21:00, Sun 13:00–17:00, Royal Avenue and Bank Street). Picnic on the City Hall green.

Eating near Shaftesbury Square and Botanic Station

Maggie May's serves hearty, simple, cheap meals (£4–7, Mon–Sat 8:00–22:30, Sun 10:00–22:30, 50 Botanic Avenue, 1 block south of Botanic station, tel. 028/9032-2662). **Bishop's** is the locals' choice for fish and chips (daily 10:00–24:00, pasta and veggie options, classier side has table service, CC, Bradbury Place, just south of Shaftesbury Square, tel. 028/9043-9070).

Villa Italia packs in crowds hungry for linguini and *bistecca*. With its checkered tablecloths and a wood-beamed ceiling draped with grape leaves, it's a little bit of Italy in Belfast (£7–10, Mon–Sat 17:00–23:30, Sun 16:00–22:30, CC, 39 University Road, 3 long blocks south of Shaftesbury Square, at intersection with University Street, tel. 028/9032-8356).

Sleeping in Bangor
(£1 = about $1.50, country code: 44, area code: 028)

To stay in a laid-back seaside hometown—with more comfort per pound—sleep 30 minutes east of Belfast in Bangor (pron. BANG-grr). Formerly a slick Belfast seaside escape, Bangor now has a sleepy and almost residential feeling. But with easy train connections to downtown Belfast (2/hr, 30 min, £3.50), elegant old homes facing its newly spruced-up harbor, and the lack of even a hint of big-city Belfast, Bangor appeals. The harbor is a five-minute walk from the train station. Bangor's **TI** is at 34 Quay Street (tel. 028/9127-0069).

MODERATELY PRICED

Royal Hotel is a fine old place right on the harbor with good weekend rates for its 50 rooms (Db-£75 weekdays, £65 weekends, view rooms are £10 pricier, CC, 26 Quay Street, BT20 5ED, tel. 028/9127-1866, fax 028/9146-7810, www.the-royal-hotel.com, e-mail: info@the-royal-hotel.com).

LOWER PRICED

Pierview House B&B is a chandeliered winner, with three of its five spacious rooms overlooking the sea (D-£37, grand Db-£42, family room, CC, 28 Seacliff Road, tel. 028/9146-3381, Mr. and Mrs. Watts).

Eating in Bangor

For good £7 meals, try **Lord Nelson** (in the Marine Court Hotel (facing harbor, 18–20 Quay Street) or the bar next door at the **Royal Hotel**. Consider **Ganges** for Indian food (9 Bingham Street).

Transportation Connections—Bangor

By train to Belfast: Trains go from Bangor station (the end of the line, don't use Bangor West) into Belfast via Cultra (Ulster Folk and Transport Museum). The journey (2/hr, 30 min) gives you a good close-up look at the giant Belfast harbor cranes. Get off at Belfast Central, which has a free Rail-Link shuttle bus to the town center (4/hr, not Sun), or stay on until the Botanic train station for the Ulster Museum, the Golden Mile, and Sandy Row.

Transportation Connections—Belfast

By train to: Dublin (8/day, 2 hrs, £21), **Larne** (hrly, 1 hr), **Portrush** (8/day, 2 hrs). Service is less frequent on Sundays. Train info: tel. 028/9066-6630.

   By bus to: Portrush (6/day, 2 hrs, £7), **Glasgow** (2/day, 5 hrs, £20), **Edinburgh** (2/day, 6 hrs, £25), **London** (2/day, 12 hrs, £44). The Europa Bus Centre is behind Hotel Europa (Ulsterbus tel. 028/9033-7003 for destinations in Scotland and London, tel. 028/9066-6630 for destinations in Northern Ireland, CC).

   By plane: Belfast has two airports. Belfast City Airport is a five-minute taxi ride from town (near the docks), while Belfast International Airport is 18 miles west of town, connected by buses from the Europa Bus Centre behind the Europa Hotel. British Airways flies to **Glasgow** (3/day, 45 min, as low as £60 round-trip, British Airways' Belfast office tel. 0845-606-0747 or central booking at tel. 0345-222-111) and bmi british midland flies to **London's** Heathrow Airport (12/day, £35, tel. 0870-6070-555).

   By ferry to Scotland: There are a number of options, ports, and companies. You can sail between Belfast and **Stranraer** (1.75-hr crossing, on Stena Line ferry—£22, tel. 028/9074-7747, www.stenaline.com) or between Belfast and **Troon** (2/day, 2.5-hr crossing, year-round, £20, also takes cars for £100–150, CC, Troon–Glasgow trains 2/hr, 30 min; easy connections from Glasgow to most anywhere in Britain, British tel. 0870-552-3523, www.seacat.co.uk). P&O Ferry goes from **Larne** (20 miles north of Belfast, 1 train/hr, TI tel. 028/2826-0088) to **Cairnryan** (5/day, 1 hr, £25, tel. 0870-2424-777).

   By ferry to England: You can sail overnight from Belfast to **Birkenhead** (10 min from Liverpool)—with dinner and breakfast—for £35 (plus £40 for a cabin that sleeps 4) on North Merchant Ferries (8 hrs, nightly at 22:00, CC, tel. 0870-600-4321).

ANTRIM COAST AND PORTRUSH

The Antrim Coast—the north of Northern Ireland—is one of the most interesting and scenic coastlines in Ireland. Within a few miles of the Portrush train terminal, you can visit some evocative castle ruins, tour the world's oldest whiskey distillery, risk your life on a bouncy rope bridge, and hike along the famous Giant's Causeway.

The homey seaside resort of Portrush used to be known as "the Brighton of the North." While it's seen its best days, it retains the atmosphere and architecture of a genteel, middle-class seaside resort. Portrush fills its peninsula with family-oriented amusements, fun eateries, and B&Bs. Summertime fun-seekers promenade along the toy harbor and tumble down to the sandy beaches, which extend in sweeping white crescents on either side.

Superficially, it has the appearance of any small British seaside resort, but its history and high population of young people (students from the University of Coleraine) give Portrush a little more personality. Along with the usual arcade amusements, there are nightclubs, restaurants, summer theater in the town hall, and convivial pubs that attract customers all the way from Belfast. At the end of the train line and just a few miles from several important sights, it's an ideal base for exploring the highlights of the Antrim Coast.

Planning Your Time

You need a full day to explore the Antrim Coast, so allow two nights in Portrush. An ideal day might be a bike tour lacing together Dunluce Castle, Old Bushmills Distillery, and the Giant's Causeway, followed by nine holes on the Portrush pitch-and-putt course.

Consider this side-trip north from Dublin.

Day 1: 11:00–16:00-Train from Dublin to Portrush.

Day 2: All day for Antrim Coast sights and Portrush.

Day 3: 8:00–10:00-Train to Belfast, all day in Belfast; 19:00–21:00-Train back to Dublin.

Orientation (area code: 028)

Portrush's pleasant and easily walked town center features sea views in every direction. On one side are the harbor and restaurants, and on the other are Victorian townhouses and vast salty views. The tip of the peninsula is marked by a lighthouse and a park filled with tennis courts, lawn-bowling greens, and putting greens.

The city is busy with students during the school year. July and August are beach-resort boom time. June and September are laid-back and lazy. Families pack Portrush on Saturdays, and revelers from Belfast crowd its hotels on Saturday nights.

Tourist Information: The TI, more generous and helpful than those in the Republic, is in the big, modern Dunluce Centre (July–Aug daily 9:00–19:00, otherwise Mon–Fri 9:00–17:00, Sat–Sun 12:00–17:00, closed Nov–Feb, tel. 028/7082-3333). Get the free North Ireland driving map, the "Stop & Visit" brochure, and a free Belfast map if you're Belfast-bound.

Arrival in Portrush: The train tracks stop at the base of the tiny peninsula that Portrush fills (no baggage check at station). The TI is three long blocks from the train station (follow signs down Eglinton Street and turn left at fire station). All listed B&Bs are within a 10-minute walk of the train station (see "Sleeping," below). The bus stop is two blocks from the train station.

Getting around the Antrim Coast

By Bus: In July and August, a couple of all-day bus passes are available (but one doesn't include Portrush). The more useful is the £4 Bushmills Open Topper, connecting Portrush, Old Bushmills Distillery, and the Giant's Causeway every two hours. The £3 "Causeway Rambler," which links Old Bushmills Distillery, the Giant's Causeway Visitors Centre, and the Carrick-a-Rede Rope Bridge hourly, is less convenient because it doesn't include Portrush in its circuit (to get from Portrush to Bushmills, take a £5 taxi, or those who want to see the Rope Bridge—along with the other sights—could even consider getting both passes). For either pass, pick up a schedule at the TI and buy the ticket from the driver (in Portrush, the Bushmills Open Topper bus stops at Dunluce Avenue, next to public WC, a 2-min walk from TI).

By Car: Distances are short and parking is easy. Don't miss the treacherous yet scenic coastal route down to the Glens of Antrim.

By Taxi: Groups (up to 4) go reasonably by taxi, which costs only £7 from Portrush to the Giant's Causeway.

Portrush

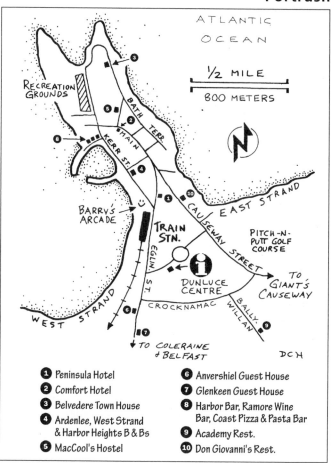

1 Peninsula Hotel
2 Comfort Hotel
3 Belvedere Town House
4 Ardenlee, West Strand
& Harbor Heights B & Bs
5 MacCool's Hostel
6 Anvershiel Guest House
7 Glenkeen Guest House
8 Harbor Bar, Ramore Wine
Bar, Coast Pizza & Pasta Bar
9 Academy Rest.
10 Don Giovanni's Rest.

Sights—Portrush

Barry's Old Time Amusement Arcade—This is a fine chance
to see Northern Ireland at play (open weekends and summer only).
Just below the train station on the harbor, it's filled with candy
floss (cotton candy) and little kids learning the art of one-armed
bandits, 2p at a time. Get £1 worth of 2p coins from the machine
and go wild (daily 13:00–22:30).

Pitch-and-Putt at the Royal Portrush Golf Course—Irish
courses, like those in Scotland, are highly sought after for their
lush but dry greens in glorious settings. While serious golfers

can get a tee time at the Royal Portrush, rookies can get a smaller dose of this wonderful golf setting at the neighboring Skerry 9 Hole Links pitch-and-putt range. You get two clubs and balls for £4.50, and they don't care if you go around twice (daily 8:30–19:30, 10-min walk from station, tel. 028/7082-2311).

Portrush Recreation Grounds—For some easygoing exercise right in town, this well-organized park offers lawn-bowling greens (£3/hr with gear), putting greens, tennis courts, a great kids' play park, and a café (tennis shoes, balls, and rackets can all be rented for a small price; Easter–Sept Mon–Sat 10:00–dusk, Sun 13:00–19:00, tel. 028/7082-4441).

Other major Portrush amusements include the **Dunluce Centre** (kid-oriented fun zone) and **Waterworld** (£4.75, daily 10:00–19:00 Easter–Aug, Sept only 10:00–18:00 on weekends, pool, waterslides, bowling, wedged between Harbor Restaurant and Ramore Wine Bar).

Sights—Antrim Coast

▲**Dunluce Castle**—These romantic ruins, perched dramatically on the edge of a rocky headland, are testimony to this region's turbulent past. During the Middle Ages the castle resisted several sieges. But on a stormy night in 1639, dinner was interrupted as half of the kitchen fell into the sea, taking the servants with it. That was the last straw for the lady of the castle. The countess of Antrim packed up and moved inland, and the castle "began its slow submission to the forces of nature." While it's one of the largest castles in Northern Ireland and is beautifully situated, there's precious little to see among its broken walls.

The 16th-century expansion of the castle was financed by the salvaging of a shipwreck. In 1588 the Spanish Armada's *Girona* sank on her way home after an aborted mission against England, laden with sailors and the valuables of three abandoned sister ships. More than 1,300 drowned, and only five washed ashore. (The shipwreck was excavated in 1967, and a bounty of golden odds and silver ends wound up in Belfast's Ulster Museum.)

Castle admission includes an impromptu guided tour of the ruins that's interesting for its effort to defend the notion of "Ulster, a place apart—facing Scotland, cut off from the rest of Ireland by dense forests and mountains . . . " (£2, April–Sept Mon–Sat 10:00–18:00, Sun 12:00–18:00; winter Mon–Sat 10:00–16:00, shorter hrs Sun, tel. 028/2073-1938).

▲▲**Old Bushmills Distillery**—Bushmills claims to be the world's oldest distillery. Though King James I (of Bible fame) only granted its license to distill "Aqua Vitae" in 1608, whiskey has been made here since the 13th century. Distillery tours waft you through the

Northern Ireland's Antrim Coast

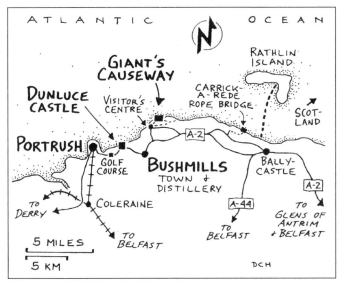

process, making it clear that Irish whiskey is triple distilled—and therefore smoother than Scotch whisky (distilled merely twice and minus the *e*). The 45-minute tour starts with the mash pit, which is filled with a porridge that eventually becomes whiskey. (The leftovers of that porridge are fed to the county's particularly happy cows.) You'll see thousands of oak casks—the kind used for Spanish sherry—filled with aging whiskey. The finale, of course, is the tasting in the 1608 Bar—the former malt barn. When your guide asks for a tasting volunteer, raise your hand quick and strong. Four volunteers per tour get to taste-test eight different whiskeys (Irish versus Scotch and bourbon). Everyone else gets a single glass of his or her choice. Non–whiskey enthusiasts might enjoy a cinnamon-and-cloves hot toddy. To see the distillery at its lively best, visit when the 100 workers are manning the machinery— Monday morning through Friday noon (weekend tours see a still still). Tours are limited to 35 people and book up. In summer, call in your name to get a tour time before you arrive (£4, Easter– Oct daily, tours are on the half-hr from 9:30, last tour at 16:00, Sun from 12:00; winter Mon–Fri only, 5 tours daily at 10:30, 11:30, 13:30, 14:30, and 15:30, tel. 028/2073-1521). You can get a decent lunch in the tasting room after your tour. The distillery is signposted a quarter mile from Bush-mills town center. For an overnight, consider **Valley View Farm B&B** (Sb-£25, Db-£40,

6a Ballyclough Road, Bushmills, tel. 028/2074-1608, fax 028/ 2074-2739, www.valleyviewbushmills.com, e-mail: valerie.mcfall @btinternet.com).

▲▲**Giant's Causeway**—This four-mile-long stretch of coastline is famous for its bizarre basalt columns. The shore is covered with hexagonal pillars that stick up at various heights. It's as if the earth were offering god his choice of 37,000 six-sided cigarettes.

Geologists claim the Giant's Causeway was formed by volcanic eruptions 60 million years ago. As the lava surface cooled, it contracted and cracked into hexagonal shapes. As the layer of hardened but alligatored rock settled, it broke into its many stair steps.

In actuality, the Giant's Causeway was made by a giant Ulster warrior named Finn MacCool who wanted to reach his love on the Scottish island of Staffa. Way back then the causeway stretched to Scotland, connecting the two lands. Today, while the foundation has settled, the formation still extends undersea to Staffa, just off the Scottish coast. Finn's causeway was ruined (into today's "remnant of chaos") by a rival giant. As the rival fled from ferocious Finn back to his Scottish homeland, he ripped up the causeway so Finn couldn't chase him.

For cute variations on the Finn story, as well as details on the ridiculous theories of modern geologists, start your visit in the Visitors Centre. The real information is on the walls of the exhibition, while a video gives a worthwhile history of the Giant's Causeway, with a regional overview (£1, 4/hr, 12 min). A gift shop and cafeteria are standing by.

A minibus (60p each way, 4/hr) zips tired ones a half-mile directly to the Grand Causeway, the highlight of the entire coast.

For a better dose of the causeway, consider this plan. Follow the high cliff-top trail from the Visitors Centre 10 minutes to a great viewpoint, then five minutes farther to reach the Shepherd's Stairway. Zigzag down to the coast; at the T junction, go 100 yards right to the towering pipes of "the Organ." Then retrace your steps and continue left to the "Giant's Boot" for some photo fun and the dramatic point where the stairs step into the sea. Just beyond that, at the asphalt turnaround, you'll see the bus stop for a lift back to the Visitors Centre. You could walk the entire five-mile Giant's Causeway. The 75p hiking guide points out the highlights named by 18th-century guides (Camel's Back, Giant's Eye, and so on). The causeway is free and always open (Visitors Centre open daily 10:00–17:00, July–Aug until 19:00, £5 to park, tel. 028/2073-1855).

▲▲**Carrick-a-Rede Rope Bridge**—For 200 years fishermen have strung a narrow 80-foot-high bridge (planks strung between wires) across a 65-foot-wide chasm between the mainland and a tiny island. The bridge (not the original) still gives access to the salmon nets that are set during the summer months to catch the fish turning the coast's corner. (The complicated system is described at the gateway.) The island affords fine views and great seabird-watching, especially during nesting season (free, April–Sept daily 10:00–18:00, July–Aug until 20:00, gone in winter, 15-min walk from £3 parking lot).

▲**Antrim Mountains and Glens**—Not particularly high (never more than 1,500 feet), the Antrim Mountains are cut by a series of large glens running northeast to the sea. Glenariff, with its waterfalls (especially the "Mare's Tail"), is the most beautiful of the nine glens.

Sleeping in Portrush
(£1 = about $1.50, country code: 44, area code: 028, zip code: BT56 8DG unless otherwise noted)

Sleep Code: **S** = Single, **D** = Double/Twin, **T** = Triple, **Q** = Quad, **b** = bathroom, **s** = shower only, **CC** = Credit Cards accepted, **no CC** = Credit Cards not accepted.

To help you easily sort through these listings, I've divided the rooms into three categories, based on the price for a standard double room with bath:

Higher Priced—Most rooms £70 or more.

Moderately Priced—Most rooms £50–70.

Lower Priced—Most rooms £50 or less.

Portrush has decent hotels, but its B&Bs seem well-worn. August and Saturday nights can be tight. Otherwise it's a "you take half a loaf when you can get it" town. Rates vary with the view and season—probe for softness. Each listing faces the sea, though sea views are worth paying for only if you get a bay window. Ask for a big room (some doubles can be very small; twins are bigger). Lounges are invariably grand and have bay-window views. All places listed have lots of stairs but most are perfectly central and within a few minutes' walk of the train station. Parking is easy.

HIGHER PRICED

Peninsula Hotel is a big, new place right in the town center with huge, fresh rooms, modern decor, and comforts. Ask for a room far from its disco, which can be a problem on party nights (Sb-£50, Db-£70, Tb-£90, breakfast-£5, CC, elevator, 15 Eglinton Street, BT56 8DX, tel. 028/7082-2293, fax 028/7082-4315, www .peninsulahotel.co.uk, e-mail: reservations@peninsulahotel.co.uk).

MODERATELY PRICED

Comfort Hotel, in the middle of town, is a glitzy, modern, 50-room establishment with a good restaurant (Db-£60, breakfast-£7.50 per person, children up to 12 free with adults, CC, elevator,

73 Main Street, BT56 8BN, tel. 028/7082-6100, fax 028/7082-6160, www.comforthotelportrush.com).

Harbour Heights B&B rents 10 cozy rooms and serves £12 dinners, too (Sb-£30, Db-£50–55, 10 percent discount with cash and this book, CC, 17 Kerr Street, Portrush, tel. 028/7082-2765, fax 028/7082-2558, www.harbourheightsportrush .com, e-mail: info@harbourheightsportrush.com, Anne and Robin Rossborough).

LOWER PRICED
Belvedere Town House, a stately place on the quiet side of town with 13 spacious, relatively well-appointed rooms, is the best value in town (S-£19, Sb-£25, D-£34, Db-£40, 5 percent extra for CC, farthest from station but with easy parking is ideal for drivers, at 15 Lansdowne Crescent, Portrush BT56 8AY, tel. 028/7082-2771, e-mail: belvedere16@hotmail.com, Sammy and Winnie Dunn).

Ardenlee B&B is enthusiastically run by Rodney Montgomery and has five bigger-than-average rooms and a fine location near the station (Db-£40–45, £5 discount for 2-night stays, 10 percent discount with this book, 19 Kerr Street, Portrush, tel. 028/7082-2639).

West Strand Guest House has 15 tight, musty rooms, none with private bathrooms (S-£18, D-£35, no CC, fine view lounge, 18 Kerr Street, Portrush, tel. 028/7082-2270, Muriel Robinson).

MacCool's Portrush Youth Hostel is a friendly and laid-back place with 20 beds in four rooms (2, 4, 6, and 8 beds each, £8 per bed, 1 tiny £16 double, no CC, one all-girls room, lockers, guests' kitchen, game-stocked lounge, non-smoking, Internet access, laundry service £3 per load, 5 Causeway View Terrace, midway between station and tip of peninsula, tel. 028/7082-4845).

Anvershiel Guest House, with five non-smoking rooms, is a five-minute walk from the train station (Sb-£25, Db-£40, Tb-£60, £5 discount for 2-night stays and cash, 10 percent discount with this book, CC, easy parking, 16 Coleraine Road, tel. 028/7082-3861, www.anvershiel.co.uk, e-mail: enquiries@anvershiel.co.uk, Victor and Erna Bow). Down the same road is **Glenkeen Guest House** (10 rooms, Sb-£30, Db-£48, Tb-£57, some smoke-free rooms, CC, 10-min walk from station, plenty of parking, 59 Coleraine Road, tel. & fax 028/7082-2279, Mrs. Little).

Eating in Portrush
Being close to a university town (Coleraine) and a get-away-from-Belfast town, Portrush has more than enough chips joints. Eglinton Street is lined with cheap and cheery eateries. For pub grub, consider the **Peninsula Hotel,** or try **Don Giovanni** for decent

Italian (£7–12 pasta dishes, daily 12:30–14:30 & 17:30–23:00, tel. 028/70825516).

The following three restaurants, located within 50 yards of each other, all under the same ownership and overlooking the harbor on Harbour Road, are just about everyone's vote for the best food values in town.

Sharing a building with the Coast Pizza Pasta Bar, the salty, modern, and much-loved **Ramore Wine Bar** is upstairs, bursting with happy eaters. They're enjoying the most inviting menu I've seen in Ireland, featuring huge £6–12 meals ranging from steaks to vegetarian food (daily 12:15–14:15 & 17:00–22:00, CC, tel. 028/7082-4313). Downstairs is the energetic **Coast Pizza Pasta Bar** with good red wine (from £2/glass) as a welcome break after all the Guinness. Come early for a table or sit at the bar (Mon–Fri 17:00–22:00, Sat 16:00–22:30, Sun 15:00–21:30, CC, tel. 028/7082-3311).

The **Harbour Bistro** (run by the Ramore folks, with the same winning formula) offers a more subdued, darker, bistro ambience than the wine bar and meals for a few pounds more (£6 lunches 12:15–14:30, £8–15 dinners, 17:30–22:00, closed Mon, no CC, tel. 028/7082-2430).

The adjoining **Harbour Bar** has an old-fashioned pub downstairs and a plush, overstuffed lounge with a toasty fire and grand views upstairs—a great place to enjoy a drink.

A surprisingly good dining alternative is the **Academy Restaurant** at the Catering College, where local students knock themselves out to give you a great meal (£9 lunches 12:30–14:30, £15 set-menu 5-course dinners 19:00–21:00, closed Mon July–Aug, closed Sun–Mon Sept–June, Ballywillan Road, reservations advised, tel. 028/7082-6201).

Transportation Connections—Portrush

By train to: Coleraine (2/hr, 12 min, sparse on Sunday morning, £1.50), **Belfast** (9/day, 4/Sun, 2 hrs, transfer in Coleraine, £7), **Dublin** (6/day, 1/Sun, 5 hrs, transfer in Coleraine, £23.50). In July and August get a £5 "Day Tracker" ticket, good for all-day train use in Northern Ireland.

By bus to: Belfast (along scenic coast, 2/day, 4 hrs, £7), **Dublin** (1/day, 4.5 hrs).

DERRY

The town of Derry (or Londonderry to Unionists) is the mecca of Ulster Unionism. When Ireland was being divvied up, the Foyle River was the logical border between the North and the Republic. But, for sentimental and economic reasons, the North kept Derry, which is on the Republic's side of the river. Consequently, this predominantly Catholic city has been much contested throughout the Troubles. Still, the conflict is only one dimension of Derry; this pivotal city has a more diverse history and a prettier setting than Belfast. And with a quarter the population, it feels more manageable to visitors.

Planning Your Time

Travelers heading north from Westport or Galway should get an early start (Donegal town makes a good lunch stop), so they can spend a couple hours in Derry and see the essentials. In Derry, visit the Tower Museum and catch some views from the town wall before continuing on to Portrush for the night.

With more time, spend the night in Derry, so you can see the powerful murals of the Bogside and take a walking tour around the walls to gain an appreciation of this underrated city.

Orientation (area code: 028)

The Foyle River flows north, slicing Derry into eastern and western chunks. The old town walls and worthwhile sights are all on the west side. Waterloo Place and the adjacent Guildhall Square, just outside the north corner of the old city walls, are the pedestrian hubs of city activity. The Strand Road area extending north from Waterloo Place makes a comfortable home base, with the majority of lodging and restaurant suggestions within a block or

Derry

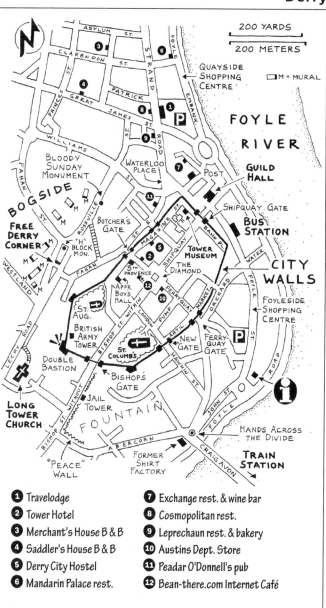

200 YARDS

200 METERS

☐ M = MURAL

FOYLE RIVER

QUAYSIDE SHOPPING CENTRE

GUILD HALL

Post

SHIPQUAY GATE

BUS STATION

CITY WALLS

FOYLESIDE SHOPPING CENTRE

TOWER MUSEUM

THE DIAMOND

BOGSIDE

FREE DERRY CORNER

BLOODY SUNDAY MONUMENT

WATERLOO PLACE

BUTCHER'S GATE

"H" BLOCK MON.

5TH PROVENCE

APPR. BOYS' HALL

ST. AUG.

BRITISH ARMY TOWER

DOUBLE BASTION

ST. COLUMB'S

BISHOP'S GATE

JAIL TOWER

LONG TOWER CHURCH

FOUNTAIN

NEW GATE

FERRY QUAY GATE

HANDS ACROSS THE DIVIDE

TRAIN STATION

FORMER SHIRT FACTORY

"PEACE" WALL

Streets: ASYLUM ST., CLARENDON ST., STRAND, FOYLE ST., PATRICK, GREAT JAMES ST., PRINCES, WILLIAMS, FAHAN, ROSSVILLE, WESTLAND, EMBANK, ROAD, MAGAZINE ST., SHIPQUAY, BANK PL., WATER ST., ORCHARD, FOYLE, MARKET, FERRYQUAY, PUMP ST., LONDON ST., WITHIN, ARTIL, HAWKIN ST., BISHOP ST. WITHOUT, JOHN ST., LECKY ROAD, ABERCORN, CRAIGAVON

❶ Travelodge
❷ Tower Hotel
❸ Merchant's House B & B
❹ Saddler's House B & B
❺ Derry City Hostel
❻ Mandarin Palace rest.
❼ Exchange rest. & wine bar
❽ Cosmopolitan rest.
❾ Leprechaun rest. & bakery
❿ Austins Dept. Store
⓫ Peadar O'Donnell's pub
⓬ Bean-there.com Internet Café

Derry History

Once an island in the Foyle River, Derry (from *daire*, Irish for "oak grove") was chosen by St. Colmcille around 546 for a monastic settlement. He later banished himself to the island of Iona in Scotland out of remorse for sparking a bloody battle over the rights to a holy manuscript he had secretly copied.

A thousand years later, after defeating the last powerful Ulster-based Gaelic chieftains in the battle of Kinsale in 1601, the English took advantage of the power vacuum to begin the "plantation" of Ulster with loyal Protestant subjects imported from Scotland and England. The native Irish were displaced to less desirable rocky or boggy lands (sowing the seeds of the modern-day Troubles). A dozen wealthy London guilds took on Derry as an investment and changed its name to Londonderry. They built the last great walled city in Ireland to protect their investment from the surrounding hostile Irish locals. The walls proved their worth in 1688–1689 when the town's Protestant defenders, loyal to King William of Orange, withstood a prolonged siege by the forces of Catholic King James II. "No surrender" is still a passionate rallying cry among Ulster Unionists determined to remain part of the United Kingdom.

The town became a major port of emigration to the New World in the early 1800s. Then when the Industrial Revolution provided a steam-powered sewing factory, the city developed a thriving shirt-making industry, employing mostly Catholic women who had honed their skills in rural county Donegal in what was initially a cottage industry. Although Belfast grew larger

two on either side. The Diamond and its War Memorial statue mark the heart of the old city within the walls.

Tourist Information: The TI sits on the riverfront and has a room-finding service, books, walking tours, and free city maps (Mon–Fri 9:00–17:00, Sat 10:00–17:00, closed Sun, tel. 028/7126-7284, www.derryvisitor.com).

Arrival in Derry: Derry is compact enough to see on foot, so drivers stopping for a few hours can park at the Foyleside parking garage across from the TI (£0.70/hr, £1.80/4 hrs, Mon–Tue 8:00–19:00, Wed–Fri 8:00–22:00, Sat 8:00–20:00, Sun 12:00–19:00, tel. 028/7137-7575). Drivers staying overnight can ask about parking at their B&B or try the Quayside parking garage behind the Travelodge (£0.50/hr, £1.80/4 hrs, £1/hr after first 6 hours, Mon–Fri 8:00–21:30, Sat 8:00–20:30, Sun 12:30–18:30).

and wealthier, Unionists cherished Londonderry and in 1921 insisted that it be included in Northern Ireland when it was partitioned from the new Irish Free State (later to become the Republic of Ireland). A bit of gerrymandering ensured that the Unionist Protestant minority maintained control of the city despite the Nationalist Catholic majority.

Londonderry was a key escort base for U.S. convoys headed for Britain in World War II, and dozens of German U-boats were instructed to surrender here at the end of the war. Poor Catholics unable to find housing took over the abandoned military barracks, with multiple families living in each dwelling. Only homeowners were allowed to vote and the Unionist minority controlling city government was not eager to build more housing that would tip the voting balance away from them. Sectarian pressures built over years until 1972, when the ugly events of Bloody Sunday brought worldwide attention to the Troubles (see "Murals of Bogside," below).

Today, life has stabilized in Derry, and the population has increased by 25 percent in the last 30 years to about 105,000. The modern Foyleside Shopping Centre, bankrolled by investors from Boston, was completed in 1995. The 1998 Good Friday Peace Accord has provided a two-steps-forward, one-step-back progress, and the British Army has become less visible. With a population that is 70 percent Catholic, the city has agreed to alternate Nationalist and Unionist mayors. There is a feeling of cautious optimism as Derry, the scene of bombs and bloody conflicts in the 1960s and 1970s, now boasts a history museum that airs all viewpoints.

Derry's end-of-the-line little train station is on the east side of town (15-min walk across Craigavon Bridge from the TI) with service to Portrush, Belfast, and Dublin. The Ulsterbus station is a couple minutes' walk from Guildhall Square.

Helpful Hints

Phone Tips: To call the Republic of Ireland from Northern Ireland, dial 00-353, then the area code without its initial 0, then the local number. To call Northern Ireland from the Republic of Ireland, dial 048, then the local eight-digit number.

Post Office: The main post office is just off Waterloo Place behind the Guild Hall (Mon–Fri 9:00–17:30, Sat 9:00–12:30, closed Sun, Custom House Street).

Banks: Northern Bank, First Trust Bank, Ulster Bank, and

Bank of Ireland cluster around Waterloo Place and Guildhall Square (all Mon–Fri 9:30–16:30).

Laundry: City Clean can do a load of laundry for £5 (drop off in morning to pick up later that day, Mon–Sat 9:00–17:30, closed Sun, Waterloo Place, tel. 028/7126-7100).

Internet Access: Bean-there.com Internet Café is on the Diamond in the center of the old walled city (£2.50/30 min, Mon–Sat 9:30–18:30, Sun 14:00–18:00, tel. 028/7128-1303).

Bike Rental: Try Happy Days Cycle Hire (tel. 028/7128-7128, www.happydays.ie).

Taxi: Try Maiden City Taxi (tel. 028/7126-1666) or Sackville Taxi (tel. 028/7135-4442).

Walking Tours

The **TI** offers solid 90-minute tours (£4, July–Aug Mon–Fri 11:15 and 15:15, June and Sept Mon–Fri until 14:30 only, tel. 028/7126-7284). **Derry City Hostel** operates 90-minute tours from the old town wall (£4, daily 10:00, 14:00, 16:00, and 19:00, call to confirm schedule, tel. 028/7128-0280, www.irishtourguides.com).

Self-Guided Walking Tours

Walk the Walls

Squatting determinedly in the city center, the old city walls of Derry (built 1613–1618 and still intact except for wider gates to handle modern vehicles) hold an almost mythic place in Irish history. It was here in 1688 that a group of brave apprentice boys (many of whom had been shipped to Londonderry as orphans after the Great Fire of London in 1666) galvanized the city's indecisive Protestant defenders by slamming the city gates in the face of the approaching Catholic forces of deposed King James II. Months of negotiations and a grinding 105-day siege followed, during which a third of the 20,000 refugees and defenders crammed into the city perished. The siege was finally broken in 1689 when supply ships broke through a boom stretched across the Foyle River. The sacrifice and defiant survival of the city turned the tide in favor of newly crowned Protestant King William of Orange, who arrived in Ireland soon after and defeated James at the pivotal Battle of the Boyne.

To fully appreciate the walls, take a walk on top of them (free and open dawn to dusk). Almost 20 feet high and at least as thick, the walls form a mile-long oval loop that you can cover in less than an hour. But the most interesting section is the half-circuit facing away from the river, starting at Magazine Gate (stairs face the Tower Museum inside the walls) and finishing at Bishop's Gate.

From Magazine Gate, walk the wall as it heads uphill, snaking along the earth's contours like a mini–Great Wall of China. In the row of buildings on the left (just before crossing over Castle Gate), you'll see an arch entry into the **Craft Village,** an alley lined with a cluster of cute shops that showcase the recent economic rejuvenation of Derry (Mon–Sat 9:30–17:30, closed Sun). After crossing over Butcher Gate, you'll pass a large square pedestal on the right that once supported a column in honor of Governor George Walker, the commander of the defenders during the famous siege. The column, which had 105 steps to the top (one for each day of the siege), was blown up in 1973 by the IRA.

Ahead on the left at the corner of Society Street is the **Apprentice Boys Memorial Hall** (built 1873), which houses the private lodge and meeting rooms of this all-male Protestant organization dedicated to the memory of the original 13 apprentice boys. The end of the siege is celebrated each year with a controversial march atop the walls by the modern-day Apprentice Boys Society on the Saturday closest to the August 12 anniversary date. A few more steps take you past the small Anglican **St. Augustine Chapel** set in a pretty graveyard where some believe the original sixth-century monastery of St. Colmcille stood.

As you walk ahead, it's hard to miss the British Army surveillance tower on the left. It's situated here for the bird's-eye view it affords of the once-turbulent Catholic **Bogside** district below. Stop at the Double Bastion fortified platform that occupies this corner of the city walls. The old cannon is nicknamed "Roaring Meg" for the fury of its firing during the siege.

From here you can see across the Bogside to the not-so-far-away hills of county Donegal in the Republic. Derry was once an island, but as the river gradually changed its course, the area below began to drain. Over time, and especially after the Potato Famine (1845–1849), Catholic peasants from rural Donegal began to move into Derry to find work and settled on this least desirable land... on the bog side of the city. Directly below and to the right are Free Derry Corner and Rossville Street, where the tragic events of Bloody Sunday took place in 1972 (see "Murals of the Bogside," below). Below on the left is the 18th-century Long Tower Catholic church, named after the medieval round tower that once stood in the area (see "Long Tower Church," below). The building behind you (next to the army tower) is a former Presbyterian school that now houses the **Verbal Arts Centre,** which promotes the development of poetry, drama, writing, and storytelling.

Continuing another 50 yards around the corner, you'll reach Bishop's Gate, from which you can look down Bishop Street Without (outside the walls) and Bishop Street Within (inside the walls), while another, shorter British Army surveillance tower peeks over your shoulder. Take a moment to look at the wall topped by a high mesh fence running along the left side of Bishop Street Without. This is a "peace wall," built to ensure the security of the Protestant enclave living behind it in the Fountain neighborhood. When the Troubles reignited 30 years ago, there were 20,000 Protestants living on this side of the river. Sadly, today this small housing estate of 1,500 people is all that remains of that proud community. The rest have chosen to move across the river to the Waterside district. The old brick tower halfway down the peace wall was part of the old jail that briefly held doomed rebel Wolfe Tone, after the 1798 revolt against the English.

From Bishop's Gate, those short of time can descend from the walls and walk 15 minutes directly back through the heart of the old city, along Bishop Street Within and Shipquay Street to Guildhall Square. With more time, consider visiting St. Columb's Anglican Cathedral, the Long Tower Catholic Church, and the Murals of the Bogside (all described below).

Murals of the Bogside

The Catholic Bogside area was the tinderbox of the modern Troubles in Northern Ireland. A terrible confrontation 30 years ago sparked a sectarian inferno and the ashes have not yet fully cooled. Today, the murals of the Bogside give visitors an accessible glimpse of this community's passionate perception of those events.

Inspired by civil rights marches in America in the mid-1960s and the 1968 Prague Spring uprising, civil rights groups began protest marches in Northern Ireland. Their goals were to gain better housing, secure fair voting rights, and end employment discrimination for Catholics in the North. Tensions mounted, and clashes with the predominantly Protestant Royal Ulster Constabulary police force became frequent. Eventually the British Army was called in to keep the peace. On January 30, 1972, a group protesting internment without trial held an illegal march through the Bogside neighborhood. They were fired upon by members of a British regiment, who claimed that snipers had fired on them first. The tragic result of the clash, now remembered as **Bloody Sunday,** was the death of 14 civilians and a flood of fresh IRA volunteers.

The events are memorialized in eight murals painted on the ends of residential flats along a 200-yard stretch of Rossville Street and Lecky Road where the march took place. You can reach them from Waterloo Place via William Street, from the old city walls at Butcher's Gate down the long set of stairs on the grassy hillside,

Murals of the Bogside

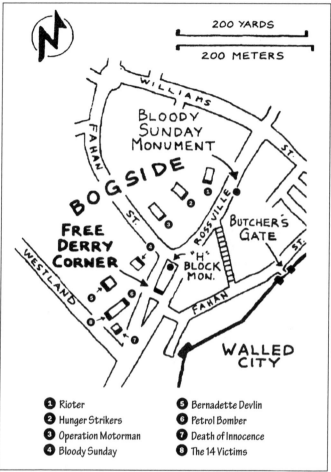

200 YARDS

200 METERS

WILLIAMS

BLOODY
SUNDAY
MONUMENT

BOGSIDE

FAHAN

ST.

❶ ❷ ❸

ST.

ROSSVILLE

FREE
DERRY
CORNER

WESTLAND

❹

❺ ❻

❽

❼

"H"
BLOCK
MON.

BUTCHER'S
GATE

ST.

FAHAN

WALLED
CITY

❶ Rioter   ❺ Bernadette Devlin
❷ Hunger Strikers   ❻ Petrol Bomber
❸ Operation Motorman ❼ Death of Innocence
❹ Bloody Sunday   ❽ The 14 Victims

or by the stairs leading down from the Long Tower Church.
These days, this neighborhood is quiet and safe.

The murals were begun in 1994 by two brothers and their
childhood friend, all of whom grew up in the Bogside during the
tragic events. One of the brothers, Tom Kelly, gained a reputation as
a "heritage mural" painter, specializing in scenes of life in the old
days. In a surprising and hopeful development, Kelly was invited to
Derry's Protestant Fountain neighborhood to work with a youth
club there to paint three heritage murals over paramilitary graffiti.

Political Murals

The dramatic and emotional murals you'll encounter in Northern Ireland will likely be one of the enduring travel memories you'll take home with you. They evolved from the colorful annual displays of flags and streamers that were hung each July in Protestant neighborhoods during the 18th century to commemorate the victory of King William III at the Battle of the Boyne. With the advent of industrial paints, these temporary seasonal displays became permanent territorial statements during the extended debate that eventually led to the partitioning of the island in 1921 and the creation of Northern Ireland. Murals expressing opposing views in Catholic neighborhoods were outlawed until the eruption of the modern Troubles, when staunchly Nationalist Catholic communities isolated themselves behind barricades, excluding state control and gaining freedom to express their pent-up passions.

In Derry, this form of symbolic, cultural, and ideological resistance first appeared in 1969 with the simple "You are now entering Free Derry" message that you'll still see painted on the surviving gable wall at Free Derry corner.

Found most often in working-class neighborhoods of Belfast and Derry, today's political murals have become a dynamic form of popular culture, blurring the line between art and propaganda, and giving visitors a striking glimpse of each community's history, identity, and values.

The Bogside murals face a few directions (and some partially hidden by buildings not shown on map), so they're not all visible from a single viewpoint. Plan on walking about three blocks along Rossville Street (which becomes Lecky Road) to see them all. Locals are used to visitors and don't mind if you photograph the murals.

The best place to start is at the **Bloody Sunday Monument** on Rossville Street. This small, fenced-off stone obelisk lists the names of those who died that day, most within 50 yards of this spot. From here, walk south toward Free Derry Corner (described below) and the murals will all be on your right.

Look for *The Rioter*, which depicts a youth holding a stone while a British armored vehicle approaches (echoing the famous Tiananmen Square photo of the lone man facing the tank).

The next mural, *Hunger Strikers*, features two long-haired men wearing blankets. It represents the IRA prisoners who refused to wear the uniforms of common criminals in an attempt to force the British to treat them instead as political prisoners (who were allowed to wear their own clothes).

Next, in *Operation Motorman*, a soldier wields a sledgehammer, depicting the massive push by the British Army to open up the Bogside's barricaded "no-go" areas that the IRA had controlled for three years.

Cross over to the grassy median strip that runs down the middle of Rossville Street. At one end is the white wall of **Free Derry Corner,** announcing "You are now entering Free Derry" (imitating a similar defiant slogan at the time in West Berlin). At the other end of the median strip stands a concrete letter *H* inscribed with the names of the 10 IRA hunger strikers who died in H-block of the Maze prison in 1981.

From here, you can see *Bloody Sunday,* in which a small group of men are carrying a body from the civil rights march. It's taken from a famous photo of Father Daly waving a white handkerchief requesting safe passage. The soldier standing on the blood-stained civil rights banner was inserted into the scene for extra emphasis.

Nearby is *Bernadette Devlin.* The woman with the megaphone is Bernadette Devlin McAliskey, an outspoken civil rights leader who became the youngest elected member of Parliament. Behind her kneels a woman supporter banging a trash-can lid against the ground in a traditional expression of protest in Republican neighborhoods.

Petrol Bomber, with the teen wearing a gas mask, captures the Battle of the Bogside, when locals barricaded off their community, effectively shutting out British rule.

Leave the grassy median strip and cross back over to the sidewalk, walking farther south along what is now Lecky Road.

In *The Death of Innocence,* a young girl stands in front of the bomb wreckage. She is Annette McGavigan, a 14-year-old who was killed in crossfire in the Bogside. The gun beside her points to the ground, no longer lethal. The large butterfly above her shoulder symbolizes the hope for peace. The artists have said they will return to add a rising sun when they feel confident that the peace process has succeeded.

Finally, around the corner, you'll see a circle of male faces. This mural, painted in 1997 to observe the 25th anniversary of the tragedy, is called *Bloody Sunday Commemoration* and shows the 14 victims.

Nationalist leader John Hume (Nobel Peace Prize co-winner in 1998 with Unionist leader David Trimble) still has a house in the Bogside. He once borrowed an old quote to explain his non-violent approach to the peace process when he said: "An eye for an eye just ends up leaving everyone blind."

Sights—Derry

▲▲**Tower Museum Derry**—Housed in a modern reconstruction of a fortified medieval towerhouse belonging to the local O'Doherty clan, this well-organized museum provides an excellent introduction to the city and sorts out some of the tangled historical roots of Northern Ireland's Troubles. Combining modern audiovisuals with historical artifacts, the displays tell the story of the city from a skillfully unbiased viewpoint. Starting with the city's monastic origins 1500 years ago and moving through pivotal events such as the 1688–1689 siege and unexpected blips like Amelia Earhart's emergency landing, they'll give you a better handle on what makes this unique city tick. Catch the thought-provoking 14-minute film in the small theater, which gives an evenhanded local perspective on the tragic events of the sectarian conflict. As you exit the small theater, scan the displays of paramilitary paraphernalia in the hallway lined with colored curb stones—red, white, and blue Union Jack colors for Loyalists; and green, white, and orange Irish tricolor for Republicans. There, you'll find tiny notes written by IRA hunger-striker Bobby Sands, that were smuggled out of the Maze prison (£4.50, July–Aug Mon–Sat 10:00–17:00, Sun 14:00–17:00, Sept–June Tue–Sat 10:00–17:00, closed Sun–Mon, Union Hall Place, tel. 028/7137-2411).

Guild Hall—This neo-Gothic building, complete with clock tower, is the ceremonial seat of city government. It first opened in 1890 on reclaimed lands that were once the mudflats of the Foyle River. Destroyed by fire and rebuilt in 1913, it was massively damaged by IRA bombs in 1972. In an ironic twist, Gerry Doherty, one of those convicted of the bombings, was elected as a member of the City Council a dozen years later. Inside are the Council Chamber, party offices, and an assembly hall featuring stained-glass windows showing scenes from Derry history. Check to see when tours are available—usually when civic and cultural events are not taking place inside (Mon–Fri 9:00–17:00, tel. 028/7137-7335).

Hands across the Divide—Designed by local teacher Maurice Harron after the fall of the Iron Curtain, this powerful metal sculpture of two figures extending their hands to each other was inspired by the growing hope for peace and reconciliation in Northern Ireland (located in a roundabout at the west end of Craigavon Bridge).

The abandoned Tillie & Henerson's shirt factory (opened in 1857) looms above the figures. The Derry shirt industry once employed over 15,000 workers (90 percent were women) in sweathouses typical of the human toll of Industrial Revolution. Karl Marx mentioned the factory in *Das Kapital* as an example of women's transition from domestic to industrial work lives.

The Fifth Province—This dreamy Celtic theme ride tries hard but ends up being just for kids. It's a quirky 45-minute multimedia romp through Ireland's heritage that has you sitting in a "time chariot" wondering how New Age mysticism connects with the NASA space program (£3, Mon–Fri at 11:30 and 14:30, Calgach Centre, 4–22 Butcher Street, tel. 028/7137-3177).

St. Columb's Cathedral—Marked by the tall spire inside the walls, this Anglican Cathedral was built from 1628 to 1633 in a style called "Planter's Gothic." Its construction was financed by the same London companies that backed the plantation of Londonderry. This was the first Protestant cathedral built in Great Britain after the Reformation. It played an important part in the defense of the city during the siege, when cannons were mounted on its roof and the original spire was scavenged for lead to melt into cannon shot. In the entryway, you'll find a hollow cannonball that was lobbed into the city, containing the besiegers' surrender terms. Inside along the nave hangs a musty collection of battle flags and Union Jacks that once inspired troops during the siege, the Crimean War, and World War II. The American flag hangs among them, from the time when the first GIs to enter the European theater in World War II were based in Northern Ireland. Check out the small chapter-house museum in the back of the church to see the original locks of the gates of Londonderry and more relics of the siege (£1, Mon–Sat 9:00–17:00, closed Sun, tel. 028/7126-7313).

Long Tower Church—Built below the walls on the hillside above the Bogside, this modest-looking church is worth a visit for its stunning high alter. The name comes from a stone monastic round tower that stood here for centuries but was destroyed for city building materials in the 1600s. The oldest Catholic church in Derry, it was finished in 1786 during a time of enlightened relations between the city's two religious communities. Protestant Bishop Hervey gave a generous-for-the-time £200 donation and had the four Corinthian columns shipped in from Naples to frame the neo-Renaissance altar (free, Mon–Sat 7:30–20:30, Sun 7:30–19:00, tel. 028/7126-2301). Hidden outside behind the church and facing the Bogside is a simple shrine beneath a hawthorn tree marking the spot where outlawed Masses were held secretly before this church was built, during the infamous Penal Law period of the early 1700s. Through the Penal Laws, the English attempted to weaken Catholicism's influence by banishing priests and forbidding Catholics from buying land, attending school, voting, and holding office.

Sleeping in Derry
(£1 = about $1.50, country code: 44, area code: 028)
Sleep Code: **S** = Single, **D** = Double/Twin, **T** = Triple, **Q** = Quad, **b** = bathroom, **s** = shower only, **CC** = Credit Cards accepted, **no CC** = Credit Cards not accepted.

To help you easily sort through these listings, I've divided the rooms into three categories, based on the price for a standard double room with bath:

Higher Priced—Most rooms £70 or more.
Moderately Priced—Most rooms £40–70.
Lower Priced—Most rooms £40 or less.

HIGHER PRICED

Travelodge has 40 comfortable rooms in a great location with a handy adjacent parking garage (Db-£50 Mon–Thu, Db-£43 Fri–Sun, CC, 22–24 Strand Road, Derry BT47 7AB, tel. 028/7127-1271, fax 028/7127-1277, www.travelodge.co.uk).

The **Tower Hotel** is the only hotel actually inside Derry's historic walls. It's a real splurge, with 90 modern and immaculate rooms, a classy bistro restaurant, and private basement parking (Sb-£69, Db-£89, cheaper Fri–Sun, CC, Butcher Street, Derry BT48 6HL, tel. 028/7137-1000, fax 028/7137-1234, www.towerhotelgroup.com, e-mail: reservations@thd.ie).

MODERATELY PRICED

Merchant's House, on a quiet street a 10-minute stroll from Waterloo Place, is a fine Georgian townhouse with marble fireplaces, ornate plasterwork, and a grand, colorful drawing room (S-£20, Sb-£25, D-£40, Db-£45, CC, 16 Queen Street, Derry BT48 7EQ, tel. 028/7126-9691, fax 028/7126-6913, www.thesaddlershouse.com, Joan & Peter Pyne).

Saddler's House, run by the owners of Merchant's House, is a charming Victorian townhouse with seven rooms located a couple blocks closer to the old town walls (Sb-£25, Db-£45, CC, 36 Great James Street, Derry BT48 7DB, tel. 028/7126-9691, fax 028/7126-6913, www.thesaddlershouse.com).

LOWER PRICED

Derry City Hostel sits just inside the old city walls with decent dorm beds (4–10 beds per room) and some private rooms run by a helpful, friendly staff (dorm beds-£10–13, S-£15, Db-£36, non-smoking, kitchen, continental breakfast-£1.50, full Irish breakfast-£3, 4–6 Magazine Street, Derry BT48 6HJ, tel. 028/7128-0280, fax 028/7128-0281, e-mail: derrycitytours@aol.com).

Eating in Derry

The **Mandarin Palace** serves up good £8–12 Chinese dinners in a crisp dining room facing the river (daily 16:30–23:30, Queens Quay at Lower Clarendon Street, tel. 028/7137-3656).

The trendy **Exchange Restaurant & Wine Bar** offers

quality dinners with a hip flair for £10–12, in a central location near the river behind Waterloo Place (Mon–Sat 12:00–22:00, Sun 17:00–21:30, Queen's Quay, tel. 028/7127-3990).

The **Cosmopolitan Restaurant,** above the lively Strand Bar, serves up hearty pub grub (daily 17:00–22:30, 31–35 Strand Road, tel. 028/7126-6400).

For a dependable cafeteria-style lunch, try the **Leprechaun Restaurant & Bakery** (Mon–Sat 9:00–17:30, closed Sun, 21–23 Strand Road, tel. 028/7136-3606).

Right on the Diamond in the center of the old city, **Austins Department Store** has a top-floor café with some nice views and £6 lunch specials (Mon–Sat 9:30–17:30, closed Sun, 2–6 The Diamond, tel. 028/7137-7727).

Chat with locals in pubs that rarely see a tourist. Try **Peadar O'Donnell's** pub on Waterloo street for Derry's best nightly ballad sessions (53 Waterloo Street, tel. 028/7137-2318).

Supermarkets: Tesco has everything for picnics and road munchies (Mon–Thu 9:00–21:00, Fri 8:30–21:00, Sat 8:30–20:00, Sun 13:00–18:00, corner of Strand Road and Clarendon Street). Super Valu meets the same needs with the same hours (Waterloo Place).

Transportation Connections—Derry

From Derry it's less than an hour's drive to Portrush, a town much more clearly British.

By train to: Portrush (9/day, 1 hr), **Belfast** (9/day, 2 hrs), **Dublin** (6/day, 5 hrs).

By bus to: Galway (4/day, 6 hrs), **Portrush** (4/day, 1.25 hrs), **Belfast** (16/day, 1.75 hrs), **Dublin** (5/day, 4.5 hrs).

Sights between Galway and Derry

Allow a long day for the drive from Galway to Derry (or Portrush) with these interesting stops along the way (leave Galway heading north on N17):

Knock—In this tiny town in 1879, locals saw the Virgin Mary and Joseph appear against the south gable of the church. Word of miraculous healings turned the trickle of pilgrims into a flood and put Knock solidly on the pilgrimage map. Today you can visit the shrine. At the edge of the site, a small but interesting folk museum shows "evidence" of the healings, photos of a papal visit, and interesting slices of traditional life.

Belleek Pottery Visitors Centre—After a stretch of scenic coastline and just over the Northern Ireland border, you reach the cute town of Belleek, famous for its pottery. The Belleek Parian China factory welcomes visitors with a small gallery and museum (Mon–Fri 9:00–18:00, less on weekends and off-season), a 20-minute video, a cheery cafeteria, and fascinating 30-minute tours of its working factory (tours £3, Mon–Sat 9:30–16:15, call to confirm schedule and reserve a spot, tel. 028/6865-8501).

Ulster American Folk Park—North of Omagh, this museum shows life before emigration, on the boat, and in America for the many Irish who left their homeland during the hard times in the 19th century (£4, £2.50 for children, seniors, students; April–Sept Mon–Sat 10:30–16:30, Sun 11:00–17:00, Oct–March Mon–Fri 10:30–15:30, closed Sat–Sun, tel. 028/8224-3292, e-mail: uafp@iol.ie.

IRELAND: PAST AND PRESENT

One surprising aspect of Ireland is the richness of its history, art, and language. And the country continues to transform and grow today, building on an ever-stronger economy, searching for peace, and reexamining some of its long-held social customs.

Irish History

Hunters, Farmers, and Mysterious Mounds (Prehistory)

Ireland became an island when rising seas covered the last land bridge (7000 B.C.), a separation from Britain that the Irish would fight to maintain for the next 9,000 years. By 6000 B.C., Stone Age hunter-fishers had settled on the East Coast, followed by Neolithic farmers (from the island of Britain). These early inhabitants left behind impressive but mysterious funeral mounds (passage graves) and large Stonehenge-type stone circles.

The Celts: Language and Legends (500 B.C.–A.D. 500)

The Celtic peoples from Central Europe (particularly the tribe called the Gaels) settled in Ireland, where they would rule for a thousand years. A warrior people with over a hundred petty kings, they feuded constantly with rival clans and gathered in ring forts for protection. The island was nominally ruled by a single high king at the Hill of Tara (near Dublin), though there was in fact no centralized nation.

Druid priests conducted pagan, solar-calendar rituals among the megalithic stones erected by earlier inhabitants. The Celtic people peppered the countryside with thousands of Iron Age monuments. While most of what you'll see will be little more than rock piles that take a vigorous imagination to reconstruct (ring forts, wedge tombs, monumental stones, and so on), just standing next to a megalith that predates the pharaohs is evocative.

The Celtic world lives on today in the Gaelic language and in legends of Celtic warriors such as Finn McCool—the "Gaelic King Arthur"—who led a merry band of heroes in battle and in play. Tourists marvel at large, ritual stones decorated with ogham (rhymes with "poem") script, the peculiar Celtic-Latin alphabet that used lines as letters. The Tara Brooch and elaborately inscribed, jewel-encrusted daggers attest to the sophistication of this warrior society (see the National Museum in Dublin).

In 55 B.C., the Romans conquered the Celts in Britain, but Ireland remained independent, its history forever skewed in a

What's a Celt?

The Irish are a Celtic people. The Celts, who came from Central Europe, began migrating west around 1500 B.C. Over time, many settled in the British Isles and western France. When the Angles and Saxons came later, grabbing the best land in the British Isles (which became Angle-land...or England), the Celts survived in Brittany, Cornwall, Wales, Scotland, and Ireland. Today this "Celtic Crescent" still nearly encircles England. The word Celtic (pronounced with a hard *C*) comes from the Greek "Keltoi," meaning barbarian.

From about 700 B.C. on, various Celtic tribes mixed, mingled, and fought in Ireland. The last and most powerful of the Celtic tribes to enter the fray were the Gaels, who probably came from Scotland. The Irish language, Gaelic, is named for them. The fact that the Celts never had a written language meant that they had to pass their history, laws, and folklore down verbally from generation to generation. This may well account for the "gift of gab" attributed to today's Irish.

Celtic society revolved around warrior kings who gathered groups of families into regional kingdoms. These small kingdoms combined to make the five large provincial kingdoms of ancient Ireland (whose names survive on maps today): Leinster, Munster, Connacht, Ulster, and the Middle Kingdom (now County Meath).

For defensive purposes, these early Irish lived in small thatched huts built on man-made islands or on high ground surrounded by ditches and a stone or earthen wall. A strictly observed hierarchy governed Celtic societies: the king on top, followed by poets, Druid

different direction—Gaelic, not Latin. The Romans called Ireland Hibernia, or Land of Winter; it was apparently too cold and bleak to merit an attempt at colonization. The biggest nonevent in Irish history is that the Romans never invaded. While the mix of Celtic and Roman is part of what makes the French French and the English English, the Irish are purely Celtic. If France is *boules* and England is cricket, then Ireland is hurling. This wild Irish national pastime (like airborne hockey with no injury time-outs) goes back more than 2,000 years to Celtic days.

Christianity: Monks and Scholars (A.D. 500–800)

When Ancient Rome fell and took the Continent with it, Gaelic Ireland remained. There was no Dark Age here, and the island priests, doctors, legal men, skilled craftsmen, freemen, and slaves. Rarely did a high king rule the entire island. Loyalty to one's clan came first and alliances between clans were often temporary until a more advantageous alliance could be struck with a rival clan. This fluid system of alliances ebbing and flowing across the Celtic-warrior cultural landscape meant that the Celts would never unite as a single nation.

While Celtic society was male-dominated, a king needed a warrior-goddess queen to ensure the kingdom's fertility and power. One major goddess was Brigit, later adopted by Christians as St. Brigid. She was worshiped as goddess of healing, fertility, and poetry. Her sacred fire burned in Ireland (on a site in modern-day County Kildare) from ancient times until the English extinguished it.

Unlike the Celtic tribes living in Western Europe and Britain, the Celts in Ireland were never conquered by the Romans. This gives Ireland a cultural continuity and uniqueness rare in Europe. Their culture—which evolved apart from Europe—remained strong and independent for centuries. Then, in the 12th century, English dominance began leading to suppression of Gaelic language and Celtic traditions. With Irish independence—won only in the 20th century—Irish ways are no longer threatened. The most traditional areas (generally along the West Coast, such as the Dingle Peninsula) are protected as Gaeltachts. Gaeltachts (literally, places where the Gaelic language is spoken) are a kind of national park for the traditional culture. If much of Ireland's charm can be credited to its Celtic roots, you'll find that charm most vivid in a Gaeltacht.

was a beacon of culture for the rest of Europe. Ireland (population c. 750,000) was still a land of many feuding kings, but the culture was stable.

Christianity and Latin culture arrived first as a trickle from trading contacts with Christian Gaul, then more emphatically in A.D. 432 with St. Patrick, who persuasively converted the sun-worshiping Celts. Perhaps St. Patrick had an easy time converting the locals because they had so little sun to worship. Patrick (c. 389–461), a Latin-speaking Christian from Roman Britain, was kidnapped as a teenager and carried off into slavery for six years in Ireland. He escaped back to Britain, then, inspired by a dream, returned to Ireland, determined to convert the pagan, often-hostile Celtic inhabitants. Legends say he drove Ireland's snakes (symbolic of pagan beliefs) into the sea and explained the Trinity with a shamrock (three leaves on one stem).

Later monks (such as St. Columba, 521–597) continued Christianizing the island, and foreign monks flocked to isolated Ireland. They withdrew to scattered, isolated monasteries, living in Celtic-style beehive huts, translating and illustrating (illuminating) manuscripts. Perhaps the greatest works of art of Dark Age Europe are these manuscripts, including the ninth-century Book of Kells, which you'll see at Dublin's Trinity College (see "Irish Art," page 245). Irish monks—heads shaved cross-wise from ear to ear, like former Druids—were known throughout Europe as ascetic scholars.

St. Columbanus (c. 600) was one of several traveling, missionary monks who helped to bring Christianity back to Western Europe, which had reverted to paganism and barbarism when Rome fell. The monks established monastic centers of learning that produced great Christian teachers and community builders. One of the monks, St. Brendan, may have even sailed to America (see page 120).

By 800, Charlemagne was importing Irish monks to help run his Frankish kingdom. Meanwhile, Ireland remained a relatively cohesive society based on monastic settlements rather than cities. Impressive round towers from those settlements still dot the Irish landscape—silent reminders of this glorious age.

Viking Invasion and Defeat (800–1100)
In 795, Viking pirates from Norway invaded, the first of many raids that wreaked havoc on the monasteries and shook Irish civilization. In two centuries of chaos, the Vikings raped, pillaged, and burned Christian churches. Monks stood guard from their round towers to spy approaching marauders, ring the warning bells, and protect the citizens. In 841, a conquering Viking band settled inland, building Ireland's first permanent walled cities, Dublin and Waterford. Viking raiders slowly evolved into Viking traders who, among other things, introduced the concept of coinage to the Irish.

Finally, High King Brian Boru led a Gaelic revival, defeating a mercenary Viking army allied with rebellious Leinster clans, at the Battle of Clontarf (1014), near Dublin. Boru died in the battle, however, and his unified kingdom quickly fell apart. Over the centuries, Viking settlers married Gaelic gals and slowly blended in.

Anglo-Norman Arrival (1100–1500)
The Normans were Ireland's next uninvited guests. In 1169, a small army of well-armed and fearless soldiers of fortune invaded Ireland under the pretense of helping a deposed Irish king regain his lands. A Welsh conquistador named Strongbow (c. 1130–1176) took Dublin and Waterford, married the local king's daughter,

then succeeded his father-in-law as king of Leinster. This was the spearhead of a century-long invasion by the so-called Anglo-Normans—the French-speaking rulers of England, descended from William the Conqueror and his troops, who had invaded and conquered England at the Battle of Hastings (1066).

King Henry II of England soon followed (1171) to remind Strongbow who was boss, proclaiming the entire island under English (Anglo-Norman) rule. By 1250, the Anglo-Normans occupied three-quarters of the island, clustered in walled cities surrounded by hostile Gaels. These invaders, who were big-time administrators, ushered in a new age in which society (government, cities, and religious organizations) was organized on a grander scale. Riding on the coat tails of the Normans, monastic orders (Franciscans, Augustinians, and Cistercians) came over from the Continent and eclipsed Ireland's individual monastic settlements, once the foundation of Irish society in the Age of Saints and Scholars.

But English rule was weak and distant. Preoccupied with the Hundred Years' War with France and its own internal Wars of the Roses, England "ruled" through deputized locals such as the earls of Kildare. Many English landowners actually resided in England, a pattern of absentee-landlordism that would exist for centuries. England only physically occupied the tiny southeast corner around Dublin (The Pale). A century after invading, the Anglo-Normans had seen their area of control shrink to only The Pale—with the rest of the island "beyond the Pale."

Even as their power eroded, the English kings considered Ireland to be theirs. They passed the Statutes of Kilkenny (1366) which outlawed all things Gaelic, including intermarriage with the English settlers, the Gaelic language, and the sport of hurling. In practice, the statutes were rarely enforced.

The End of Gaelic Rule (1500s)

In 1534, angered by Henry VIII's break with Catholicism (and taking advantage of England's Reformation chaos), the earls of Kildare rebelled, led by Silken Thomas. Henry crushed the revolt, executed the earls, and confiscated their land. Henry's daughter, Queen Elizabeth I, gave the land to colonists ("planters"), mainly English Protestants. The next four centuries would see a series of rebellions by Catholic, Gaelic-speaking Irish farmers fighting to free themselves from rule by Protestant, English-speaking landowners.

Hugh O'Neill (1540–1616), a noble angered by planters and English abuses, led a Gaelic revolt in 1595. The rebels were joined by the Spanish, who were fellow Catholics and England's archrival on the high seas. At the Battle of Yellow Ford (1598), guerrilla tactics led to an Irish victory.

But the Battle of Kinsale (1601) ended the revolt. The exhausted Irish, who had marched the length of Ireland in winter, arrived to help Spanish troops, who were pinned down inside the town. But the English crushed the Irish before they could join the Spanish, who then surrendered. O'Neill knelt before the conquering general, ceding half a million acres to England. Then he and other proud, Gaelic, Ulster-based nobles unexpectedly abandoned their land and sailed to the Continent (The Flight of the Earls, 1607), an event seen as the symbolic end of Gaelic Irish rule.

English Colonization and Irish Rebellions (1600s)

King James I took advantage of the Gaelic power vacuum and sent 25,000 English and Scottish planters into the confiscated land (1610–1641), making Ulster (in the northeast) the most English area of the island. The Irish responded with two major rebellions.

In 1642, with England embroiled in Civil War between a Catholic king and a Protestant Parliament, Irish rebels capitalized on the instability. Tenant farmers took up pitchforks against their English landlords, slaughtering 4,000 in the Massacre of the Planters (1641). Irish society was split between an English-speaking landed gentry (descendants of the first Anglo-Norman invaders, called "Old English") and the local Irish-speaking landless, or nearly landless, peasantry. But with Catholicism as their common bond, the Irish forces allied with the Old English against Oliver Cromwell's Protestant Parliament.

Cromwell responded by invading Ireland (1649–1654) with 20,000 men. He conquered the country—brutally. Thousands were slaughtered, priests were tortured, villages were pillaged, and rebels were sold into slavery. Most Catholic Irish landowners, given the choice of "to hell or to Connaught," were exiled to the rocky land west of the River Shannon. Cromwell confiscated 11 million acres of Catholic land to give to English Protestants. (In 1641, Catholics owned 59 percent of Ireland—by 1714 they owned 7 percent.) Cromwell's scorched-earth invasion was so harsh (the "curse of Cromwell"), it still raises hackles in Ireland.

In 1688–1689, rebels again took advantage of England's political chaos. They rallied around Catholic King James II, who was deposed by Parliament in the "Glorious Revolution" of 1688, then fled to France, and wound up in Ireland where he formed an army to retake the crown. In the Siege of Londonderry, James' Catholic army surrounded the city but some local apprentice boys locked them out, and after months of negotiations and a 105-day stand-off, James went away empty-handed.

The showdown came at the massive Battle of the Boyne (1690), north of Dublin. Catholic James II and his 25,000 men were defeated by the 36,000 troops of Protestant King William III of Orange. From this point on, the color orange became a symbol for pro-English, pro-Protestant forces.

As the 17th century came to a close, England had successfully put down every rebellion. To counter Irish feistiness, English legislation became an out-and-out attack on the indigenous Gaelic culture. The English punished the mostly Catholic nation with the Penal Laws. Catholics couldn't vote, hold office, buy land, join the army, play the harp, or even own a horse worth more than £5. Catholic education was banned and priests were outlawed. But the Penal Laws were difficult to enforce, and many Catholics continued to worship in private or at "Mass rocks" in the countryside.

Protestant Rule (1700s)

During the 18th century, Ireland thrived under the English. Dublin in the 1700s (pop. 50,000) was Britain's second city, one of Europe's wealthiest and most sophisticated. It's still decorated in Georgian (neoclassical) style, named for the English kings of the time.

But beyond The Pale surrounding Dublin, rebellion continued to brew. Over time, greed on the top and dissent on the bottom led to more repressive colonial policies. The Enlightenment provided ideas of freedom, and the Revolutionary Age emboldened the Irish masses. Irish nationalists were inspired by budding democratic revolutions in America (1776) and France (1789). Increasingly, the issue of Irish independence was less a religious question than a political one, as poor disenfranchised colonists demanded a political voice.

In Dublin, Jonathan Swift (1667–1745), the dean of St. Patrick's Cathedral, published his satirical *Gulliver's Travels*, with veiled references to English colonialism. He anonymously wrote pamphlets advising, "Burn all that's British, except its coal."

The Irish Parliament was an exclusive club, and only Protestant, male landowners could be elected to a seat (only 1 percent of the population qualified). In 1782, led by Henry Grattan (1746–1820), the Parliament negotiated limited autonomy from England (while remaining loyal to the king) and fairer treatment of the Catholics. England, chastened by the American Revolution (and soon preoccupied by the French Revolution), tolerated a more-or-less independent Irish Parliament for two decades.

Then in 1798 came the bloodiest Irish Rebellion. The United Irishmen (who wanted to substitute the word "Irishman" in place of the labels Protestant or Catholic) revolted against Britain, led by Wolfe Tone (1763–1798), a Protestant Dublin lawyer. Tone, trained in the French Revolution, had gained French aid for the Irish cause. (Though a French naval invasion in 1796 already had failed due to a freakish "Protestant wind" that blew the ships away from Ireland's shores.) The Rebellion was marked by bitter fighting—30,000 died over six weeks—before British troops crushed the revolt.

England tried to solve the Irish problem politically by forcing Ireland into a "Union" with England as part of a "United Kingdom" (Act of Union, 1800). The 500-year-old Irish Parliament was dissolved, becoming part of England's Parliament in London. Catholics were not allowed in Parliament. From then on, "Unionists" have been those who oppose Irish independence, wanting to preserve the country's union with Britain.

Votes, Violence, and the Famine (1800s)

Irish politicians lobbied in the British Parliament for Catholic rights, reform of absentee-landlordism, and for Home Rule—i.e., independence. Meanwhile, secret societies of revolutionaries pursued justice through violence.

Daniel O'Connell (1775–1847), known as The Liberator, campaigned for repeal of the Union (independence) and for Catholic equality. Having personally witnessed the violence of the Irish Rebellion and the French Revolution, O'Connell chose peaceful, legal means. He was a charismatic speaker, drawing over half a million people to one of his "monster meeting" demonstrations at the Hill of Tara (1843). But any hope of an Irish revival was soon snuffed out by the biggest catastrophe in Irish history: The Famine.

The Great Potato Famine (1845–49) was caused by a fungus *(Phytophthora infestans)* that destroyed Ireland's main food crop. Roughly a million people starved to death or died of related diseases (estimates range between 500,000 and 1.1 million). Another one to two million emigrated—most to America, and others to Canada and Australia.

The poorest were hardest hit. Potatoes were their main food source, and any other crops were far too expensive—grown by tenant farmers on their landlords' land to pay the rent and destined for export. (If this makes you mad at the English landlords, consider American ownership of land in Central America, where the landlord takes things one step beyond by not growing the local staple at all. He devotes all the land to more profitable cash crops for export and leaves the landless farmer no alternative but to buy his food—imported from the United States—at plantation wages, in the landlord's grocery store.)

Britain—then the richest nation on earth, with an empire stretching around the globe—could seemingly do nothing to help its starving citizens. A toxic combination of laissez-faire economic policies, racial bigotry, and self-righteousness conspired to blind the English to the plight of the Irish. While the English tend to blame the famine on overpopulation (Ireland's population doubled in the 40 years leading up to the famine), many Irish say there actually was no famine—just a calculated attempt to starve down the local population. Over the course of five long years, Ireland was ruined. The population was cut by nearly a third (from 8.4 million to 6 million), many of their best and brightest had fled, and the island's economy—and spirit—took generations to recover. The Irish language, spoken by the majority of the population before the Famine, became a badge of ignorance and was considered useless to those hoping to emigrate. Ireland, which remained one of Europe's poorest countries for over a century, was slow to forget Britain's indifference. Ireland's population has only recently begun to grow again. Irish Nationalists point out that Britain's population, on the other hand, has grown from 12 million in 1845 to around 60 million today.

Before the famine, land was subdivided—each boy got a piece of the family estate (which grew smaller with each generation). After the famine, the oldest son got the estate and the younger siblings, with no way to stay in Ireland, emigrated to Britain, Australia, Canada, or the United States. Because of the huge emigration to the United States (today there are 45 million Irish Americans), Ireland began to face west, and American influence increased. (As negotiations between Northern Ireland and the Irish Republic continue, American involvement in the talks is welcomed and considered essential by nearly all parties.)

Occasional violence demonstrated the fury of Irish nationalism, with the tragedy of the Famine inflaming the movement. In 1848, the Young Ireland armed uprising was easily squelched. In 1858, the Irish Republican Brotherhood was formed (the forerunner of the IRA). Also called the Fenians, they launched a never-ending campaign for independence by planting terrorist bombs. Irish Americans sent money to help finance these revolutionaries. Uprising after uprising made it clear that Ireland was ready to close this thousand-year chapter of invasions and colonialism.

On the political front, Home Rule Party leader Charles Stuart Parnell (1846–1891), an Irishman educated in England, made "the Irish problem" the focus of London's Parliament. Parnell lobbied for independence and for the rights of poor tenant farmers living under absentee landlords, pioneering the first boycott tactics. Then, in 1890, at the peak of his power and about to achieve Home Rule for Ireland, he was drummed out of politics by a scandal involving his mistress, scuttling the Home Rule issue for another 20 years.

Culturally, the old Gaelic, rural Ireland was being swamped by the Industrial Revolution and dominated by Protestant England. Writers and educators formed the Gaelic League (1883) to preserve the traditional language, music, and poetry. A year later, the Gaelic Athletic Association was founded to resurrect pride in ancient Irish sports such as hurling. Building on the tradition of old Celtic bards, Ireland produced some of the great early-modern writers: W. B. Yeats, Oscar Wilde, G. B. Shaw, and James Joyce, whose rambling modern novel *Ulysses* chronicles a day in the life of Dublin.

Easter Rising, War of Independence, Partition, and Civil War (1900–1950)

As the century turned, Ireland prepared for the inevitable show-down with Britain.

The Sinn Fein party (meaning "We, Ourselves") lobbied politically for independence. The Irish Volunteers were more Catholic and more militant. And the Irish Republican Army (IRA), a secret organization formed in 1916 to fight for independence was more militant still. Also on the scene was the Irish Citizens Army, with a socialist agenda to clean up Dublin's hideous tenements.

Of course, many Irish were Protestant and pro-British. The Ulster Volunteers (Unionists, and mostly Orangemen) feared that Home Rule would result in a Catholic-dominated state that would oppress the Protestant minority.

Meanwhile, Britain was preoccupied with World War I, where it was "fighting to protect the rights of small nations," and so delayed granting Irish independence. The increasingly militant Irish rebels, believing that England's misfortune was Ireland's opportunity, decided to rise up and take independence on their own.

On Easter Monday, April 24, 1916, 1500 Irish "Volunteers," along with members of the Irish Citizens Army, marched on Dublin, occupied the Post Office, and raised a green-white-and-orange flag. The teacher and poet Patrick Pearse stood in front of the Post Office and proclaimed Ireland an independent republic.

British troops struck back—in a week of street fighting, some 300 died. By Saturday, the greatly outnumbered rebels had been arrested. The small-scale uprising—which failed to go national and was never even popular in Dublin—was apparently over.

However, the British government overreacted by swiftly executing the 15 ringleaders, including Pearse. Ireland was out-raged, no longer seeing the rebels as troublemakers but as martyrs. From this point on, Ireland was resolved to win its independence at all costs. A poem by W. B. Yeats, "Easter 1916," memorialized the event and its effect on the Irish with the refrain: "All changed, changed utterly:/A terrible beauty is born."

In the 1918 elections, the Sinn Fein party won big, but the new Members of Parliament refused to go to London, instead forming their own independent Irish Parliament in Dublin. The following year, Irish rebels ambushed and shot two policemen, sparking two years of confrontations called the War of Independence. The Irish Republican Army faced 40,000 British troops, including the notorious "Black and Tans" (named for their uniforms). A thousand people died in this war of street-fighting, sniper-fire, jailhouse beatings, terrorist bombs, and reprisals.

Finally, Britain agreed to Irish independence. But Ireland itself was a divided nation—the southern part of the island was mostly Catholic, Gaelic, rural, and for Home Rule; the northern part was Protestant, English, industrial, and Unionist. The solution? In 1920, in the Government of Ireland Act, the British Parliament partitioned the island into two independent, self-governing countries within the British Commonwealth—Northern Ireland, and the Irish Free State. While the northern six counties (the only ones without a Catholic majority) voted to stay with Britain as Northern Ireland, the remaining 26 counties became the Irish Free State. (For a review of the ongoing Troubles between the North and the Republic, see the Northern Ireland chapter.)

Ireland's various political factions wrestled with this compromise solution, and the island plunged into a yearlong Civil War (1922–1923). The hard-line IRA opposed the partition, unwilling to accept a divided island, an oath of loyalty to the queen, or the remaining British Navy bases on Irish soil. They waged a street war on the armies of the Irish Free State, who supported the political settlement. Dublin and the southeast were ravaged in a year of bitter fighting before the Irish Free State emerged victorious. The IRA went underground, moving its fight north and trying for the rest of the century to topple the government of Northern Ireland.

In 1937, the Irish Free State severed all ties with the British Commonwealth, taking an old name—Eire (a Gaelic word apparently derived from the early Greeks' name for the island, Ierne). In 1947 it became officially known as the Republic of Ireland.

Celtic Tiger in the South, Troubles in the North (1950–2000)

Beginning in 1960, the Republic of Ireland—formerly a poor, rural region—was transformed into a modern, economic power, thanks to foreign investors and, in 1973, membership in the European Union. Through the mid-1990s, Ireland's booming, globalized economy grew a whopping 40 percent, earning the Republic the nickname "The Celtic Tiger."

Meanwhile, Northern Ireland—with a 55 percent Protestant

majority and a large, 45 percent disaffected Catholic minority—
was plagued by the Troubles. In 1967, the Northern Ireland Civil
Rights Movement, inspired by America's black civil rights movement, organized marches and demonstrations demanding equal
treatment for Catholics (better housing, job opportunities, and
voting rights). Protestant Unionist Orangemen, countered by
marching through Catholic neighborhoods, provoking riots.
In 1969, Britain sent troops to help Northern Ireland keep the
peace, and met resistance from the IRA, which saw them as an
occupying army supporting the Protestant pro-British majority.

From the 1970s to the 1990s, the North was a low-level bat-
tlefield, with the IRA using terrorist tactics to achieve their political ends. The Troubles, claiming some 3,000 lives, continued
with bombings, marches, hunger strikes, rock-throwing, and
riots (notably Derry's Bloody Sunday in 1972), interrupted by
cease-fires, broken cease-fires, and a string of peace agreements.

Then came the 1998 Good Friday Peace Accord, which has
proven to be a flawed but durable breakthrough in the process of
getting bitter, hard-line opponents to seek common ground.

Global Nations (2000 and beyond)

Today, both Northern Ireland and the Republic of Ireland have
every reason to be optimistic about the future, as their economies
boom and the political and cultural Troubles lessen. The formerly
isolated island is welcoming tourists with open arms, and reaching
out to the rest of the globe.

Visitors returning to Ireland are amazed at the country's
transformation. Although there are still some tense areas in
the North—as there are in all big cities—the peace process is
grinding forward.

Now, for the first time in history, the Irish are importing
labor, and they've surpassed the English in per-capita income.
Since 1980, when Apple Computer set up shop here, a stream
of multinational and American corporations have opened offices
in Ireland. Ireland has one of the youngest populations in Europe.
And those young Irish, beneficiaries of one of Europe's best edu-
cational systems, provide these corporations with a highly skilled
and educated workforce. Powered by this youthful and energetic
workforce, Ireland's pharmaceutical, chemical, and software industries are booming. In fact, little Ireland is second only to the
United States in the exportation of software.

Of course, this rapid growth comes with problems. Urban
sprawl, rising housing prices, water and air pollution, and the
homogenous nature of globalization all left their mark on Ireland.
Still, the Celtic Tiger continues to roar.

While the Irish are embracing the new economies and industries of the 21st century, when it comes to sex and marriage, they still see their island as an oasis of morality and traditional values. The Catholic Church continues to exert a major influence on Irish society. But since the Church no longer controls the legislature, the Irish government—driven by the popular demands of the youngest population in Europe—will undoubtedly push for some changes on the following issues.

Birth Control: Americans take for granted that birth control is readily available. But Ireland only began allowing the widespread sale of condoms in 1993.

Abortion: In Ireland, women who choose to terminate their pregnancies must go to England for help. Abortion is still illegal in Ireland. And it's only been legal since 1993 to counsel Irish women to go to England for abortions. This was a big issue in 2001, when the Dutch anchored their "abortion ship" in Dublin's harbor, and again in 2002, when a referendum legalizing abortion was narrowly defeated. Watch for more referendums proposing the legalization of abortion. Locals refer to this as their next Civil War.

Divorce: Ireland voted to legalize divorce in 1995—but only on very strict conditions, and with little compensation offered to Irish women who work as homemakers.

Irish Art

Megalithic tombs, ancient gold- and metalwork, illuminated manuscripts, high crosses carved in stone, paintings of rural Ireland, and provocative political murals—Ireland comes with some fascinating art. To best appreciate this art in your travels, kick off your tour in Ireland's two top museums (both in Dublin): The National Museum and the National Gallery. Each provide a good context to help you enjoy Irish art and architecture—from ancient to modern and both rural and urban. Here's a quick survey:

Megalithic Period: During the Stone Age 5,000 years ago, farmers living on the Boyne River north of Dublin built a "cemetery" of approximately 40 burial mounds. The most famous of these mound tombs is the passage tomb at Newgrange. More than 300 feet in diameter and composed of 200,000 tons of loose stone, Newgrange was constructed so that the light from the winter solstice sunrise (Dec 21) would pass through the eastern entrance to the tomb, travel down a 60-foot passage, and illuminate the inner burial chamber. Not bad engineering for Stone Age architects. The effect is now recreated daily so visitors can experience this ancient ritual of renewal and rebirth.

Some of Europe's best examples of megalithic (big rock) art are at Newgrange. Carved on the tomb's stones are zigzags, chevrons, parallel arcs, and concentric spirals. Scholars think these designs symbolize a belief in the eternal cycle of life and the continuation of the life force, or that they pay homage to the elements in nature on which these ancient peoples depended for their existence.

Exploring these burial mounds (only Newgrange and Knowth are open to the public), you begin to understand the reverence that these people had for nature and the need they felt to bury their dead in these great mound tombs, returning their kin to the womb of Mother Earth.

Bronze Age: As ancient Irish cultures developed from 2000 B.C., so did their metalworking skills. Gold and bronze were used to create tools, jewelry, and religious objects. The National Museum in Dublin houses the most dazzling of these works. Gold neck rings worn by both men and women, cufflink-like dress fasteners, bracelets, and lock rings (to hold hair in place) are but a few of the personal adornments fashioned by the ancient Irish.

Most of these objects were deliberately buried, often in bogs, as votive offerings to their gods or to prevent warring tribes from stealing them. Like the earlier megaliths, they're decorated with geometric and organic motifs.

Iron Age: The Celts, a warrior society from Central Europe, arrived in Ireland perhaps as early as the seventh century B.C. With their metalworking skills and superior iron weaponry, they soon overwhelmed the native population. And, though the Celts may have been bloodthirsty, they wreaked havoc with a flair for the aesthetic. Shields, swords, and scabbards were embellished with delicate patterns, often enhanced with vivid colors. The dynamic energy of these decorations must have reflected the ferocious power of the Celts.

The Age of Saints and Scholars: Christianity grew in Ireland, from St. Patrick's first efforts in the fifth century A.D. In the sixth and seventh centuries, its many great saints (such as St. Columba) established monastic settlements throughout Ireland, Britain, and the Continent, where learning, literature, and the arts flourished. During this "Golden Age" of Irish civilization, monks, along with metalworkers and stonemasons, created imaginative designs and distinctive stylistic motifs for manuscripts, metal objects, and crosses.

Monks wrote out and richly decorated manuscripts of the Gospels. These manuscripts—which preserved the written word in Latin, Greek, and Irish—eventually had more power than the oral tales of the ancient pagan heroes.

The most beautiful and imaginative of these illuminated manuscripts is the Book of Kells (c. A.D. 800), on display in the Old Library at Trinity College in Dublin. Crafted by Irish monks at a monastery on the Scottish island of Iona, the book was brought to Ireland for safekeeping from rampaging Vikings. The skins of 150 calves were used to make the vellum which is painted with rich pigments from plants and minerals. The entire manuscript is colorfully decorated with flat, stylized human or angelic forms and intricate, interlacing animal and knot patterns. Full-page illustrations depict the life of Christ and many pages are given over to highly complex yet symmetrical designs that resemble an Eastern carpet. Many consider this book the finest piece of art from Europe's Dark Ages.

The most renowned metalwork of this period is the Ardagh Chalice, dating from the eighth century. Now on display at the National Museum in Dublin, the silver and bronze gilt chalice is as impressive as the Book of Kells. Ribbons of gold wrap around the chalice stem, while intricate knot patterns ring the cup. A magnificent gold ring and a large glass stone on the chalice bottom reflect the desire to please God (He would see this side of the chalice when the priest drank during the Mass).

The monks used Irish high crosses to celebrate the triumph of Christianity and provide a means of educating the illiterate masses through simple stone carvings. The Cross of Murdock (Muiredach's Cross, A.D. 923) is 18 feet tall, towering over the remains of the monastic settlement at Monasterboice (north of Dublin). It is but one of many monumental crosses that visitors will discover throughout Ireland. Typically, stone carvers depicted Bible stories and surrounded these with the same intricate patterns seen in the Book of Kells and the Ardagh Chalice.

Early Irish art focused on organic, geometric, and linear designs. Unlike Mediterranean art, Irish art of this early period was not preoccupied with a naturalistic representation of people, animals, or the landscape. Instead, it reflects Irish society's rituals and the elements and rhythms of nature.

The Suppression of Native Irish Art: The English, after invading Ireland in 1169, suppressed Celtic Irish culture. English traditions in architecture, painting, and literature replaced native styles until the late 19th century, when revivals in Irish language, folklore, music, and art began to surface.

Since the Book of Kells, Ireland's greatest contributions to the world of art have been in literature and drama. Irish notables include Jonathan Swift, Oscar Wilde, George Bernard Shaw, W. B. Yeats, James Joyce, and Samuel Beckett.

Painters in the late 19th and early 20th centuries went to the west of Ireland, which was untouched by English dominance and influence, in search of traditional Irish subject matter.

Jack B. Yeats (1871–1957, brother of the poet W. B. Yeats),

Belfast-born painter Paul Henry (1876–1958), and Sean Keating (1889–1977) all looked to the west for inspiration. The National Gallery in Dublin holds many of these artists' greatest works, with an entire gallery dedicated to Jack Yeats. Many of his early paintings illustrate scenes of his beloved Sligo. His later paintings are more expressionistic in style and patriotic in subject matter.

Henry's paintings depict the rugged beauty of the Connemara region and its people, with scenes of rustic cottages, mountains, and bog lands. Keating, the most political of the three painters, featured patriotic scenes from Ireland's struggle against the English for independence.

Contemporary Irish art is often linked to the social, political, and environmental issues facing Ireland today. Themes include the position of the Church in the daily lives of the modern Irish, the effects of development on the countryside, the changing roles of women in Ireland, and the Troubles. Look for this provocative art at the Irish Museum of Modern Art in Dublin and at city galleries.

In Northern Ireland, murals in sectarian neighborhoods (such as Shankill and Falls Roads in Belfast) are stirring public testaments to the martyrs and to the heroes, to resistance and to confrontation, and to the reconciliation that continues to elude the people of Northern Ireland. (For more on these murals, see the Derry chapter).

The Irish Language

The Irish have a rich oral tradition that goes back to their ancient fireside storytelling days. Part of the fun of traveling here is getting an ear for the way locals express themselves. Ask an Irish person for directions and you'll more often than not have an interesting, memorable experience.

Irish Place Names

Here are a few words that appear in Irish place names. You'll see these on road signs or at tourist sights.

Alt cliff
An Lar city center
Ard high, height, hillock
Baile (pron. BALL-yah), **Bally** (pron. BAH-lee) town, townland
Beag (pron. beg) little
Bearna (pron. bar-na) gap
Boireann (pron. burr-en) large rock, rocky area
Bothar (pron. boh-er) road
Bun end, bottom
Caiseal (pron. cash-el) castle, circular stone fort
Caislean castle
Cathair circular stone fort, city

Cill (pron. kill) church
Cloch stone
Doire (pron. DER-ry) wooded area
Droichead (pron. DROH-ed) bridge
Drumlin small hill
Dun (pron. doon) fort
Fionn (pron. fin) white, fair-haired person
Gaeltacht Irish language district
Gall (pron. gaul) foreigner
Gaol (pron. jail) jail
Garda police
Gort field
Innis (pron. in-ish) island
Kil church; monk's cell
Mileac (pron. mee-luch) low marshy ground
Mor large
Oifig an Phoist (pron. UFF-ig un fwisht) post office
Poll hole, cave
Rath ancient earthen fort
Si (pron. shee) fairy mound, bewitching
Sli (pron. slee) route, way
Sliabh (pron. sleeve) mountain
Sraid (pron. shrawd) street
Teach (pron. tagh) house
Trá (pron. thraw) beach, strand
Tur tower

Irish Pleasantries

When you reach the more remote western fringe of Ireland, you're likely to hear folks speaking Irish. Although locals in these areas can readily converse with you in English, it's fascinating to hear their ancient Celtic language spoken. Here are some basic Irish phrases:

Dia dhuit (pron. JEE-a dich) Good day, Hello
Dia's muire dhuit (pron. JEE-as MWUR-a dich)
    response to *dia dhuit*
Fáilte (pron. FAHLT-shuh) Welcome
Conas ta tu? (pron. CUNN-us thaw too) How are you?
Go raibh maith agat (pron. guh roh moh UG-ut) Thank you
Slán agat (pron. slawn UG-ut) Goodbye

Irish Pub and Music Words

The Irish love to socialize. Pubs are like public living rooms, where friends gather in a corner to play tunes and everyone is a welcome guest. Here are some useful pub and music words:

Poitín (pron. po-CHEEN) moonshine, homemade liquor

Craic (pron. crack) fun atmosphere, good conversation
Bodhrán (pron. BOUR-ohn) traditional drum
Uilleann (pron. ILL-in) elbow (*uilleann* pipes are elbow bagpipes)
Trad traditional Irish music
Ceili (pron. KAY-lee) Irish dance gathering
Fleadh (pron. flah) music festival
Slainte (pron. SLAWN-chuh) cheers, to your health
Táim súgach! (pron. thaw im SOO-gakh) I'm tipsy!
Lei thras (pron. LEH-hrass) toilets
Mná (pron. min-AW) women's room
Fir (pron. fear) men's room

Irish Politics

Politics is a popular topic of conversation in Ireland. Whether you pick up a local newspaper or turn on your car radio, you'll often encounter these Irish political terms in the media:
Taoiseach (pron. TEE-shock) Prime Minister of Irish Republic
Seanad (pron. SHAN-ud) Irish Senate
Dáil (pron. DOY-ill) Irish House of Representatives
TD, Teachta Dála (pron. TALK-ta DOLL-a)
    Member of Irish Parliament

Irish-Yankee Vocabulary

advert advertisement
afters dessert
anticlockwise counterclockwise
aubergine eggplant
banger sausage
bank holiday legal holiday
bap hamburger-type bun
billion a thousand of our billions (a trillion)
biro ballpoint pen
biscuit cookie
black pudding sausage made from dried blood
bloody damn
bog slang for toilet
bonnet car hood
boot car trunk
braces suspenders
bridle way path for walkers, bikers, and horse riders
brilliant cool
bum bottom or "backside"

busker street musician
candy floss cotton candy
car boot sale temporary flea market with car trunk displays (a good place to buy back your stolen goods)
caravan trailer
cat's eyes road reflectors
champ mashed potatoes and onions
cheap and nasty cheap and bad quality
chemist pharmacist
chicory endive
chips french fries
chockablock jam-packed
cider alcoholic apple cider
clearway road where you can't stop
coach long-distance bus
concession discounted admission

cotton buds cotton swabs
courgette zucchini
cos romaine lettuce
crisps potato chips
cuppa cup of tea
dear expensive
dicey iffy, risky
digestives round graham crackers
dinner lunch or dinner
diversion detour
donkey's years until the cows come home
draughts checkers
draw marijuana
dual carriageway divided highway (four lanes)
en suite bathroom attached to room
face flannel washcloth
fanny vagina
fell hill or high plain
first floor second floor
football Gaelic football
fortnight two weeks
full monty The whole shebang. Everything.
GAA Gaelic Athletic Association
gallery balcony
gammon ham
gangway aisle
give way yield
glen narrow valley
goods wagon freight truck
grand good, well ("How are you?" "I'm grand, thanks")
gurrier hooligan
half eight 8:30 (not 7:30)
heath open treeless land
holiday vacation
homely likable or cozy
hoover vacuum cleaner
hurling Irish field hockey/rugby

ice lolly Popsicle
interval intermission
ironmonger hardware store
jacket potato baked potato
jelly Jell-O
jumble sale, rummage sale
jumper sweater
just a tick just a second
keep your pecker up be brave
kipper smoked herring
knackered exhausted
knickers ladies' panties
knocking shop brothel
knock up wake up or visit
ladybird ladybug
left luggage baggage check
let rent
lorry truck
mac mackintosh coat
mate buddy (boy or girl)
mean stingy
mews courtyard stables, often used as cottages
minced meat hamburger
mobile (pron. MOH-bile) cell phone
nappy diaper
natter talk and talk
nought zero
noughts & crosses tic-tac-toe
off license store selling take-away liquor
pasty crusted savory (usually meat) pie
pavement sidewalk
petrol gas
pissed (rude), paralytic, bevvied, wellied, popped up, ratted, pissed as a newt drunk
pitch playing field
plaster Band-Aid
publican pub manager
punter partygoer
put a sock in it shut up

quay waterside street, ship offloading area
queue line
queue up line up
quid pound (money in Northern Ireland, worth about $1.50)
RTE Irish Republic's broadcasting network
ramps speed bumps
randy horny
redundant, made fired
return ticket round-trip
ring up call (telephone)
roundabout traffic circle
rubber eraser
sanitary towel sanitary pad
sausage roll sausage wrapped in a flaky pastry
Scotch egg hard-boiled egg wrapped in sausage meat
self-catering apartment with kitchen
sellotape Scotch tape
serviette napkin
single ticket one-way ticket
slag to ridicule, tease
smalls underwear
snogging kissing, cuddling
solicitor lawyer
starkers buck naked
starters appetizers
stone 14 pounds (weight)

strand beach
subway underground pedestrian passageway
sultanas golden raisins
surgical spirit rubbing alcohol
sort out figure out
swede rutabaga
taxi rank taxi stand
theatre live stage
tick a checkmark
tight as a Scotsman cheapskate (water-tight)
tights panty hose
tipper lorry dump truck
tin can
to let for rent
top up refill a drink
torch flashlight
towpath path along a river
Travellers itinerants, once known as tinkers
turf accountant bookie
underground subway
verge grassy edge of road
victualler butcher
way out exit
Wellingtons, wellies rubber boots
wee urinate
whacked exhausted
witter on gab and gab
zebra crossing crosswalk
zed the letter *z*

APPENDIX

Let's Talk Telephones

Here's a primer on making phone calls. For information specific to Ireland, see "Telephones" in the introduction.

Making Calls within a European Country: About half of all European countries use area codes (like we do); the other half uses a direct-dial system without area codes.

To make calls within a country that uses a direct-dial system (Belgium, the Czech Republic, Denmark, France, Italy, Portugal, Norway, Spain, and Switzerland), you dial the same number whether you're calling across the country or across the street.

In countries that use area codes (such as Austria, Britain, Finland, Germany, Ireland, Netherlands, and Sweden), you dial the local number when calling within a city, and you add the area code if calling long-distance within the country.

Making International Calls: You always start with the international access code (011 if you're calling from the U.S. or Canada, or 00 from Europe), then dial the country code of the country you're calling (see chart below).

What you dial next depends on the phone system of the country you're calling. If the country uses area codes, drop the initial 0 of the area code, then dial the rest of the number.

Countries that use direct-dial systems (no area codes) vary in how they're accessed internationally by phone. For instance, if you're making an international call to the Czech Republic, Denmark, Italy, Norway, Portugal, or Spain, simply dial the international access code, country code, and the local phone number. But if you're calling Belgium, France, or Switzerland, drop the initial 0 of the local phone number.

International Access Codes

When making international calls, first dial the international access code of the country you're calling from. For the United States and Canada, it's 011. Virtually all European countries use "00" as their international access code; the only exceptions are Finland (990) and Lithuania (810).

Country Codes

After you've dialed the international access code, dial the code of the country you're calling.

Austria—43	Canada—1
Belgium—32	Czech Rep.—420
Britain—44	Denmark—45

European Calling Chart

Just smile and dial, using this key:
AC = Area Code, LN = Local Number.

European Country	Calling long distance within...	Calling from the U.S.A./ Canada to...	Calling from another European country to...
Austria	AC (Area Code) + LN (Local Number)	011 + 43 + AC (without the initial zero) + LN	00 + 43 + AC (without the initial zero) + LN
Belgium	LN	011 + 32 + LN (without initial zero)	00 + 32 + LN (without initial zero)
Britain	AC + LN	011 + 44 + AC (without initial zero) + LN	00 + 44 + AC . (without initial zero) + LN
Czech Republic	LN	011 + 420 + LN	00 + 420 + LN
Denmark	LN	011 + 45 + LN	00 + 45 + LN
Estonia	LN	011 + 372 + LN	00 + 372 + LN
Finland	AC + LN	011 + 358 + AC (without initial zero) + LN	00 + 358 + AC (without initial zero) + LN
France	LN	011 + 33 + LN (without initial zero)	00 + 33 + LN (without initial zero)
Germany	AC + LN	011 + 49 + AC (without initial zero) + LN	00 + 49 + AC (without initial zero) + LN
Gibraltar	LN	011 + 350 + LN	00 + 350 + LN From Spain: 9567 + LN
Greece	LN	011 + 30 + LN	00 + 30 + LN

European Country	Calling long distance within...	Calling from the U.S.A./ Canada to...	Calling from another European country to...
Ireland	AC + LN	011 + 353 + AC (without initial zero) + LN	00 + 353 + AC (without initial zero) + LN
Italy	LN	011 + 39 + LN	00 + 39 + LN
Morocco	LN	011 + 212 + LN (without initial zero)	00 + 212 + LN (without initial zero)
Nether-lands	AC + LN	011 + 31 + AC (without initial zero) + LN	00 + 31 + AC (without initial zero) + LN
Norway	LN	011 + 47 + LN	00 + 47 + LN
Portugal	LN	011 + 351 + LN	00 + 351 + LN
Spain	LN	011 + 34 + LN	00 + 34 + LN
Sweden	AC + LN	011 + 46 + AC (without initial zero) + LN	00 + 46 + AC (without initial zero) + LN
Switzer-land	LN	011 + 41 + LN (without initial zero)	00 + 41 + LN (without initial zero)
Turkey	AC (if no initial zero is included, add one) + LN	011 + 90 + AC (without initial zero) + LN	00 + 90 + AC (without initial zero) + LN

- The instructions above apply whether you're calling a fixed phone or cell phone.
- The international access codes (the first numbers you dial when making an international call) are 011 if you're calling from the U.S.A./Canada, or 00 if you're calling from virtually anywhere in Europe. Finland and Lithuania are the only exceptions. If calling from either of these countries, replace the 00 with 990 in Finland and 810 in Lithuania.
- To call the U.S.A. or Canada from Europe, dial 00 (unless you're calling from Finland or Lithuania), then 1 (the country code for the U.S.A. and Canada), then the area code and number. In short, 00 + 1 + AC + LN = Hi, Mom!

Country Codes (continued)

Estonia—372	Morocco—212
Finland—358	Netherlands—31
France—33	Norway—47
Germany—49	Portugal—351
Gibraltar—350	Spain—34
Greece—30	Sweden—46
Ireland—353	Switzerland—41
Italy—39	United States—1

Dial Away . . .

Note that the Republic of Ireland (country code: 353) has a different country code than Northern Ireland, which is part of Britain (country code: 44). The Republic of Ireland has a special way to dial Northern Ireland (048, then the local number without the area code).

From the United States/Canada to the Republic of Ireland: Dial 011-353, then the area code without its initial 0, then the local number.

From European countries (including Northern Ireland) to the Republic of Ireland: Dial 00-353, then the area code without its initial 0, then the local number.

From the United States/Canada to Northern Ireland: Dial 011-44-28 (28 is Northern Ireland's area code without its initial 0), then the local number.

From the Republic of Ireland to Northern Ireland: Dial 048, then the local number. (In this case, Northern Ireland's area code, "028," is omitted entirely.)

From any European country (except the Republic of Ireland) to Northern Ireland: Dial 00-44-28 (Northern Ireland's area code without its initial 0), then the local number.

From anywhere in Ireland (north or south) to the United States or Canada: 00-1, then the area code and local number.

Useful Numbers

Ireland

Emergency: 999

Operator Assistance: 10 for Ireland, 114 to call outside Ireland

Directory Assistance within Ireland: 11811 (free from phone booth, or 34p from anywhere else)

International Info: 11818 (free from phone booth)

Note that calls beginning with 1-800 are free throughout Ireland, but 1-850 calls cost the same as local calls.

Northern Ireland
Emergency (police and ambulance): 999
Operator Assistance: 100 for Britain, 155 to call outside Britain
Directory Assistance within Britain: 192 (20p from phone booth, otherwise £1.50)
International Info: 153 (20p from phone booth, otherwise £1.50)

Airlines
These are phone numbers for the Republic of Ireland. (To call the special 1-800 numbers from the States, dial 011-353, then the 800 number without the initial 1).
Aer Arann Express (Aran Islands & Co. Kerry): 01/814-1058 (www.aerarannexpress.com)
Aer Lingus: 01/886-8888 (www.aerlingus.com)
Air Canada: 1-800-709-900 (www.aircanada.ca)
American: 01/602-0550 (www.aa.com)
British Airways: 1-800-626-747 (www.british-airways.com)
bmi british midland: 01/407-3036 (www.flybmi.com)
Continental Airlines: 1-890-925-252 (www.continental.com)
Delta: 1-800-768-080 (www.delta-air.com)
Lufthansa: 01/844-5544 (www.lufthansa.co.uk)
Ryanair (cheap fares): 01/609-7878 (www.ryanair.com)
Scandinavian Airlines System (SAS): 01/844-5888 (www.scandinavian.net)
United Airlines: 01/819-1760 (www.ual.com)
Virgin Atlantic: 01/500-5500 (www.virginatlantic.com)

Dublin Car Rentals
Avis: 1 Hanover Street East, 01/605-7502; airport 01/605-7500 (www.avis.ie)
Hertz: 149 Upper Leeson Street, 01/660-2255; airport 01/844-5400 (www.hertz.com)
Budget: 151 Lower Drumcondra Road, 01/837-9611; airport 01/844-5150 (www.budget.com)
Europcar: Baggot Street Bridge, 01/614-2840; airport 01/812-0410 (www.europcar.ie)

U.S. Embassies
In the Republic of Ireland: 42 Elgin Road, Dublin, tel. 01/668-7122 or 01/668-8777, www.usembassy.ie
In Northern Ireland: 14 Queen Street, Belfast, tel. 028/9032-8239, www.usembassy.org.uk

2003

JANUARY						
S	M	T	W	T	F	S
			1	2	3	4
5	6	7	8	9	10	11
12	13	14	15	16	17	18
19	20	21	22	23	24	25
26	27	28	29	30	31	

FEBRUARY						
S	M	T	W	T	F	S
						1
2	3	4	5	6	7	8
9	10	11	12	13	14	15
16	17	18	19	20	21	22
23	24	25	26	27	28	

MARCH						
S	M	T	W	T	F	S
						1
2	3	4	5	6	7	8
9	10	11	12	13	14	15
16	17	18	19	20	21	22
23/30 24/31	25	26	27	28	29	

APRIL						
S	M	T	W	T	F	S
		1	2	3	4	5
6	7	8	9	10	11	12
13	14	15	16	17	18	19
20	21	22	23	24	25	26
27	28	29	30			

MAY						
S	M	T	W	T	F	S
				1	2	3
4	5	6	7	8	9	10
11	12	13	14	15	16	17
18	19	20	21	22	23	24
25	26	27	28	29	30	31

JUNE						
S	M	T	W	T	F	S
1	2	3	4	5	6	7
8	9	10	11	12	13	14
15	16	17	18	19	20	21
22	23	24	25	26	27	28
29	30					

JULY						
S	M	T	W	T	F	S
		1	2	3	4	5
6	7	8	9	10	11	12
13	14	15	16	17	18	19
20	21	22	23	24	25	26
27	28	29	30	31		

AUGUST						
S	M	T	W	T	F	S
					1	2
3	4	5	6	7	8	9
10	11	12	13	14	15	16
17	18	19	20	21	22	23
24/31	25	26	27	28	29	30

SEPTEMBER						
S	M	T	W	T	F	S
	1	2	3	4	5	6
7	8	9	10	11	12	13
14	15	16	17	18	19	20
21	22	23	24	25	26	27
28	29	30				

OCTOBER						
S	M	T	W	T	F	S
			1	2	3	4
5	6	7	8	9	10	11
12	13	14	15	16	17	18
19	20	21	22	23	24	25
26	27	28	29	30	31	

NOVEMBER						
S	M	T	W	T	F	S
						1
2	3	4	5	6	7	8
9	10	11	12	13	14	15
16	17	18	19	20	21	22
23/30	24	25	26	27	28	29

DECEMBER						
S	M	T	W	T	F	S
	1	2	3	4	5	6
7	8	9	10	11	12	13
14	15	16	17	18	19	20
21	22	23	24	25	26	27
28	29	30	31			

Festivals and Public Holidays

This is a partial list of holidays and festivals. Some dates have yet to be set. For more information, contact the National Tourist Offices (listed in this book's introduction) and check out these Web sites: www.whatsonwhen.com, www.whatsgoingon.com, and www.festivals.com.

March 17	St. Patrick's Day throughout Ireland (parades, drunkenness, 5-day festival in Dublin)
May 5	May Day (some closures), Ireland and U.K.
June 2	June Holiday (banks closed), Ireland and U.K.
July 12	Orange Day (Protestant marches, protests), Northern Ireland
July 16	Bloomsday (James Joyce festival), Dublin
July– last half	Galway Arts Festival, Galway
Aug 4	August Holiday (banks closed), Ireland
Aug– 2nd weekend	Dingle Races (boat races), Dingle
Aug– 3rd weekend	Dingle Regatta, Dingle
Mid-Aug	Rose of Tralee International Festival, Tralee
Aug 25	Late Summer Holiday (banks closed), U.K.

Late Aug–	Blessing of the Boats (maritime festival), Dingle
early Sept	
Mid-Sept	Matchmaking Festival (2 weeks), Lisdoonvarna
Late Sept	Galway Oyster Festival (4 days), Galway
Late Oct	Belfast Queens Festival (music, 12 days), Belfast
Oct 27	October Holiday (banks closed), Ireland
Dec 25	Christmas, Ireland and U.K.
Dec 26	St. Stephen's Day (religious festival), Ireland
Dec 26	Boxing Day, U.K.

Climate

The first line is the average low, the second line is the average high, and the third line is number of days with no rain. Note that temperatures are moderate throughout the country, so use the Dublin temperatures listed below as a model.

J	F	M	A	M	J	J	A	S	O	N	D
DUBLIN											
34°	35°	37°	39°	43°	48°	52°	51°	48°	43°	39°	37°
46°	47°	51°	55°	60°	65°	67°	67°	63°	57°	51°	47°
18	18	21	19	21	19	18	19	18	20	18	17

Numbers and Stumblers

- Europeans write a few of their numbers differently than we do. 1 = 1 , 4 = 4 , 7 = 7 . Learn the difference or miss your train.
- In Europe, dates appear as day/month/year, so Christmas is 25/12/03.
- Commas are decimal points and decimals commas. A dollar and a half is $1,50, and there are 5.280 feet in a mile.
- When pointing, use your whole hand, palm down.
- When counting with fingers, start with your thumb. If you hold up your first finger to request one item, you'll probably get two.
- What Americans call the second floor of a building is the first floor in Europe.
- Europeans keep the left "lane" open for passing on escalators and moving sidewalks. Keep to the right.

Metric Conversion (approximate)

1 inch = 25 millimeters	32 degrees F = 0 degrees C
1 foot = 0.3 meter	82 degrees F = about 28 degrees C
1 yard = 0.9 meter	1 ounce = 28 grams
1 mile = 1.6 kilometers	1 kilogram = 2.2 pounds
1 centimeter = 0.4 inch	1 quart = 0.95 liter
1 meter = 39.4 inches	1 square yard = 0.8 square meter
1 kilometer = .62 mile	1 acre = 0.4 hectare

Faxing Your Hotel Reservation

Use this handy form for your fax or find it online at
www.ricksteves.com/reservation. Photocopy and fax away.

One-Page Fax

To: _____ @ _____
         hotel   *fax*

From: _____ @ _____
         name   *fax*

Today's date: ____ /_____ /____
                day   *month* *year*

Dear Hotel _____,

Please make this reservation for me:

Name: _____

Total # of people: _____   # of rooms: _____   # of nights: _____

Arriving: ____ /_____ /____ My time of arrival (24-hr clock): _____
            day *month* *year*

(I will telephone if I will be late)

Departing: ____ /_____ /____
             day *month* *year*

Room(s): Single___ Double___ Twin___ Triple___ Quad___

With: Toilet___ Shower___ Bath___ Sink only___

Special needs: View___ Quiet___ Cheapest___ Ground Floor___

Credit card: Visa___ MasterCard___ American Express___

Card #: _____

Expiration date:_____

Name on card: _____

You may charge me for the first night as a deposit. Please fax, e-mail, or
mail me confirmation of my reservation, along with the type of room
reserved, the price, and whether the price includes breakfast. Please also
inform me of your cancellation policy. Thank you.

_____
Signature

_____
Name

_____
Address

_____
City   *State*   *Zip Code*   *Country*

_____
E-mail Address

Road Scholar Feedback for
IRELAND 2003

We're all in the same travelers' school of hard knocks. Your feedback helps us improve this guidebook for future travelers. Please fill this out (or use the online version at www.ricksteves.com/feedback), attach more info or any tips/favorite discoveries if you like, and send it to us. As thanks for your help, we'll send you our quarterly travel newsletter free for one year. Thanks! Rick

Of the recommended accommodations/restaurants used, which was:

Best _____

      Why? _____

Worst _____

      Why? _____

Of the sights/experiences/destinations recommended by this book, which was:

Most overrated _____

      Why? _____

Most underrated _____

      Why? _____

Best ways to improve this book:

_____

_____

I'd like a free newsletter subscription:

_____ Yes   _____ No   _____ Already on list

_____
Name

_____
Address

_____
City, State, Zip

_____
E-mail Address

Please send to: ETBD, Box 2009, Edmonds, WA 98020

INDEX

FREE TRAVEL GOODIES FROM

Rick Steves

EUROPEAN TRAVEL NEWSLETTER

My *Europe Through the Back Door* travel company will help you travel better *because* you're on a budget—not in spite of it. To see how, ask for my 64-page *travel newsletter* packed full of savvy travel tips, readers' discoveries, and your best bets for railpasses, guidebooks, videos, travel accessories and free-spirited tours.

2003 GUIDE TO EUROPEAN RAILPASSES

With hundreds of railpasses to choose from in 2003, finding the right pass for your trip has never been more confusing. To cut through the complexity, visit www.ricksteves.com for my online *2003 Guide to European Railpasses.* Once you've narrowed down your choices, we give you unbeatable prices, including important extras with every Eurailpass, **free:** my 90-minute *Travel Skills Special* video or DVD and your choice of one of my 24 guidebooks.

RICK STEVES' 2003 TOURS

We offer 20 different one, two, and three-week tours (200 departures in 2003) for those who want to experience Europe in Rick Steves' Back Door style, but without the transportation and hotel hassles. If a tour with a small group, modest family-run hotels, lots of exercise, great guides, and no tips or hidden charges sounds like your idea of fun, ask for my 48-page 2003 Tours booklet.

YEAR-ROUND GUIDEBOOK UPDATES

Even though the information in my guidebooks is the freshest around, things do change in Europe between book printings. I've set aside a special section at my website (www.ricksteves.com/update) listing *up-to-the-minute changes* for every Rick Steves guidebook.

> *Visit www.ricksteves.com to get your...*
>
> ☑ **FREE EUROPEAN TRAVEL NEWSLETTER**
> ☑ **FREE 2003 GUIDE TO EUROPEAN RAILPASSES**
> ☑ **FREE RICK STEVES' 2003 TOURS BOOKLET**

Rick Steves' Europe Through the Back Door

130 Fourth Avenue North, PO Box 2009, Edmonds, WA 98020 USA
Phone: (425) 771-8303 ■ Fax: (425) 771-0833 ■ www.ricksteves.com

Free, fresh travel tips, all year long.